THE REAL GUIDE TO

MAKING
MILLIONS
THROUGH
REAL
ESTATE

THE REAL GUIDE TO

MAKING MILLIONS THROUGH REAL ESTATE

Start Your Own Portfolio With as Little as $3000

Lisa Vander

EP
Entrepreneur.
Press

Editorial director: Jere L. Calmes
Cover design: Pay Fan
Composition and production: Eliot House Productions

This publication is designed to provide accurate and authoritative information in regard to the subject matter covered. It is sold with the understanding that the publisher is not engaged in rendering legal, accounting, or other professional services. If legal advice or other expert assistance is required, the services of a competent professional person should be sought.

Library of Congress Cataloging-in-Publication Data

Vander, Lisa.
    The real guide to making millions through real estate: start your portfolio with as little
as $3,000/by Lisa Vander.
      p.   cm.
    Includes bibliographical references.
    ISBN 1-932531-78-5 (alk. paper)
    1. Real estate investment—United States. 2. Real estate investment—United States—Finance.
3. Real estate management—United States. I. Title.
    HD255.V365 2005
    332.63'24—dc22   2005015122

Printed in Canada

11 10 09 08 07 06   10 9 8 7 6 5 4 3 2 1

Contents

PART ONE

Getting Started the Real Simple Way

PART THREE

Real Economic and Financial Environments

PART FOUR

The Real Approach to Wealth

CHAPTER 16

CHAPTER 17

CHAPTER 18

PART FIVE

Real Rewards: The Millionaire Years

Appendices

Acknowledgments

Writing this book has been an amazing adventure filled with bumps, turns, and twists in the road to help investors across the country create and *keep* millions of dollars for themselves through investment real estate. It all began when I chose to leave the comfort of a job I knew selling real estate to follow my passion for helping people to be financially prepared for their futures. I was scared about making the move to writer and national speaker, especially as a single mother. The process has been nerve wracking and frustrating at times and exciting and exhilarating at others. But one thing is certain, I could not have done this alone. An incredible network of supportive people encouraged me to keep moving forward when I was tired and wanted to quit. I thank each and every one of you from the bottom of my heart, and the readers of this book will also be grateful as they begin to implement their personal real estate plans.

I must first recognize my immediate family: my daughter Jessica for her incredible strength, dignity, and belief in what is good and right; my daughter Megan for her light-hearted wisdom and her unending love and companionship; and my daughter Marette who is an inspiration that the impossible is always possible when love is present. I want to thank my grandparents, Grace and Chris Cheevers, and my mother, Carol Siedenburg, for their love, encouragement, and vision, which are now being passed on to another generation with my daughters. I want to also acknowledge my dad, Bo Siedenburg, who continues to be my hero by helping me endlessly with technology and everything else that comes up. A special thanks must also go to my brothers and sister: John for believing that real estate can be his dream as well; Chris and his family, Rachel and the kids, for their example of what family really means; Eric for being an example of hope, living a good life, and kindness; Kevin for telling the truth and being patient; and my sister, Carrie, for being strong against the odds and defending what's right.

I thank my aunts and uncles: Aunt Julie who listens and loves me in my mother's absence; Aunt Kathy who has been my mentor since my grandmother Grace passed away; Aunt Nancy for loving my daughters during the summers to give me a break; Aunt Christine for her free-spirited attitude; Uncle Doug for his examples of conservative living and the numerous discussions trying to predict economic markets, and to the many cousins, nieces, and nephews who make up my wonderful family.

Next, I thank my amazing friends: starting with Candice Hinds, who has been "family" for years; I could not have done this without you. Keep doing your magic, it really works; Presley, Dominique, and Danica Cross for their tremendous friendship, strength, and love; John Reardon who got me started investing in real estate and always makes me laugh about being an entrepreneur; Darby Barclay for coaching me while out on the "skinny branches;" Mike Yagley for his timely "showing up" to assist with grace and ease; Peter Black for his continual humor and teasing that keeps me on my toes; Annette Kilmer for her quiet wisdom; Lisa Dunham for growing up with me; Wendy and Sarah for continually believing in me; and Susan Meyers-Pyke for her vision, wisdom, and friendship throughout the years.

I also want to thank Kip Nicol, Betsy Macomber, Steve Dillaway, and Rick Halperin for all their time and effort; Gayle Goldman for her stories of gifts and grace; Greg Brooks for "hanging in there;" for the "girls," Noemi, Barbara, Sherry, and Laurie; Bob Ryan for fun on the radio; and his colleagues for listening to a new wave of investors; Marty Stone and Spenser Strauss for first introducing me to the ideas of ROE and for the numerous conversations about investment strategies.

I cannot let pass without mention the numerous clients and colleagues who encouraged me to continue writing and speaking, especially Leslie Smith who is an example of how this program really works, and also Tina Lifford, Jim Dutka, Lou Meza, Ravi and

Margaret Bhola, Mike Davis, Danny Glessner, Roxie Graham, Theresa Johansing, Dan Moore, Donna Marie Fisher, Cissy Brady-Rogers, Gayle Walker, and Laura Peterson.

Without my book agent Irene Webb and her persistence and belief in me, this book would not exist. Gail Gillman's clear thinking and numerous hours of editorial support brought my words to life in a way for people everywhere to understand. Entrepreneur Press, Jere Calmes, and the rest were willing to take this book to more people than we could imagine.

Finally, I thank everyone not listed who has changed my life for the better, especially all the investors who graciously listened and took action on these teachings.

Prosperity and richness to all of you,
Lisa Vander

Preface

I think I've always recognized the value in real estate. Growing up as the third of six children in a close-knit Irish Catholic family, I quickly learned how important and necessary it was to stake out my territory. My earliest memories are of my mother in the kitchen, cooking with a house full of children, friends, and family. With that many kids running around all the time, there was never a dull moment. In addition to the fun and love mixed in with the chaos, I learned by example to be entrepreneurial, because both my parents ran their own businesses. My mother's business was called "our family." She learned to keep many plates in the air and run a household on a tight budget. I challenge you to convince me that running a household with six kids is not a business! My father was an engineer early in his life and later decided to start his own small computer company. My family fought a lot, shared a lot, and always listened to and encouraged each other to be the best that we could. Our mantra was and still is "be whatever you want to be; just be responsible and go for your dreams, whatever they are."

I think the best example of living that mantra was my grandmother Grace. She was a feisty, redheaded Irish woman who ran a corporation in Chicago, Illinois, in the early 1940s (well before women were accepted in the corporate environment) while still managing to raise seven children with my grandfather, Chris. As a young child, I remember going to my grandparents' large home for holiday visits and being frightened of "Gracey." She had a sharp tongue and always asked a lot of questions, many of which I couldn't answer. Despite her rough edges, she had a warm heart and was always interested in all her grandchildren's business ideas and interests, encouraging us to follow our dreams.

All of the members of my family were encouraged to appreciate education, take on new challenges, and love the adventure of learning. With this in mind, many years later my husband and I left Santa Barbara, California, with our undergraduate degrees and our six-week old daughter to venture off to the University of Idaho for my husband's graduate work in psychology. After arriving in this small town and realizing that I could only work in a fast food chain restaurant, I decided graduate school was the best option for me as well. I enrolled in a masters program for Counseling and Human Services in the College of Education. It was here in graduate school that I first learned how to understand what motivates people and help them make life-changing decisions. I learned how to encourage people to break through the barriers that kept them stuck and get started with a new way of thinking and living.

In 1989, right after graduate school, we moved to San Diego and for the first time started investing in real estate. It was not long before my Grandma Gracey flew out from Chicago to see what I was up to. Recognizing a chip off the old block, she gave me my first money to invest in real estate and then continued to send business articles to support the success of my first adult business venture. Each time I saw her on holidays, she wanted a full report on my plan to increase the profits and make my property more valuable. Nothing ever got beyond her watchful eye. Through her questions and support, I was better able to make financial and business decisions that would last over time. I realize now that she wasn't investing in my real estate endeavors; she was investing in me, my family, the success of my children into the future, and finally in my ability to share these insights with hundreds of thousands of other investors across the country.

That first investment sparked my interest in real estate. I instinctively knew that I could use real estate as a way of securing my future so that I could afford to live the life I had always wanted, but I had not known how to achieve. I bought several properties, fixed them up, and then sold each for a profit, but rarely kept any as investments. Inspired to learn more, I got my real estate license in 1993. I was tremendously motivated and soon built up a large clientele. I started paying attention to the habits of my wealthiest clients, and it wasn't long before I started recognizing a pattern. Unlike the get-rich-quick methods promoted on TV and in bookstores of buying, fixing up, and selling real estate, I noticed that almost all of my wealthiest clients rarely sold their real estate. They all proclaimed that holding onto real estate for the long haul was what had created their wealth. It turned out that keeping property through the ups and downs of the real estate market was the wealth-building secret I had been looking for.

It was during this time that I experienced the unexpected. After ten years of marriage, my husband and I separated, and I found myself raising two young children on my own. It was suddenly even more crucial that I create a plan to invest for both my children and myself. The demands of being a single mother combined with time restrictions and the tremendous outlay of expenses were obstacles that would ordinarily stop any investor, but with Gracey's example and guidance, I persisted with my dreams of being financially secure. Following the lead of those wealthy clients, I started buying raw land, developing duplexes, and buying investment property, sometimes in other states. Amazingly, my plan began working, first for my clients as I advised them, and slowly for myself as I managed to put money away to grab opportunities as they came my way.

After years of being a residential real estate agent and investing for myself, I decided to take my personal successes to a new level and began teaching the techniques I saw work for my clients throughout the years. I started giving workshops, hosting a radio show, making TV appearances, and writing columns for newspapers and magazines. I found myself living not only by my family's mantra, but also by the words of Stephen Jobs, CEO and co-founder of Apple Computers: "*If you are working on something exciting that you really care about, you don't have to be pushed. The vision pulls you.*"

What has inspired me to keep moving forward when the odds seemed to be against me is the tremendous number of phone calls and letters I receive that proclaim the amazing impact my workshops have had on investors' personal and financial lives. Many of my clients are average, everyday Americans who love their families and enjoy their jobs. They are not looking to real estate as their new full-time jobs, but as a wealth-building tool. Most of my clients lead active lives. Some have children that keep them busy and are stretched both financially and with their time. Others are well-to-do and want to strategically invest their money for more wealth and prosperity.

My clients are hard working, financially savvy, and interested in making sound investment decisions that will get their children through school, will not hamper their lifestyles too much, and will keep the stability and values of their families intact. These clients are brave, they are courageous, and they keep telling me what is working and what is not working in the strategies that we are implementing. Their generosity and commitment to hard work have continued to inspire me through the years. It is not uncommon for me to have lunch with clients who tell me that they have made $1 million in a couple of years or increased the profitability of their holdings to undreamed of levels. It is because of the many people who continue to seek greater lives for themselves and who want to stay in the game of investment real estate that I keep teaching, speaking, and learning. It is because of them that I am writing this book.

Chances are you are one of these hard working, busy, and courageous people, or you would not have picked up this book. You are probably curious about investing in real estate, but just don't know how to go about it. Or maybe you've already started your real estate portfolio and are looking for a solid way to expand your investments. Perhaps you have what I call "lazy money" in your investments—money that is not working very hard for you. If any of these scenarios sound like you, then you've come to the right place!

There is a vast array of information that beginner and seasoned investors need to sift through in order to create solid real estate plans that will lead to building safe, long-lasting wealth for themselves and their families. My goal with this book is to take this sometimes overwhelming amount of investment information and put it into a format that is tangible, practical, easy to use, and useable over and over again for you and for generations to come.

It is easy to get lost in all of the conflicting theories about real estate or become confused about where to begin or how to improve the profits in your already existing real estate portfolios. To address those concerns, I have put together a safe and secure system that looks at who you are as an individual so that you make the best choices for YOU. No one plan is right for everyone; so through the information and exercises in this book, you'll learn how to create a customized real estate plan that suits your personal needs. It's important to remember that PLAN is not a four-letter word! Real estate investment successes are directly linked to having an accurate and specific route or course of action. Planning can be intimidating to some people, mostly because they tend to think of a plan as something that is set in stone. That couldn't be farther from the truth with your real estate plan. In fact, it's just the opposite; your plan will change as you do. Staying focused on the overall goal and being able to adjust your plan when your goals or the market changes increase your odds of producing successful results and real estate fortunes.

In addition to mastering how to put together a powerful real estate plan, in this book you'll learn how to analyze and reanalyze your real estate portfolio year after year for the duration of your investing years. You'll also discover how to approach those millionaire years you've been working so hard to reach and the importance of learning when you have enough and begin to give back from what you have created and developed.

In my mind, making real money is more than accumulating dollars. It's about earning the freedom to live the life you deserve and spending more time with the ones you love. After years of being a successful real estate agent and a real estate investor, I have grown to appreciate the special times I had with my grandmother. I now realize what an amazing gift it was for me to have such a committed and listening adult concerned with teaching me how to succeed at business.

I would like you to also experience this pattern of support and training. I know how valuable it was for me to sit with my grandmother at her kitchen table, receiving her wisdom and insights about my concepts and ideas. I would like this book to be an extension of that kitchen table, a safe place to ask yourself questions, seek some answers, and be able to play around as you work out the details of your dream. I hope that this book will guide and direct you into real estate wealth and that you come to love real estate as much as I do. I have enjoyed my decades of ups and downs in the real estate market. I have made lots of money and lost some too. I've experienced headaches, heartaches, frustrations, triumphs, and successes. Still, my will to succeed and faith in my proven strategies keep me investing. I have found the adventure to be invigorating and worth all the time that I have spent creating it. I'm thrilled to have the opportunity to share these truths with you so that you will have the freedom to dream—and dream large. It's time to start making those dreams a reality.

PART ONE

Getting Started the Real Simple Way

Why Real Estate?

"Life gives us exactly what we expect from it. No more, no less. We tend to forget,
however, that it's generally ready to give us much more than we realize."
—Mark Fisher

It seems that you can't open a magazine or newspaper or turn on the television or radio these days without being bombarded by terrible news about the state of the American economy. With everyone talking about the loss of jobs to outsourcing, social security instability, and the downturn of the stock market, is it any wonder that people are concerned about the financial future of the United States? Americans are desperate for tangible solutions to their investment and financial worries. They will do whatever it takes to have financial security for themselves and their families. But what can they do?

If I asked you what investment has made more millionaires than any other throughout history, what would your answer be? Oil? Transportation? Technology? Nice guesses, but you'd be wrong on all counts. The answer is simple: real estate. Real estate is so powerful that anyone can start, even well into their 40s and 50s, and still end up in 10 to 15 years with millions of dollars of real estate equity that can provide a comfortable retirement lifestyle. It is one of the most powerful and competitive alternative investment answers for those seeking financial security.

Consider this: the majority of the world's wealth, over 80 percent, is held in real estate, but it is owned by less than 20 percent of the population. That hardly seems fair, does it? The time has come to educate people on how easy it is to create sustainable wealth and reap the rewards and benefits of long-term real estate investing. Real estate offers hope for all generations of investors who want to get started today on a clear and concise plan that will bring them real financial security forever.

BUILDING LONG-TERM, SUSTAINABLE WEALTH WITH REAL ESTATE

Americans work and play hard, striving tenaciously toward improving all areas of their lives. They invest aggressively, expect instant results, and worry continuously about their financial affairs. They are problem solvers seeking information that will give them immediate solutions for difficult situations. The more data and instructions they get, the better off they feel, and the more willing they are to leap into action to solve problems.

With that in mind, here is some information that most Americans don't know. Despite the fact that in 2000, 68.4 percent of Americans owned their personal residences and have untapped equity in their homes, less than 22 percent have used real estate as an investment option. This is in contrast to the over 49 percent of Americans who invest in the stock market and/or mutual funds. In general, there is still little understanding of how a home and the equity built up in it can transition a person into being a powerful investor in the real estate market. Yet as the wealthiest people know, real estate has been a profitable and solid performer for wealth accumulation since the beginning of recorded history.

This valuable and life-changing information has been kept a secret, despite the phenomenal amount of traditional investment literature published. Visit any bookstore in the last 20 years, and you're likely to have gotten lost in the rows and rows of books on financial strategies and investment information. Amazingly, few of these books addressed real estate as a powerful investment alternative to the stock market. In fact, you can barely even find real estate mentioned. No wonder people haven't been investing in real estate. Fortunately, the tide is turning and more people are using real estate as a viable investment alternative.

Contrary to popular belief, real estate is not difficult to understand or assign value to. There is little difference between learning how to interpret and evaluate a stock portfolio in the securities markets and learning to understand the rates of return on the equity built up in the real estate market. Just like anything, the more you know, the more comfortable you will feel about investing your money in real estate. Through education and (with all due respect to Nike) just doing it, real estate investors have an opportunity to produce substantial wealth for themselves. Now who doesn't want that?

A BRIEF (AND PAINLESS) HISTORY LESSON

For most Americans, the stock market and mutual funds have been the only investment option they have utilized, and fortunately, for the last 20 years, the stock market has gained steadily and performed well for those who invested. Many who invested thought they were financially set and did not investigate any other investment options. Unfortunately, they did not diversify their growing portfolios away from the stock market to take advantage of other investments, such as real estate. They kept all their investment efforts in one basket, exposing themselves to the fluctuating conditions of the stock market. In the late 1990s and early 2000s, the stock market fell through the floor, and almost everyone saw their retirement portfolios cut drastically. There was an expectation that the stock market would rebound quickly, and they would be able to go back to investing in that arena. But it did not happen quite so swiftly and easily.

In the early 2000s, fear and panic set in. In record numbers, investors began removing their hard-earned investment dollars from the stock market and mutual funds and, without knowing much about the ebb and flow of the real estate markets, began investing in real estate. With little or no financial information to guide and direct their investment strategies and plans, they flooded real estate offices and bookstores and, much to their chagrin, found that solid real estate investment books that taught long-term, conservative strategies were rare, if not nonexistent. Those investors who wanted to win big, yet still craved some of the safety and guidance available through the securities market, were out of luck.

Most of the real estate books promoted get-rich-quick schemes, buying and selling without an agent, and property management tips and techniques. It was assumed that real estate was for renegades who wanted to create wealth through cleaning up yards, working on plumbing, and managing unruly tenants. Few suggested using real estate as an alternative to the stock market by using the proven methods of analysis and diversified accounts found within managed stock portfolios and retirement planning circles. Despite the lack of information, real estate produced amazing results for a small and wealthy group of people. Real estate investments quietly and steadily paid their investors handsome rewards for their time and money.

AMERICANS ARE RUNNING OUT OF TIME

Over 73 million Americans will be trying to retire within the next 20 years, but only 5 percent of them will be financially prepared to live with the freedom and choices they are accustomed to having. These numbers are astonishingly low, given the overall wealth of the nation and the fact that most wealth is held in people's underleveraged personal residences. The traditional dream of retiring by age 65 has been replaced by the necessary reality of working into our 70s and even 80s. To make matters worse, the funds in social security are being depleted at a rate that won't keep pace with the surge of recipients coming of age. The social security system may not be able to withstand the volume of claims that will be filed in the next 20 to 30 years.

If that isn't scary enough, the U.S. Congress continues to discuss and propose plans of action that will reduce the benefits and medical coverage available through Medicare and other federally funded programs. Health-care costs continue to rise above national inflation rates. People are living healthier and longer lives because of improvements in medical care, pharmaceuticals, diets, and exercise. These conditions add to the national crisis of how to fund Americans who may not have sufficiently prepared for the future and will live well beyond the age of their parents.

So what, you may be thinking. I'm not even CLOSE to retirement age. Why do I need to worry about all of that? I've got plenty of time to save. To that I say, lucky you! Still, chances are you are part of the over 50 percent of the security market investors who lost at least a *third* of their entire portfolios when the market dropped in the early 2000s. That would be like paying full price for this book and then watching someone tear out the last couple of sections. You'd be upset, wouldn't you? I don't blame you (and not only because you'd be missing valuable information). No one likes to lose something they've come to rely on. So, what are you going to do? Should you continue to simply drop money into mutual funds with the amount of instability in these markets? Or is it time to start looking for other investment alternatives?

THE STOCK MARKET HAS CHANGED. NOW WHAT?

Since the 1970s, the trend is for Americans to begin investing later in life, oftentimes waiting until their mid-40s or 50s before getting started. Most have used the stock market and mutual funds as their primary (and sometimes only) investment option for retirement. In 1980, 5.7 percent of American households had $57 billion invested in mutual funds. By the year 2000, the number of investors increased to over 49 percent of American households with over $2.6 *trillion* invested. This is an amazing 43 percent increase in households investing in mutual funds and the stock market in this 20-year period.

The remarkable amount of wealth generated in the last 20 years will still not be enough to provide real financial security to upcoming generations. The national economic forecast is shaky. It is predicted that the financially unprepared will negatively impact the future economic stability of society. The generation Xers and Yers will not be able to contribute enough funds to sustain the lifestyles to which Americans have grown accustomed. What is the average American going to do when it is his/her turn to retire in 10, 20, or 30 years? If you're like me, you are frustrated by the seemingly limited number of viable investment opportunities available to you. You want a way to invest where you can control the profits and influence the outcomes more closely.

SHOULD I SAVE OR SHOULD I INVEST?

The beauty of real estate investing is that it allows the investor to use leverage (other peoples' money, either private or institutional, to acquire and multiply investment opportunities and returns), and compounded interest (where the growth from your investment works together with your original down payment to create more equity) to produce exponential results that far surpass the traditional methods of long-term savings plans. Figure 1.1 shows the difference between saving and investing rates of returns.

FIGURE 1.1: **How Much Money Do You Need to Save for Each Year of Retirement?**

Step Number 1
Decide what percentage of your annual salary you will need in retirement on top of traditional company pension, if any, and social security. Then use this table to find the percentage of salary you need to save each year, depending on how long you have until retirement.

Income as a Percent of Annual Salary	Years to Retirement					
	10	15	20	25	30	35
30%	36%	21%	13%	9%	6%	4%
40%	48%	27%	18%	12%	8%	6%
50%	60%	34%	22%	15%	10%	7%
60%	72%	41%	26%	28%	12%	9%
70%	84%	48%	31%	21%	14%	10%

FIGURE 1.1: **How Much Money Do You Need to Save for Each Year of Retirement?**

Step Number 2

Adjust the required savings rate to take account of your current savings by finding the appropriate number in this table and subtracting it from the percentage determined in Step 1.

Current Savings as a Percent of Annual Salary	Years to Retirement					
	10	**15**	**20**	**25**	**30**	**35**
100%	13%	10%	8%	7%	7%	6%
200%	25%	19%	16%	14%	13%	13%
300%	38%	29%	24%	22%	20%	19%
400%	51%	38%	32%	29%	27%	25%
500%	64%	48%	40%	36%	33%	32%

Example

If you are 25 years from retirement and want a retirement income equal to 70 percent of your salary, the first table suggests you need to save 21 percent a year. But if you already have savings equal to 200 percent of your salary, you would reduce that number by 14 to get a 7 percent annual savings rate.

The table above assumes a 9 percent annual investment gain prior to retirement; 8 percent annual gains after retirement; 3 percent inflation retirement income lasting for 30 years at which point your portfolio is depleted.

THERE'S STILL HOPE!

As I said earlier, real estate investing has made more millionaires than any other investment vehicle throughout history. The average rate of return on real estate equity is 20 percent to 35 percent annually when calculating all the benefits of using real estate (cash flow, appreciation, loan reduction, and tax benefits). Compared with the 12 percent average rate of return on long-term stock investments, it's not hard to see why real estate is one of the most powerful ways to develop long-term, sustainable wealth.

The true power in real estate comes through the art of leverage (an art you'll master in later chapters) and regularly evaluating your real estate portfolio to maintain targeted rates of return year after year according to your real estate plan. In the next chapter, you'll learn the three phases of that plan and discover the differences between active, portfolio, and passive income. I'll also reveal the benefits of long-term investing and show how the "get-rich-quick" concept behind short-term investing is sometimes more hype than reality and does not always lead to lasting wealth development.

• • •

Real estate is the sleeping investment giant of the 21st century. Whether you're looking to start investing in your future or are well along the path towards financial freedom, all it takes is a little initiative and someone to show you the way. Since you're reading this book, it looks like you've got both. Now let's start making some real money!

$$

Analysis Paralysis Can Be Forever Thwarted

I am an engineer and love looking at data. The more data you give me the better. But after awhile I started to realize that I wasn't actually making any investment decisions. I was stuck in what is called "analysis paralysis." Today, that is not the case at all. After looking at all of the benefits to real estate, the decision to invest was a no-brainer. I realize that I can't continue to rely on the stock market alone for my financial future, and social security won't provide enough for my retirement plans. After evaluating both investment options, I have come to the conclusion that you just can't beat the rates of return you get on real estate. I have now bought two investment properties and continue to enjoy researching and analyzing, but it is coupled with the important ingredient of purchasing and implementing my well-thought-out plans. I am no longer paralyzed and am on my way to becoming a millionaire.

—TOM L., VICE PRESIDENT OF TELECOMMUNICATIONS CONSULTING FIRM

CHAPTER 2

Start Making Real Money

"Whatever you do or dream you can, begin it; for boldness has
genius, power and magic in it."
— Johann Wolfgang von Goethe

Most people begin their real estate investment portfolios by accident. I call them "accidental investors." Sometimes it's a house they've put on the market but have been unable to sell by the time their new home purchase closed escrow. Other times, they may have trouble unloading a home or some property inherited from a parent. At first, they begrudgingly keep the properties, hoping that one day soon they will be able to sell them and use the proceeds immediately. It doesn't take long, however, before these investors start to grumble about the cash drain the property is having on them and their families. Maybe they'll even experience a temporary decline in property value as well. Complaining and frustration is the normal first reaction for these unintentional investors. The temptation is to take a financial loss and run for the hills, but let me assure you that is generally not the best decision to make in the long run, despite the initial unhappiness caused by these properties.

You've probably heard the expression, "patience is a virtue." Nowhere does this apply more than in the world of real estate. Patience in real estate investing is the number-one key to success. The secret is being willing to wait for the rewards and benefits that come in the latter and more mature phases of a diverse real estate portfolio, as well as having the patience to ride out a downturn in the market. It is very important to understand that time is your friend. The more time you have, the more capable you are of creating what you have designed. Market conditions are cyclical and they *will* improve, if they follow historical patterns. The time frame for these returns can be up to ten years and on rare occasions sometimes longer. More frequently, the time frame to experience a successful and profitable return is less than six years. It turns out the best things *do* come to those who wait!

THE REAL ESTATE PLAN PHASES

Before I explain the three phases of real estate investing, I should first congratulate you on getting in the real estate game. Whether you are an unintentional investor, contemplating your first investment, or well on your way to building your portfolio, jumping into the real estate market is no small step. You should be proud of yourself. Feel good? Great. Let's move on.

There are three distinct real estate plan phases about which all investors should be aware when they are making real estate investment decisions. These three phases are the acquisition phase, the equity management phase, and the exit strategy phase. It is critical that you have a clear understanding of where you are in your real estate plan, and how your investment strategies must adjust accordingly.

The Acquisition Phase

The acquisition, or beginning, phase of real estate investing is most characterized by fear, confusion, and analysis paralysis. If you are both excited and scared, you're right where you are supposed to be. Most beginner investors have either acquired their first property unintentionally or are using money from their primary residences to get started. It is perfectly natural for investors to be overwhelmed when they begin to invest, especially if they are unfamiliar with the language, vocabulary, and concepts of real estate.

Typical first-time investors are often naïve about the positive sides of investment real estate and cautious about investing money in something they know little about.

Because of this, investors tend to read lots of books and attend many real estate investment seminars in order to learn as much as they can. As a result, they begin to understand terms such as escrow, the loan process, real estate contracts, property management, tenant selection, tax reporting, and managing expenses. Still, typical first-time investors are usually very reactive and easily excited, with a tendency to make rash decisions without getting the proper guidance and direction. However, they are also the most flexible about what strategies they are going to use to create their long-term wealth.

The Equity Management Phase

The equity management phase can also be called the mastery phase. Investors enter this phase when they have already accumulated at least three to four investment properties. By this point, they will have a firm understanding of all of the people and institutions involved in the process of investment real estate, comprehend the terminology, and have begun to solidify an investment strategy. At this stage, investors have usually experienced some successes as well as some failures or unexpected upsets from owning investment real estate.

With some experience under their belts, investors should determine whether they are comfortable with the growth and profit of their real estate portfolio as it currently stands or if they are ready to increase or improve it. I highly recommend that you obtain help from professional financial services experts to determine this. Generally, investors are reluctant to try new investment theories because they have developed ones that are working just fine. They are usually aware that they could improve the rates of returns on their investments, but shy away from the work required to learn a new skill or take on a different style of investing or managing. I see this as a form of stagnation and not always in the best interest of the investor.

Once you have gotten into the habit of running your properties, you may need to start looking at how to improve the management that is in place. You might also start thinking about how you will diversify your real estate portfolio to even out the mix of assets you've acquired. This is the time when mastery of different tax strategies and planning is important, and improvements to profit are calculated for the property. The equity management phase is where investors begin to understand the mathematics and tax implications of investing more proficiently.

Having reached this phase, it is important to have advisors, what I call "team players," that know more than you do. This might seem like stating the obvious, but it is amazing how many people I've seen who think they can figure it out all on their own. The truth is, a good team can save you thousands of dollars. With its advice, you should learn how to take and hold title, how to finance each property, how much to leverage your real estate holdings, and how to protect the equity that has been built up in your real estate portfolio. You'll learn more about choosing your team in Chapter 9.

I'll be honest with you, the mastery phase is the most time consuming and often the most frustrating because you must be constantly evaluating your investments and making decisions about how to produce the results you desire. It is the most active phase of all phases.

OK, you're thinking. I start out scared and I graduate to being frustrated. Is this real estate stuff really worth it? My reply is a resounding YES! And it's all because of the next phase.

The Exit Strategy Phase

The exit strategy phase is the least spoken about and, I believe, the least understood. Planning for financial security is a billion-dollar industry, but if I asked the average Joe to explain how he will live his life once he has attained his financial goals, I'd most likely be met with a blank stare. Most Americans are primarily interested in thinking about how to accumulate wealth and don't take the time to plan what to do with their fortunes once they have them. Sure, making money can be fun. It's even a little sexy. But isn't figuring out what to do with it once you have it even *more* fun? If you've done a good job of managing expenses and costs during the equity management phases of your real estate plan, now is the time to start asking yourself some important questions.

The exit phase of the plan begins about three to five years before you are completely retired from having to depend on your salary to support your lifestyle. This period is when most investors begin to ask themselves whether they want to live in their current homes for the next 10 to 15 years. Quite often, it is the suddenly-too-large home they used to raise their children, or is in a location that does not serve them any more. About five years before they retire, investors who have sufficiently prepared for retirement begin to purchase the home they plan to live in.

Please try to remember that *retirement* is not a dirty word. Just because you are retired doesn't mean you are dead. What you are is financially secure and free to live the life you've worked for. More and more people these days are living what I call an active retirement. They travel. They volunteer. Some even continue to consult or hold part-time jobs. The difference is that they are no longer dependent on the income work brings in.

Investors in the exit phase have more freedom in their choices because they have sufficient equity built up and do not have to push the risk factors of their portfolios. Many investors choose to completely sell off all their real estate holdings during this phase. They may decide that owning and managing real estate is too much work at this point in their lives. Instead, they would rather take all the equity they have accumulated over time and place it in the stock market or into a more conservative and passive investment vehicle. Any of these options are great. The choice is yours!

During this final phase of your real estate plan, it is important to start looking at how and when you will distribute your real estate portfolio to your heirs. People usually do not hit the exit strategy phase of investment real estate until they are in their late 40s to early 60s. The older the people are, the more likely they will be concerned about how to pass estates on to their heirs. Proper estate planning and tax preparation is critical in this phase.

This is typically a very satisfying and happy time in the investor's life. Investors often find they have more time on their hands and can do things they haven't been able to do in years. With the freedom to live how they choose, you'd think that people might spend a little time thinking about how they would choose to live. Instead, this is the most over-looked and forgotten phase of the plan. This is what you've been working and planning for. Please don't forget to dream!

Although it is not difficult, it takes time to create a powerful and profitable real estate plan. Do not get anxious and expect that it will produce immediate wealth for you. Investors who take it slow and steady tend to do better with investment real estate in the long run because they grow with their properties and are more patient with themselves. The key is to pace yourself and stay in the game till the end.

THE THREE TYPES OF INCOME

They say that money makes the world go 'round. While this isn't 100 percent accurate (I certainly hope it takes more than that), building an income stream *is* necessary for any type of investment, particularly real estate. There are three main types of income: active, passive, and portfolio. Investors sometimes confuse one with the others, but because each type of income stream has particular intentions and strategies attached to it, it is important to understand the differences among them.

Active Income

A simple definition of active income is income that is generated by you. It is any activity in which the person must be physically present and involved to receive payment or money for services provided. Usually, this is your salary. It is very natural for people to focus on their active incomes, especially in America where it's common to be defined by what you do for a living and how much money you make. Prestige and social status are most often associated with the job that you do and the position that you hold. You might be surprised then to learn that active income is the least wealth-oriented form of income. For that reason, I do not focus on this income stream much in this book. I will refer to the use of active income in order to evaluate whether or not you can afford to sustain a property through all different kinds of real estate market conditions.

By the time people are in their late 20s, they are usually able to provide their families with the fundamental necessities in life: food, shelter, and clothing. They have developed what I call the "active income muscle." After you have learned to get a job, live on your own, and support yourself independently, it is time to look at being financially independent in a new way. It is time to begin working a different muscle: the "passive income muscle."

Passive Income

Passive income is income that is generated whether you are there or not. It is money or an investment working for you when you do not have to be present to benefit from it. Residential rental income and commercial income are some examples of passive income. Passive income is what I will be encouraging you to focus your attention on in this book. It is taxed at a different rate and in a different manner than active income, and later in life the income that is generated through passive income does not affect or diminish the benefits seniors rely on through social security. The goal of investing in real estate is the creation of more passive income than active income by the end of your real estate plan.

Focusing on passive income is not very natural for human beings. It takes concerted effort to grow and establish passive income. It is not our natural instinct to prepare and hold off a reward for something better in the future. That is why most people do not prepare for a rainy day or for when they will not be able to actively work for a living. Some people are not willing to forgo the benefits of today for the benefits of tomorrow and never develop the passive income muscle. In the long run, that is not in their best financial interest. Like any muscle, it just needs a good workout to start getting in shape. Strong muscles work more efficiently, and your passive income muscle works the same way. I always encourage investors to pay attention to their passive income muscles and to work on them whether they have a lot of active income or not.

Many of my clients want to buy real estate and begin immediately taking a reward from owning that investment. In fact, many will not buy any real estate that does not have a positive cash flow from the outset, meaning more income comes in than goes out when owning the property. This is unrealistic, especially when beginning to invest and when you are at the top of the real estate market. Remember: the real estate market is cyclical. Good investments require time. The benefits of long-term investing are not to be used now, they are designed to be used later, when you are not able to work in your career or when you have created enough real estate equity that you can choose to work or not.

You must remember to be patient. I can't stress this enough. Be careful not to want the rewards from your investment labors too soon in the investment time schedules. I have witnessed lasting wealth come to those who have been willing to wait, set their immediate desires aside, and plan for the future. Those clients who want all the rewards up front often get hit when the market adjusts or their passive income decreases as is expected and normal when investing in real estate for the long haul.

The trick is to avoid becoming too dependent on the passive income generated from your real estate portfolio before your portfolio has had a chance to season or become mature. A mature real estate portfolio can create a lifestyle that is lasting, but you must be willing to learn the lessons necessary to allow compounded interest and growth to work. Be aware that when you take money out of the investment in the early phases of the real estate plan to spend on items, you are short-changing the ability of your portfolio to create compounded growth for the future. Remember: less growth equals less wealth development.

You must always be prepared to live off your active income and avoid living a life that is dependent on the benefits of your real estate investments before they have created enough equity to sufficiently fuel that lifestyle into the future, *uninterrupted*. Trust your natural instinct to provide for yourself while you are young and live within your means while you have the time and energy through your active income efforts.

There is nothing wrong with taking a benefit from your real estate investments now and then to augment or assist your living situation. But when you do this, make sure that you understand fully the financial impact this has on your future goals. Don't fool yourself. An investment means that you put money away for a set period of time. I promote taking the original investment out only when you are at the end of your plan, unless you want to make real estate a part of your active income stream (what I'd call a real estate career). If that is the case, you must calculate your real estate plan differently.

Many of the investors that I work with want to have their cake and eat it, too. They want to pretend they are sophisticated investors, they want to prepare for the future, and they want to take the money out today and still meet their goals and objectives. Not only is this impossible, it is very shortsighted. Investors should be aware of the future value of their real estate portfolios based on decisions they are making today. Good financial business and investment decisions are critical for investors who want to protect what they have and adequately prepare for their financial futures.

Portfolio Income

The final income stream is portfolio income. This is defined as royalties, dividends from stocks, and monthly money received from annuities. Portfolio income is taxed at a different rate from active income and passive income and does not have as many tax shelters as passive income does. I will not be addressing portfolio income in this book, but it is important to remember that a solid, diversified investment portfolio should have income coming from all three income sources. I encourage my clients to move easily among the real estate investment world, the portfolio income world, and the active income world.

BEING A SHORT-TERM INVESTOR

There are many programs and get-rich-quick promotions that offer short-term investing strategies. They often promote buying homes at a discount, lease option contracts, and buying at the right time in the market. These short-term investment theories can be beneficial and, if used the right way, can create tremendous wealth, but they must be understood completely when being implemented.

To be honest, I have known very few wealthy people who have used these get-rich-quick methods of real estate. Most of the wealthy people I have known have held onto their real estate for a least one full cycle, which is typically a ten-year span. I have also noticed that many of these short-term methods spend plenty of time analyzing the buying costs, but are not very strategic or clear about the holding or selling costs. These investors often boast about their success stories and buying discounts, but they do not tell you the true net benefit to them after all costs are calculated. Oftentimes, there's more hype and bravado attached to their successes than there is real wealth development. I am much more interested in your creating lasting wealth for yourself and your family than short-term bursts of money.

Don't get me wrong, a burst of money is never a bad thing—if it is reinvested. Unfortunately, I have witnessed countless times that when investors make money in a short time, they do not know how to reinvest all of their financial gains from each real estate transaction. They will usually take the money made from these short-term strategies to improve their lifestyles and increase their expenses instead of putting their proceeds back into real estate. While this philosophy may be fun and exciting in the short-term, it will not lead to long lasting wealth development.

Short-term investing is dependent on buying property at a discount and being able to sell it in a short period of time (usually no more than one year) for a reasonable profit. Investors buy the property because it is undervalued either in purchase price or in income being generated from the rents. They will then add the least amount of capital and time to improve the investment. The short-term investor must be careful to time the purchase correctly and must quickly make the necessary repairs to put the property back on the market in order to realize any gains. The shorter the time investors have their money in the investments, the better off they are. Many of these short-term investors do not have tenants in the units, so the holding costs can be substantial.

It is a great plan—in theory. My experience personally and professionally as a real estate agent is that locating properties and making sure that they meet the necessary discounted requirements are more difficult than is being promoted. Finding discounted properties usually takes significantly more time than finding properties that are at market rate. Many of the investors that I work with do not have the extra time in their schedules to find these highly discounted properties, fill out the necessary paperwork to buy them, make the improvements, and hold the properties only to realize surprisingly small profits after selling and paying the taxes—all in less than a year.

I promote to my clients that when they find greatly discounted real estate opportunities, they should take all the actions that short-term investors make but hold onto the property. Let me say that again: don't sell the property. Keep the gains for yourself, and refinance the property. Now you can have the best of both worlds. You get the fabulous gains from locating a discounted property and get to defer the closing and sale costs to another time. You are also able to leverage this property to obtain other real estate so that you can grow your real estate portfolio slowly over time. It is really important for short-term investors to realize the true costs of spending the gains from those real estate transactions now rather than letting them accumulate in their real estate investment portfolio over time.

BEING A LONG-TERM INVESTOR

If I've said it once, I've said it a thousand times: long-term, steady investors make it big in the long run. Investors who are willing to slowly grow wealthy and are patient with their investments overwhelmingly get and *stay* wealthy.

Because the market is cyclical, long-term investors are not as dependent on timing of the real estate market. They are usually more concerned with being able to sustain and maintain the property. Long-term investors look at creating profit with the real estate that they own. They are focused on how to manage the property efficiently from a property management standpoint as well as from an equity standpoint. Good long-term investors usually do not take out a lot of the gain they have achieved in their real estate portfolios to increase their personal lifestyles. They have the benefit of learning to slowly live into their wealth, keeping their personal tastes and appetites at bay while they are accumulating wealth. They are more oriented toward being able to generate passive income for the future when they no longer want to work for a living.

Because they hold onto their properties for an extended period of time, long-term investors continually need to evaluate the properties that they have in their real estate portfolios. They should learn how to create the greatest profits from the equity that they have. The wealthiest individuals have known this for years and do not sell property frequently without knowing the impact and costs associated with these actions.

The fun part of creating wealth for clients is that if they have been conservative for 10 to 20 years, they do not realize how much money they actually have in their real estate portfolios, and what that equates to in retirement income. Oftentimes, these investors have met or exceeded their real estate investment goals, but don't yet realize it. They can now stop accumulating at such high levels and begin to live into the wealth that they have created. I get a kick out of watching the grins slide across their faces as they realize that the work part is finally over and it's time to get out there and play!

SUSTAINING YOUR WEALTH

One of the greatest concerns that I see with investors who are entering into real estate is that they do not have a healthy appreciation for what can happen when the real estate market corrects and goes into the negative. Investors who set their sights on only measuring the value of their real estate portfolio by price and appreciation panic when the market tightens up, vacancy rates increase, and rents decrease. This is often coupled with the property values dropping significantly. It is during these downward adjustments that many poorly prepared investors want to sell off or bail on their real estate investments.

I care more about investors being able to sustain their real estate investments in both the up and down markets than I do about being able to only sustain in an up market. It's easy to make money when times are good; it's when the market shifts that it becomes more of a challenge. It is nearly impossible to time the market perfectly so that you get in just at the moment it is starting to go up. The truth is, even with charts and graphs, there is no way to know exactly where you are in a market cycle until after you've been there. Instead of focusing on timing, I think that investors who look at calculating the rate of return on equity (your annual return on the money you have in the property as a percentage of the total amount you've invested) take a much steadier and reliable approach to real estate wealth development.

If there is one thing that is definite, it's that the market will adjust. Investors who have good jobs, have families to care for, and are more conservative by nature, are reluctant to use real estate as an alternative to the stock market because they feel there is not sufficient information on how to protect against these adjustments in the market. This is not necessarily true. Sustainability is related to understanding the effects of interest rates, rental prices, vacancy rates, and where you are in the cycle of your real estate plan. If you are able to sustain a property for at least five to six years and you are measuring the rate of return on equity every year, then you can begin to set up systems to protect or hedge against these normal fluctuations in the market.

Some of these tools include knowing what the ten-year historical trends in vacancy patterns are for the area where you own the real estate. This can be learned by talking with three different property management companies that have been actively managing property in the area where you are investigating. Ask them how long rents stay low and what happens when the market rebounds. Most investors panic and think that vacancies will be 50 percent for a long time. Those numbers would be unusually high for any particular area. It is important to ask a reputable property management company about these vacancies so that you can conservatively prepare.

It is also very important to determine the local drop in rental values in a down market. Usually rental values do not drop at the same rate as the property values drop, and the inverse is true when prices rebound. For example, in Southern California, a standard increase on rental rates is about 5 percent per year. In contrast, the average rate of appreciation for a ten-year cycle is about 7.5 percent, a significant difference. Even in a decline, the drop in rents is usually no more than 10 percent to 15 percent. Knowing these standard historical drops will assist the investor to be reasonably assured of how to plan for these negative adjustments. Investors who fail to look at these historical trends and strategically prepare for these drops more often than not will be forced to sell. The key is staying aware and knowing what to focus on.

> "I have missed more than 9,000 shots in my career. I have lost almost 300 games. I have been trusted to make the game winning shot and missed 26 times. I have failed over and over and over again in my life. And that is why I succeed."
>
> —Michael Jordan, winner of 5 MVPs and 6 NBA titles

I have found that people tend to exaggerate and make the loss of income on vacancies much greater than it needs to be. Therefore, they are less likely to invest in real estate because of their fear of what may happen, rather than what will probably happen. They could be reasonably assured of how far the market will adjust and plan for it accordingly. The truth is, it's easy to find reasons *not* to do something. The price is too high, the economy is unpredictable, I don't have enough money . . . . Fortunately, there are more reasons to invest in real estate than reasons not to invest. In the next chapter, I will address some of these common fears about real estate investing and how to best overcome them.

$$$

Your First Investment Property Can Be Your Primary Residence

I figured the real estate learning curve was going to be too steep for me, but I was wrong. It all began when I picked up a book on investment real estate and a whole new world opened up to me. I had never seriously thought of real estate as a good long-term investment opportunity for me. Everyone I knew seemed to be talking about "flipping" properties, but I was looking for a more conservative investment that I could sustain over time. I wasn't in a big hurry to get rich as long as I got rich in the end! The idea of living in my investment property especially appealed to me. It wasn't long before I bought my first investment property, a small condominium that I could live in for a couple of years and then convert into a rental property. I was especially proud that I could buy my first place all on my own. After a short period of time, I am now looking at purchasing more real estate outside of my area and learning how to manage and create long-term wealth with a diversified portfolio. I'm in this for the long haul!

—GAYLE GOLDMAN, PRESIDENT, QUICKBOOKS CONSULTING COMPANY

Fears, Risks, and Values

"Only those who will risk going too far can possibly find out how far one can go."
—T.S. Eliot

There are a million reasons nervous investors give to explain why they are afraid to invest in real estate, and believe me, I've heard them all. From the horror stories about what tenants can do to rental properties to doomsday reports proclaiming an impending and historic downturn in the value of real estate, there is certainly no lack of excuses for why *not* to get into the real estate market. Many investors cite the higher entrance fees and complicated paperwork as reasons for why they are unwilling to take the leap into real estate. When you couple that with the fact that real estate is not as liquid as having a stock portfolio, the concerns about investing in real estate become very real.

IDENTIFYING YOUR FEARS ABOUT INVESTMENT REAL ESTATE

Because I have a masters degree in counseling and human services and have worked with people for many years on how to overcome fear and empower themselves to do what they want, addressing the fears and concerns of investment real estate seems natural and important. With that in mind, below are six key fears I've found that explain why investors may be reluctant to invest in real estate.

1. Fear of negative cash flow. Sometimes buying investment property means you will experience negative cash flow for a short period of time. Having a negative cash flow does not mean, however, that your investment decision is wrong or that you should immediately sell your property. In order to combat your fear, you need to create a plan of action for each property that will help you get through the lean times. Investors can look at negative cash flow as a forced savings plan (as long as the rate of return on equity meets your overall investment strategy). Sometimes, contributing $100 to $500 per month to a real estate investment creates the highest possible rate of return for the money invested, maybe even higher returns than equivalent monthly contributions to other investment options such as 401(k)'s, stocks or bonds.

2. Fear that this isn't the "right time" to invest. The truth is, when you practice long-term investing, there is no right time to start investing in real estate. The good news is there is no wrong time either! When you have a real estate plan, you are looking for long-term results that consider the natural ebbs and flows of the real estate market. You can buy real estate at any time as long as you keep in mind that every year you must target a specific rate of return on the equity you have in that investment (a concept I'll discuss further in Chapter 6). Long-term investors need to consider their ability to sustain their investments over time.

3. Fear of losing your money. You may lose money in real estate and, like any invest-ment, you must be prepared for that. Real estate investing is not without loss or pain. You may lose *some* money on *some* properties at *some* time in your investment career. But those risks can be reduced. A good way to accomplish this is to have alternate ways of making your property more profitable. Some methods include increasing the rents, enhancing the property condition, and refinancing.

4. Fear of tenant and management hassles. Tenant hassles come with the territory when owning investment real estate, and most investors don't like the bother and incon-venience. When you are considering buying a property, it's important to decide whether you are going to be involved personally with the physical management of the property or if you are going to hire a property manager to do the work for you. Either way, there are plenty of good books about property management (and we'll discuss the topic in Chapter 15). Continue to educate yourself on how to manage the inconveniences of property ownership efficiently because the rewards of owning real estate far outweigh the negatives and hassles.

5. Fear of low-income areas. Your decision on where you purchase real estate will be based on your personality and comfort levels. You may not want to purchase in low-income areas although they can often be very profitable. Regardless, you should know what rate of return you want from your overall real estate plan and purchase properties accordingly.

6. "There is only one thing to fear and that is fear itself." Former President Franklin Delano Roosevelt knew what he was talking about. It's normal to be scared when trying something new. The key is to not let that fear keep you from moving forward. When you put your money in any investment tool, whether it is the stock market or real estate, you will experience a certain degree of fear. The alternative to taking action is to take no action and let taxes and inflation eat away at your retirement possibilities. Liberate yourself. Realize that investing in real estate need not be cumbersome. Be prepared for some work, but while you're working at it, you can smile and have fun all the way to the bank. You'll win some and you'll lose some. But overall, there is a high probability that you will win a lot more in the long run.

WHAT IS RISK?

You must have a healthy relationship with risk in order to be a successful investor of any type, but most assume this to be especially true in real estate. What are people referring to when they say real estate is risky? Generally, they are concerned about the possibility of losing an investment through foreclosure or not being able to pay the bills on a building in a timely manner.

It is also assumed that it is risky to have unknown tenants in your properties. Horror stories of what tenants can do to a property permeate the minds of all investors. Try to remember that these risks are the liabilities of creating great wealth for the future. Without tenants, you would not be able to build a fortune for yourself or your family. Embrace this risk!

It is more rare to hear people talk about the risks of not getting involved with any kind of investment plan. The most conservative and risk-averse people often pride themselves on knowing all the answers or catching all the downsides to investment real

$$$

John and Susan's Story

John and Susan are in their mid-50s and have owned several properties throughout the years. They have made a lot of money and have spent a lot of money, but what they failed to do was to save and invest money. The only thing they have now is their beautiful home, completely remodeled, with some equity. They are scared because they want to retire soon and have no plan of action and no savings.

I suggest that they use their home equity to get started. They balk at the idea because they feel they will be jeopardizing the sense of security that they get from their home. Plus, they want to have a low home mortgage when they retire. What John and Susan don't realize is that their unwillingness to use the money they have available to them for future wealth development is much more dangerous than strategically taking the money out of their home. Although it may seem counter-intuitive to them, using some of the built-up equity in their home and increasing their mortgage will actually improve their odds of having a successful retirement plan.

Many aging Americans, like John and Susan, are already in a very risky spot because they haven't adequately prepared themselves for retirement and don't want to admit it. They want to continue to hold onto the idea that their paid-off home is their safest investment. But how will a home that has no mortgage payment help you if you do not make enough money to pay the water, electric, or gas bills? Many Americans will not receive enough social security to keep them living the lifestyle to which they have grown accustomed and will (by default) sacrifice that lifestyle if they do not get into action soon.

estate. But the reality is, their reluctance to evenly measure risk puts them in the most vulnerable situation of not properly planning for their futures. Sometimes taking no action because of fear, or not wanting to take money out of a personal residence to start an investment portfolio is the *most risky action* to take.

Many conservatives want to stick their heads in the sand, continue to live a meager lifestyle, and complain that they don't have enough resources or money to really do the things they want to do. They are frozen by their fears. What they don't seem to realize is that although risk can't be entirely eliminated when you invest, the risks in real estate can be calculated and worked around with a solid real estate plan.

FINDING YOUR APPROACH TO REAL ESTATE

Once you've committed to investing in real estate, it's time to figure out what type of investor you want to be. With Figures 3.1 and 3.2, you'll begin to define for yourself some of your feelings about real estate by doing a short self-analysis. Don't worry, there are no wrong answers here. This is about determining what is best for you.

FIGURE 3.1: **Getting to Know Your Real Estate Investment Approach**

Have you ever invested in real estate, stocks, bonds, or mutual funds?

1. No, I would be uncomfortable with any risk if I invested.   _____

2. No, but I am comfortable with a degree of risk if I invested.   _____

3. Yes, but I was uncomfortable with the risk.   _____

4. Yes, and I was comfortable with the risk.   _____

I would classify myself as:

❑ **Very conservative.** I am uncomfortable with any degree of risk or potential loss of my principal even if it means a loss of potential return.

❑ **Moderately conservative.** Safety of principal is very important to me, but I am willing to take a small degree of risk for the potential of higher return.

❑ **Moderate.** I am willing to take a certain degree of risk to have the potential of greater growth; however, I would like a certain degree of safety against market fluctuation, even if it means a smaller return.

❑ **Moderately aggressive.** I am comfortable with a higher degree of risk in order to have the potential for greater returns.

❑ **Very aggressive.** I am willing to assume a high degree of risk for the potential of the highest return. I understand the value of my portfolio may fluctuate greatly.

FIGURE 3.2: **Comfort Levels of Investment Real Estate**

This form will help you identify the comfort level you have relative to different types of real estate. Go to the first column on the far left labeled "Condominium," then continue going right and read the levels of risk and mark the level that most closely matches your thoughts about investing in condominiums. If, for example, you believe that condominiums are high-risk investments, mark the high-risk box. Next, use check marks to indicate how interested you are in buying each type of real estate. Then, continue down the list of property types, putting a check in the box corresponding to the response that most closely matches your thoughts on each type of real estate.

	RISK			INTEREST				
	Low Risk	Medium Risk	High Risk	Yes, I'll buy	Somewhat interested in buying	I need more information	Probably not going to buy	I'll never buy
Condominium								
Single-Family Residence								
Multiple Units (2–4)								
Multiple Units (5 or more)								
Land								
Commercial Property								
Timeshares								
Vacation Homes								

WHAT IS LEVERAGE ANYWAY?

Leverage is the amount of loan or debt taken to own a piece of real estate. It is a way to use other peoples' money (private, institutional, or family) for acquiring and multiplying investment opportunities and returns. Leverage allows owners to put only 5 to 40 percent of their own money down on a property and get the full benefit of the entire asset they are purchasing. Leverage is the reason real estate investment can provide better returns than the stock market. See Figure 3.3.

For example, a homeowner can buy a property valued at $200,000 with only 10 percent of her own money for the down payment. This means that with a $20,000 investment (plus closing costs), you are able to get the tax benefits and appreciation on the whole $200,000, even though you only have put 10 percent of your own money into the deal. Pretty good deal, isn't it? The art of using leverage is what makes real estate fortunes for so many people. A little money invested gets you the benefits of the full value in real estate.

To continue this example, say you buy a home for $200,000 and put $20,000 for the down payment, which is 10 percent of the value. You would then get a loan for $180,000. The property is leveraged to 90 percent loan to value. Now say the house appreciates in the first year by 4 percent. Your investment would have increased by:

$200,000 (Purchase price) x 4% (Appreciation) = $8,000 Appreciation benefit.

You gained $8,000 in the first year with only $20,000 of your own money in the property for the down payment. In the first year, your return on investment for using the down payment is:

$8,000 (Appreciation) ÷ $20,000 (Down payment) =
40% Rate of return for appreciation benefit.

This calculation does not take into account the cost of the loan and the expenses of owning the property. I will show you how to calculate that later in the book. As you can see from this example, leverage can increase real estate fortunes at amazing rates.

YOUR HOME IS YOUR EQUITY CASTLE

It is critical that homeowners and investors use leverage wisely. You must decide how much to leverage a property and how much safety or security is desired. You want to be sure to respect and protect your nest egg (or equity in your primary residence) while at the same time using the money strategically to establish financial security and freedom for the future. It's important to note that risk and leverage are directly related. This means that the higher the leverage, the higher the risk of losing the property or damaging your

FIGURE 3.3: **The Art of Using Leverage: Stock Market vs. Real Estate Investments**

This example demonstrates the power of leverage as an investment tool, especially in investment real estate. With relatively low down payments, you can control a lot of real estate. The benefits of using real estate are even greater when you calculate all four components of the rates of return for real estate investing such as cash flow, appreciation, loan reduction and tax benefits. This is an example of just one component, appreciation.

Stock Investment	First Year	Second Year	Third Year	Fourth Year	Fifth Year
Rate of return on investment	12%	12%	12%	12%	12%
Down payment	$10,000	$10,000	$10,000	$10,000	$10,000
Current stock value	$10,000	$11,120	$12,544	$14,049	$15,735
Leverage	0	0	0	0	0
Growth value	**$1,200**	**$2,544**	**$4,049**	**$5,735**	**$7,623**

Real Estate Investment	First Year	Second Year	Third Year	Fourth Year	Fifth Year
Annual appreciation	4%	4%	4%	4%	4%
Down payment	$10,000	$10,000	$10,000	$10,000	$10,000
Current property value	$100,000	$104,000	$108,160	$112,486	$116,985
Leverage	90%	86%	82%	78%	74%
Growth value (appreciation only)	**$4,000**	**$8,160**	**$12,486**	**$16,985**	**$21,166**

Difference between stocks and real estate	**+$2,800**	**+$5,616**	**+$8,437**	**+$11,250**	**+$13,543**

credit scores when things go south on you for a period. I don't recommend investors leverage their personal residences more than 80 percent at any one time. This keeps them safe when market conditions change and allows an investor to be better able to sell the home, if necessary, in a down market.

Unfortunately, there is not one universal method for all investors to determine the right amount to leverage. People have different comfort levels and risk tolerances that need to be considered in conjunction with their family values when refinancing and leveraging their real estate portfolios. The reality with leveraging is that if you put the least amount of money in possible, you get the greatest returns on your money. Big risks equal big rewards. See Figure 3.4. Most of my beginner investors feel like they are behind when they begin investing because they don't have a lot of their own money. I remind

FIGURE 3.4: **Using Leverage to Create a Healthy Real Estate Plan**

Everything you need to know about investing you learned in kindergarten

This is a basic description of how leverage works. You can leverage your equities to get the results you are seeking when you invest in real estate.

A lower down payment or lower equity produces
{
Higher rates of return
Higher leverage
Higher risk
Lower passive income

A higher down payment or higher equity produces
{
Lower rates of return
Lower leverage
Lower risk
Higher passive income

Definition of leverage: Using someone else's money or assets to acquire the full value of an investment or asset for your own gain.

them that it is the use of other peoples money that will get them wealthy over time, so they better get used to it, understand it, enjoy it, and get rich with it.

COMMON CONCERNS ABOUT INVESTMENT REAL ESTATE

Most investors won't get involved with positive real estate investment opportunities because of their fears. People are afraid of making money. They are afraid of losing money. They are afraid of making mistakes and not doing it right. Some investors are afraid of having their offers and/or financing rejected.

Fears are real and can be overwhelming. I acknowledge my fears when I invest, but I move through the fear. I stay more true to my committment to financial freedom and wealth than to my emotions that can stop me from being great.

Everyone has fear. Those who move beyond their fears are able to produce great financial wealth. I believe Teddy Roosevelt said it marveously:

> *It is not the critic who counts, not the man who points out how the strong man stumbled, or where the doer of deeds could have done them better. The credit belongs to the man who is actually in the arena; whose face is marred by dust and sweat and blood; who strives valiantly; who errs and comes short again and again; who knows the great enthusiasms, the great devotions, and spends himself in a worthy cause; who, at best, knows in the end the triumph of high achievement; and who, at worst, if he fails, at least fails while daring greatly, so that his place shall never be with those cold and timid souls who know neither victory or defeat.*

There Will Be Problems

Real estate investing can be challenging, and any investor should be prepared to handle the discomforts and unknowns that come along with it. It is not like the stock market, something you can sometimes practically ignore, yet still make money. In contrast, real estate is a more hands-on investment, not unlike owning a small business where you are its CEO.

Do not be shortsighted and expect that you will be able to manage and run your real estate portfolio from your couch or easy chair in your living room. You will need to learn about the industry and make informed decisions. As you become more sophisticated as an investor, you will be able to make more decisions through delegation, but that comes over time. I find that it's best for you to get more involved in the early phases of your real estate plan so that you understand what to look for when you delegate these tasks. This way you will better know what areas need special attention and care as well as determine your strengths and weaknesses.

There Will Be Change

Accept the fact that changes will happen. Oftentimes, investors are disappointed because they had a rosy or unrealistic expectation of what their real estate investment would be like. They want an appreciating market to continue forever. They want those good tenants to stay in their properties forever. They want the new kitchens, carpets, and lawns to stay fresh and new forever. That would be great, but that is not going to happen with investment real estate. Things deteriorate at a faster level in investment real estate because your tenants are more likely to misuse or damage your property. Humans are not as considerate of someone else's property as they are of their own. Do not be shocked by this. This should be calculated into the expenses of owning investment real estate.

Markets change, tenants change, management changes. Change is a part of long-term living. This is also true with investment real estate. Beginner investors who get into a market when it is "hot," or appreciating, may have unrealistic expectations about how real estate actually works. They do not realize that it's those who know how to manage the downside who make wealth over time. Everyone is a real estate investment genius in a hot market, but the truly wealthy are geniuses in a down market. The trick is being prepared for the changes.

There Will Be Vacancies

Investors need to remember that vacancies are very normal in rental income. Some years you will have high vacancy rates, and some years you will have low vacancy rates. Smart investors prepare for these known facts and know how to improve the impact of vacancy by making sure they are financially prepared to manage their properties when the cash flow is decreased. Do not expect that you will be able to overcome vacancies. Instead, be prepared, be proactive, and have strategies in place to minimize the time you have vacancies.

There Will Be Years When Real Estate Values Decline

Be prepared to hang in there when the market is declining and make sure you know what you should do when that happens. (I will discuss this in great detail in Chapter 13.) Then, understand what to do when the market is inclining.

There Will Be National and Local Recessions

The real estate market is affected by both local and national economics. They are linked, but not necessarily correlated. This is important to understand as an investor because both the lending practices of banks and your ability to manage your real estate investment are regulated on a national and regional level. For example, you may have a regional depression or recession due to job losses or a natural disaster while the rest of the nation is experiencing a boom market. Or it could be just the reverse. On a national level, the nation may be experiencing slow job growth. Consequently, the federal government will lower interest rates to stimulate the economy. If you are in a local area that is experiencing economic growth, the lowering of interest rates will spur your ability to acquire more real estate. The same argument holds true when the national market is experiencing tremendous growth. The government will want to decrease inflation and will make the cost of money more expensive in order to curb spending. As a result, interest rates increase, which will affect your buying power as an investor. You may be faced with riding out some of these recessions. Just don't forget that the normal real estate cycle is about ten years, and things will turn around.

OVERCOMING THE RISKS AND FEARS OF INVESTMENT REAL ESTATE

Hopefully in this chapter I've addressed some of the fears you have about investing in real estate. I can't stress enough how normal it is to be afraid. This is a big deal. But now that I've addressed those fears, it's time to jump into action with some concrete strategies to get past them.

Read Books about Investment Real Estate

Knowledge is power. The more information and support that you have about investment real estate, the more likely you are to make smart and successful decisions to get you what you want—wealth and financial freedom. I advise my clients to read at least three to four new books about investment real estate a year. You should read books that are new on the market so that you can learn about new tax laws, new methods of property management, and to keep your mind fresh on the topics of real estate. I began my real estate investing career in 1989, and I continue to go to seminars and read books so that I stay current on the field.

Join Investment Clubs

It is critical that you surround yourself with other investors who are just as committed as you are to creating profit in their real estate holdings. When you become a member of a local investment club or apartment association, you join a "network of information," increasing your odds of being informed about important and relevant issues. These contacts will prove to be invaluable to you over time.

Create Exit Strategies for Each of Your Real Estate Investments

It is important to have an exit strategy and timeline for each of the properties in your portfolio. For example, if you own an asset that you plan to sell within five to six years and the market starts a downward turn, you could consider liquidating that asset early so that you don't have to wait for another full cycle of the market to occur. Timing the length of ownership of your real estate investments is critical for good strategy and wealth-building techniques.

Know How to Create Passive Income Streams

In the exit strategy phase of the real estate plan, investors should learn the skills to safely create passive income streams that take into consideration taxation and rate of return on equity. It is imperative that proper planning and advice is given in preparation for your years of living off the fruits of your investment real estate work.

Make Adjustments Along the Way

The more flexible investors are in reading the financial reports they keep on their properties and in responding to the changing market conditions, the more profitable the investors will be. Adjustments must occur for the profit margins to stay favorable for the investor.

DON'T FORGET ABOUT YOUR VALUES WHEN YOU INVEST

Remember why you are doing this in the first place. The goal is to benefit from all of your hard work in the future, not give yourself a heart attack while doing it. Be sure to establish goals that will stretch you and keep your real estate portfolio growing, but not stress you. Apply enough personal pressure to produce your desired results, but not so much that you become overanxious or find daily living unbearable. Life is too short for that kind of stress!

Be kind to yourself as you are building your real estate portfolio. Nobody's perfect. There will be a certain amount of expected and normal error that occurs when you own investment real estate. I have not met a real estate investor who has not lost money or made a lot of big mistakes while investing—myself included. Having a tough skin is critical when investing in real estate. Tenants will be late with their rent. It's a sad fact of life. Perhaps you'll even rent to a tenant that you know you should not and learn to regret that decision. These are the normal errors of investing. Successful people have a mature relationship with failure and with success. They look and plan for success, and they understand that all successful people fail, sometimes miserably, before they make it big with their successes. Failure is only failure if you are not able to learn and grow from your mistakes.

Being an investor means brushing yourself off when you fall and getting back up to succeed over and over again. The tough keep going; the weak stop and complain that it was a tough game. Yes, real estate can be tough. But the rewards are so tremendous that if you stick it out and learn to protect yourself for these normal downturns, wealth and your dreams are within your grasp!

§§§

Find a Role Model to Follow After

I have been in the acting field for years and it is a known fact that after women turn 40, the opportunities for making a living in movies diminish dramatically. It was clear to me early in my career that I needed to create passive income to sustain the lifestyle to which I had grown accustomed, but the thought of investing in real estate was scary and a bit overwhelming. Then I remembered my wonderful sister. As a young child, I watched her buy a small home which seemed impossible for her at the time. That small house transformed the way she felt about herself and positioned her for a better way of life. She was a great role model to help me overcome my fears. I decided that I was willing to push through my hesitations to have what others had and to really take control of my life. Today, I can proudly say that I am buying over 100+ units that will produce about $30,000 per month in passive income. That small dream that started so many years ago never died.

I love real estate and I am so glad that I had the courage to invest. Now I can maintain my great lifestyle through the investments I have made. Real estate has made everything possible in my life.

— T. LIFFORD, ACTRESS AND REAL ESTATE INVESTOR

PART TWO

The Real Estate Plan

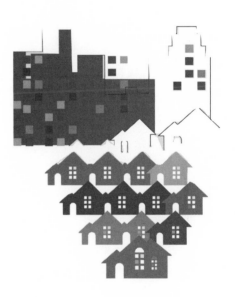

CHAPTER 4

Having a Real Budget

"Beware of little expenses; a small leak will sink a great ship."
—Benjamin Franklin

By now you're hopefully feeling confident and ready to get moving on that real estate plan. You've stared your fears straight in the face and have come out a winner. Now it's time to face something equally scary—your spending habits. Before you start investing in real estate, it's important to take a close look at the way you handle your money. The truth is, most people don't pay much attention to where their money goes. That five-day a week Starbucks habit might not seem like a big deal until you realize that you're spending almost *$1,000 a year on coffee.* And that's just the tip of the iceberg!

In this chapter, you'll take a look at your overall financial state and personal money habits. Chances are, it'll be an eye-opener. You will learn to create your own personal budget as well as a budget for each property held in your portfolio. I've also provided some worksheets that will help you calculate your net worth, prioritize any debt you have, and start figuring out some debt reduction plans. Let's get started.

CREATING YOUR PERSONAL BUDGET

When I teach my real estate plan workshop, I require all participants to fill out a personal budget worksheet before the class begins. I love watching how people react to this "homework." Some people come into the workshop with elaborate spreadsheets showcasing their numbers and how much money they are making. They sit proudly with all of their columns and rows and figures. Others come to the workshop with their forms completely blank. While I wait for the class to start, I gently encourage everyone to finish their budgets. It's incredible to see the resistance that some people have to this seemingly simple request. You'd think that I was asking them to cut off their right arms. There is something about putting your spending and savings habits down on paper that makes it *real*, and some people react negatively to this. Americans put an enormous amount of pressure on themselves to be financially responsible. Unfortunately, not everyone naturally has this gift. Don't beat yourself up over it. There is nothing wrong with not knowing how to manage your money as long as you are willing to address the problem squarely and try to resolve it competently.

Your value as a person is not related to whether you pay your bills on time, whether you spend all your income, or whether you are compulsive about how you organize and manage your money. You are more valuable than your money. Let me say that again: *You are more valuable than your money.* You can have poor money management habits and still be a great human being. The truth is, once you become familiar with how you spend your money, the easier it will be for you to make adjustments and to improve your financial situation and the quicker you will pick up these skills. You're already ten steps ahead of most Americans simply because you bought and are reading this book. You've taken a proactive stance toward improving your financial state, and for that you should be proud. Now, take the next big step, and get your budget down on paper.

I have provided an easy worksheet in Figure 4.1 that will assist you in defining the numbers that need to go into your personal budget. Figure 4.2 then allows you to determine your net worth. Take your time with this; nobody is rushing you. It is much more important that you be honest with yourself and get the numbers right. Accurate numbers are necessary for the IRS, essential for your annual review, and crucial if you are going to grow your real estate portfolio.

FIGURE 4.1: **Budget Worksheet**

Business owners and those who are self-employed should calculate personal expenses and business expenses separately. Do not combine your personal expenses with your business expenses. Those who own investment real estate should create a budget for each of the properties they own.

Monthly Income			
Active Income		**Passive Income**	
Monthly active income source A		Passive income source A	
Monthly active income source B		Passive income source B	
Monthly active income source C		Passive income source C	
Monthly active income subtotal		Monthly passive income subtotal	
Total monthly income (A+P)			

Monthly Living Expenses			
Housing		**Personal**	
Bottled water		Barber/beauty	
Association fees		Cleaners	
Domestic care		Clothing	
Improvements		Financial advice	
Insurance		Gifts	
Maintenance		Life insurance	
Mortgage or rent payment		Pocket money	
Pet care		Professional dues	
Pest service		Tax preparation	
Real estate taxes		Toiletries	
Telephone		Subtotal	
Utilities			
Yard/pool		**Installments and Payments**	
Subtotal		Alimony	
Child support		Church/charity	
Food		Credit cards	
Groceries		Credit cards	
Dining Out		Subtotal	
Subtotal			

FIGURE 4.1: **Budget Worksheet**

Monthly Living Expenses			
Health		**Entertainment**	
Disability insurance		Cable TV	
Health insurance		Hobbies	
Long-term care		Periodicals	
Doctor/dental		Recreation	
Medicines		Videos/music	
Vision		Sport/events	
Subtotal		Vacations	
		Subtotal	
Auto/Transportation			
Gas/tires		**Savings and Stock Investing**	
License		401(K)	
Insurance		Retirement plans	
Repair/maintenance		Savings accounts	
Park/wash		Mutual funds	
Loan payments		Other savings	
Subtotal		Subtotal	
Children		**Taxes**	
Allowance		Federal taxes	
Babysitter		State taxes	
Camp		FICA	
Child care		Medicare	
Education		SDI	
Subtotal		Subtotal	
Total monthly expenses			

Getting comfortable with numbers is crucial in investment real estate. Ideally, your income needs to be greater than your expenses. You will be working to create more passive income than expenses throughout your real estate plan. Creating passive income for the future is what the entire real estate plan is all about.

FIGURE 4.2: **Determining Your Net Worth**

Assets				
Cash and savings		Pension plans		
CDs, T-Bills		Collectibles		
Stocks and bonds		Personal residence		
Mutual funds		Other real estate		
Cash value life insurance		Businesses		
IRA accounts		Vehicles		
Total assets				

Liabilities				
Charge account A		Personal loans		
Charge account B		Other debt		
Charge account C		Business loans		
Auto loans		Home mortgage		
Bank loans		Other mortgages		
Student loans		Taxes owed		
Total liabilities				

Net Worth			
Subtract liabilities from assets			

Congratulations. You Now Have Your Budget Complete!

Hot Tip Creating a personal budget on paper forces you to take a good, hard look at where your money is going each month. You may not even realize how much money you actually spend. Sophisticated investors make business and personal decisions based on knowledge and information derived from the facts found in both their personal and property budgets. Setting a realistic monthly budget and sticking to it can keep you on target toward reaching your goals for wealth development and financial freedom in the future. Don't delay. Start operating from a budget today!

It is not unusual for people to be overwhelmed at first with getting their numbers down on paper. Just start the process by filling it out as best you can. If you must estimate some of the numbers in your budget, then do this, but it is important that you admit that you are not very good at being specific, and that you are currently not keeping good records. Don't worry, this sense of being overwhelmed with the numbers won't last forever. Trust me, you will improve with time. Just stay dedicated to improving, and before long you will be comfortable with knowing all of the numbers. It will happen even to you. Advanced investors who have more complicated real estate portfolios will need to hire a bookkeeper to help them with their numbers and make sure they have proper accounting procedures in place.

With your budget properly filled out, you will get some insight into your future ability to create and maintain profit from real estate holdings year after year. Figure 4.3 will help you develop these insights. Over time, the practice of paying attention to your budget will produce better profits and increase your wealth. Isn't that worth spending time on?

Now that you have completed and have reviewed your budget, you are ready to start creating wealth through real estate investing. Hopefully, you've learned something from this exercise and identified some changes you can easily make to your lifestyle. This is a huge step that you have taken. Now let's keep going. *But remember: investment real estate is a marathon, not a sprint.* It takes a long time to receive the benefits from real estate investing. You need to determine that you will be in it for the long run and endure until the end. From now on, you will be doing a budget every year. This is how you'll learn to keep your money in your own pocket, not someone else's.

Hot Tip The budget for each of your real estate properties should be reviewed at least once a year. Analyzing and evaluating your property budgets and making the necessary adjustments will boost the odds of producing ever-increasing wealth and profits. You will be able to determine which properties are managed efficiently, and which ones need more attention to increase the profits.

FIGURE 4.3: **Review of Your Budget**

1. What have you noticed about the way you spend money? _____

    _____

    Did you notice any common patterns? _____

    _____

    _____

2. What ways can you cut back on your spending? Are you being wasteful or living beyond your means? Where and how? _____

    _____

    _____

    _____

3. How can you increase your income? By working more hours? By becoming better at time manage-ment? By delegating work to less expensive personnel? By making a career move? By enhancing your education? _____

    _____

    _____

    _____

4. How can you restructure your business to give you more free time to do the things that bring you joy? _____

    _____

    _____

    _____

5. How much can you increase your income per year based on some of the ideas discussed above?

    _____

    _____

    _____

REDUCING YOUR DEBT

Chances are that through your budgeting exercise you have discovered some liabilities. Liabilities is just a fancy word for debt, something everyone has at some time or another. Debt is what makes the American economy so vibrant, but consumer debt can be a very scary and debilitating thing if not attended to correctly. Figure 4.4 is a personalized debt reduction plan that will help you identify both your current debt as well as the interest rates you are paying for that debt. You'll also create a schedule to pay off your debt within a specific time period. Be sure to include *all* liabilities, including student loans, car loans, consumer debt, personal loans, and taxes.

FIGURE 4.4: **Debt Reduction Plan**

Name of Debt	Total Amount Due	Monthly Payment	Percentage Rate (%)	Payoff Date	Payoff Plan $/Month
1.					
2.					
3.					
4.					
5.					

PRIORITIZING YOUR DEBT REDUCTION PLAN

So, how bad was it? Did all of your debt fit into the space I provided, or did you need to add lines to the chart? It would not be uncommon for many of you to need to do some clean-up work around your spending habits. Some of you might even have a great deal of consumer debt that will need to be managed before you begin your real estate investing. Please don't feel like you have to do this alone. You might consider seeking the advice of a debt relief counselor or check out the consumer debt services offered through local or government offices. These resources can be extremely helpful. Many credit counseling and debt relief services can be found by searching online.

Before you run off and pay all your debt, get good advice. Your lender may also be a good debt relief advocate for you and may be able to help you by strategically determining which debt to pay off and when. Sometimes, you can structure a real estate contract to get debt paid off when you are buying your investment real estate. Make sure you find out what simple techniques to use so you can quickly get involved with buying investment real estate and improving your financial situation.

Don't get discouraged because you have acquired the taste and skills of spending money. Look at it this way, you were a good student for the marketing companies of America. The good news is that since you already have the habit of buying and spending, all we have to do is refocus on what you are buying. Instead of spending your hard-earned cash on liabilities, it's time to start buying assets. Begin to focus that "spending habit" on some bargains in real estate so that your money starts making *you* wealthy and secures *your* future instead of lining the pockets of department stores and credit card companies.

Think of yourself as being in training. Your bad money habits won't disappear overnight, but with the right research, a positive attitude, and access to good advice, you'll be off to a great start. You won't be able to buy everything you look at (nor should you want to!). Temperance and self-control are still needed, but consider this a license to shop and find those great real estate opportunities for yourself and your family. You will be looking at a lot of real estate. If you have become good with managing your money, you will soon acquire a taste for buying investment real estate that will bring you money and wealth in the future. Now that's what I call fun shopping!

Now that you've listed your debts, it's time to prioritize them and decide which debt needs to be paid off first. Use the form in Figure 4.5 to help do this. Take a look at the interest rates of each of your debts. Are you paying more money than you should? Pay off the debt with the higher interest rates first, and if there is a small debt, pay that off right away to clear it off of your list. The key is to be realistic with your target dates for payoff and only set goals that you can achieve. As an added motivation, calculate the additional cash you will have when the debt is paid. See Figure 4.6. Once your designated debt is paid, convert these monthly payments to your investment plan or savings. In other words, instead of paying someone else, start paying yourself.

IMPLEMENTING YOUR DEBT REDUCTION PLAN

Once you have decided to get your consumer debt under control (and this is no small feat), you will need to begin implementing your debt reduction plan. There are many ways to go about this. Some investors refinance their personal residences and pay off all of their consumer debt with a second trust deed (mortgage). Other investors take a slower approach and reduce their debt on a disciplined monthly basis. You need to

FIGURE 4.5: **Debt Reduction Priorities**

Priority Number	Name of Debt	Payoff Plan $/Month	Target Date for Payoff	Cash Flow Increase/Month
1.				
2.				
3.				
4.				
5.				

FIGURE 4.6: **Review of Debt**

1. How much money (discretionary funds) will you have monthly (after paying all of your bills and planning your debt reduction) that can be utilized for wealth building? Knowing this will keep you motivated to pay off the debt. _____

   _____

   _____

2. How will you apply these discretionary funds to the real estate plan you have developed? _____

   _____

   _____

3. What are the rewards for paying off this debt? What incentives have you built into your plan, and what is going to keep you energized about your plan? _____

   _____

   _____

determine what is right for you. Once again, this is where a good lender or a debt counselor can be very useful in helping you begin to implement your plan strategically.

MANAGE YOUR REAL ESTATE PORTFOLIO LIKE A BUSINESS

As I said earlier in this book, owning investment real estate is like owning a business where you are the CEO. Actually, since each rental property is different, it's like owning several businesses. You want to create a budget for each property in your real estate portfolio. The more properties you have in your portfolio, the more important are well-kept and maintained financial records. Bookkeepers, accountants, and future buyers will want to look at how you have managed both the money in your small business and the physical property. Successful CEOs have businesses that continually produce a profit when they actively look at the bottom line and adjust income and expenses so that it runs efficiently and smoothly. Real estate is no different. Running the numbers and looking at efficiency make all the difference.

$$$

A Single Woman Wins Big with Real Estate Investing: Wendy's Story

Wendy came to one of my workshops believing there was little she could do for herself in real estate investing. As a young single mother with a couple of small children, she could barely make ends meet, but she desperately wanted to be prepared for her kids' college expenses and for her retirement (which was some day far off in the distant future). She had seen some of her friends buy and sell real estate and thought it looked like fun, not to mention profitable. She came to my workshop because her best friend told her she had a natural talent for understanding numbers. Her friend was right. Wendy arrived at the workshop with her budget completely filled out, though she was a bit nervous and scared about how to make this dream of owning real estate a reality for her. She was shy and reluctant about her budget because she did not have much money in assets and very little extra to spend. What she did have, however, was hope and a solid belief in herself. She was also willing to be uncomfortable in the beginning phases of her quest to find a better way to live. She had a better vision of what was possible than of what could go wrong or not work for her. She moved ahead despite her fears and anxieties.

After being in the class and going over her budget, Wendy started to see real estate as the small business that it is. This was familiar territory for her. Throughout her childhood, Wendy's parents had

$$$

grown a small grocery business into a two-, three-, and eventually five-store grocery chain in their city. She remembered how consistently her parents had fussed over the business budgets every month and how that discipline had eventually paid off for them. Now happily retired, her parents' grocery business is running smoothly and profitably through a good management team that was put into place through their diligent work and preparation.

Wendy was proud of her parents. She saw the work and commitment they had, but never thought she would be able to duplicate their success without a partner or any idea of what business to grow. Plus, she remembered the long hours they worked and the time the family sacrificed to build the business and was hoping to avoid that result. Suddenly, Wendy realized that she had found the small business she was looking for—real estate investing.

Wendy decided to be bold and ask people she knew if they would be her business partners in her first real estate transaction. She summoned the courage to ask her parents if they wanted to invest with her. Wendy discovered she already had a lot more than she had ever realized when she first came to the workshop. She had a vision, a dream, some great role models, and determination to make her small business work for her. She was no longer afraid of the little amount of money she had, realizing that most people start out with very little. Like most winners, Wendy had learned that when you are responsible with a little, a lot will come to you over time.

THE PSYCHOLOGY OF REAL ESTATE

This next section is for those of you who may want to look a bit deeper into some of the reasons why you spend money the way you do. I encourage you to explore this side of yourself; however, I realize it is not for everyone. If you have no interest in psychology and the study of human behavior, feel free to pass this section up and move on to the next chapter. I'll meet you there.

Imprinting and Impressions about Money and Money Management

All people grow up in the context of a family or a group of people. These people influence you in many ways. Using Figure 4.7, take the time to identify the beliefs you have formulated about money and the way you relate to money as defined by the people in your past. Have fun answering these questions. See if you discover something new about yourself that you did not know before.

FIGURE 4.7: **Your Family's Sense of Money**

1. What line of work are your parents in? _____

    _____

2. What did your father or father figure tell you about money? Did he tell you how to save it or how to invest it? _____

    _____

3. What did your mother or mother figure tell you about money? Did she tell you how to save it or how to invest it? _____

    _____

4. What significant people in your life have done really well financially? _____

    _____

5. What did they do that you admired? _____

    _____

6. How have you modeled your life after them? _____

    _____

7. Who in your past handles money the way you do? _____

    _____

8. What significant people in your life have been poor money managers? _____

    _____

9. What did they do that you didn't like or that didn't work? _____

    _____

10. What actions have you purposefully avoided after watching their bad decisions and experiences?

    _____

    _____

FIGURE 4.7: **Your Family's Sense of Money**

---

11. What have you been told about investing in real estate? _____

_____

_____

12. What bad experiences have you had or heard about that impact your ability to invest in real
estate? _____

_____

_____

13. What keeps you from using real estate as an investment tool in your overall financial plan? ____

_____

_____

14. What personal successes can you use as a foundation for healthy financial planning and growth?

_____

_____

Your Beliefs About Money

Your interaction with money is not static. It changes throughout your life. Figure 4.8 is designed to help you define the messages and beliefs you established about money when you were a child, young adult, middle-aged adult, and mature adult. Its purpose is to assist you in understanding what you learned and how you reacted to money *through-out* life.

I hope you have learned a lot about yourself in this chapter. If you liked the psychology exercises you just completed, you're sure to love Appendix D, The Psychology of Investing. Check it out for more fun ways to learn about you and your investment style. From the way you spend your money to the reasons you spend like you do, there are lots of factors to consider where money is concerned. With the insight you've gained and a concrete budget in hand, you are now ready to start finding the money you need to invest. In the next chapter, I'll introduce you to some places to begin looking for that money. You actually have more options than you might think.

FIGURE 4.8: **Your Changing Attitudes Toward Money**

	Child (4–14)	Young Adult (15–25)	Middle Adult (26–50)	Mature Adult (51–80+)
What was your family's financial position in your community during these phases of life?				
How did your family handle money matters? Were they silent, vocal, calm, or hysterical?				
What were you taught about money and investing? Who was actively involved in teaching you?				
What were your experiences with investments? When did you begin to invest personally?				
What is your overall experience and comfort with money and money management?				

Notice that how your family reacted and what they said about money changes over time. Beliefs around money does change. What happened in your past does not have to dictate what happens in the future. You can be a changing force in your own financial future.

$$

Making Real Estate Investing My Exciting New Career

I have been a sales representative for years in the corporate world. I've been lucky in that I've done well in my career and have lived a good life. However, after many years in the corporate setting, I wanted to strike out and be in charge of my destiny, especially my own schedule. I was able to finally take this plunge because my husband and I had enough passive income from our real estate investments to explore this new avenue for my life. I am now currently managing and growing my family's real estate fortunes and looking at properties around the country that fit perfectly into our real estate portfolio. The freedom I have today from our real estate investments provides my husband and me with a lifestyle filled with choices that we enjoy and value.

It all started when my husband and I both had average incomes and only about $50,000 to invest. We decided that we were going to take the risk no matter how frightened we were. We knew we would have to stay consistent and keep at it, regardless of the results. In less than seven years, we accumulated over $3.5 million in equity. Now we live near the beach in Southern California. We could not be happier with how everything has turned out for us. I tell everyone that if we could invest in real estate with our income, then anyone can do it. You just have to budget for it and make it happen for yourself.

I've learned how not only to grow our portfolio but also how to keep and sustain it so we can have a safe and secure financial future. I can't stress enough how important it is to take the time to figure out your own personal budget, reduce your debts, and then start investing. It doesn't matter how little money you have; you can *still* invest in real estate.

—CLAUDIA HANSON, SOFTWARE SALES AND ENTREPRENEUR

Where to Get Real Investment Money

"Don't marry for money, you can borrow it cheaper."
—Scottish Proverb

I love the scene in the film *Jerry Maguire* where Cuba Gooding, Jr., shouts to Tom Cruise, "Show me the money!" Of course, he was talking about salary, but the same words of wisdom can easily be applied to real estate. As you work your way through your real estate plan, you'll regularly be required to make decisions about how much money you will be investing or spending. But before you can decide how much to invest, you need a plan in place for where you can *get* the money. Fortunately, you have several options.

MONEY FROM REFINANCING

The most common way new investors begin their real estate plans is by choosing to refinance their homes and use that money to fund their real estate ventures. This usually seems like an exciting concept until they realize that refinancing typically increases the monthly expenses (i.e., the mortgage) on their homes. Most investors like the idea of making money from the equity they have built up in their homes, but they do not want to have to change their lifestyles to do it. They begin to second-guess their initial enthusiasm. Hang on a second, they think. Wasn't the point of all of this to *increase* my lifestyle? Sadly, there is no such thing as a free ride. If you remember to think in the long-term, you'll realize that in order to have the benefits of real estate investing, you need the discipline to make it work.

I wish I could promise you fabulous rewards without some inconvenience or risk, but I have not seen anyone become wealthy this way. Don't be tempted by the "get rich quick" and "create great wealth while sitting on the couch" schemes of late night TV. They are just a phantom fantasy for investors. Despite the claims of these techniques, getting rich quick almost always requires certain levels of risk. Real estate investing is not risk free as some may promote. Sure, you *might* get rich quick. But you could just as easily lose the money you acquired. I want to help you avoid that unfavorable position.

OK, so let's assume that you've decided to refinance your home or an investment property you've already purchased in order to buy a new property. How do you decide how much money to pull out of a refinance? A common mistake investors make is to pick a random number out of thin air based on what makes them feel comfortable with the increase in monthly payments. While I agree that you should feel comfortable with your payments, there should be some method to your madness. Rash decisions without strategy can be very costly. The bottom line is, unless you know how much money to take out to get your plan started, you may spend needless extra money refinancing several times when one refinance will do the job.

> **Hot Tip**
>
> The historical trends of real estate have shown that single-family residences and condominiums have typically dropped no more than 20 to 30 percent in any declining real estate market. So, if you refinance to 80 or 70 percent, you are sure to keep your property liquid (that means you will be able to sell the property without having to come up with money at the closing). This is beneficial should any unforeseen situations occur in your life such as suddenly needing to sell your home because of a job transfer, divorce, unplanned childbirth, or death.

I usually advise my clients to start by refinancing their primary residences to about 80 percent loan to value (LTV). That means that your loan is 80 percent of the value of

> **Hot Tip**
>
> More often than not, investors do not need to use all the equity out of their homes for reinvestment purposes. Sometimes all they may need to pull out is $50,000 to $300,000 from a refinance, depending on the amount of net equity they are targeting.

your property. You may choose to refinance for less if you are looking to acquire less money to invest or are unable to incur the additional monthly expenses from the refinance. I like to use the 80 percent rule because that typically secures the best possible financing rates as well as keeps the real estate somewhat liquid so that you can sell in all market conditions.

Most investors like to keep their primary residences underleveraged once they have begun to establish their real estate investment portfolios. Listening to your sense of security and peace is important. For many investors, the safety and comfort of a lower monthly home mortgage payment allows them to sleep better at night because they know they won't lose their homes in a bad real estate market. I've found that as long as safety and security is provided for their primary residences, most people are willing to leverage their investment real estate to greater degrees.

Investors who are reluctant to pull money out of their primary residences for fear of losing their money or creating an unstable situation for themselves often fail to look at what will happen to them if they *don't* use some of this equity for future planning. By keeping a lot of your equity in your home and neglecting to transfer it around to secure other investments, you are not using your money wisely. As a result, you miss out on some of the tax benefits available only to investment real estate. In the end, your refinances are the tools used to guide your investment decisions to produce the returns you planned. In Figure 5.1, you'll get a chance to calculate your own refinancing potential for each of your properties.

LENDER MONEY

As you can see in Figure 5.1, refinancing a property can be an excellent way to make cash available for real estate investing. Most people use lenders and bank financing to secure investment real estate. Some investors will need to have 100 percent bank financing for the first several transactions or until there has been some equity built up with which to reinvest. There is nothing wrong with doing this if this is the only option available to you. Everybody's got to get started somehow. Unfortunately, the downside of having no equity is that you are often forced to pay higher rates for your loan as well as experience negative cash flows on your investment properties. This often means you will need to contribute money from your job or savings to sustain these highly leveraged investments.

FIGURE 5.1: **Refinancing Your Property**

Type of Asset	A. Current Estimated Property Value	B. Loan Amount(s) 1st Title Deed 2nd Title Deed	C. Interest Rate on Each Loan	D. Current Equity A − B = D	E. Refinance Potential with 70 or 80% LTV A x 80% = (E)	F. Money from Refinance to Reinvest in Real Estate E − B = F
Example Personal residence	$600,000	1st TD = $225,000 2nd TD = $25,000 Total = $250,000	1st TD = 5.75% 2nd TD = 6.25%	$350K	80% = $480,000 75% = $450,000 70% = $420,000	80% refi. = $230,000 75% refi. = $200,000 70% refi. = $170,000
Personal residence	$	1st = $: 2nd = $: Total = $	1st = _____% 2nd = _____%	$	80% = $ 75% = $ 70% = $	80% refi. = $ 75% refi. = $ 70% refi. = $
Investment property (1)	$	1st = $: 2nd = $: Total = $	1st = _____% 2nd = _____%	$	80% = $ 75% = $ 70% = $	80% refi. = $ 75% refi. = $ 70% refi. = $
Investment property (2)	$	1st = $: 2nd = $: Total = $	1st = _____% 2nd = _____%	$	80% = $ 75% = $ 70% = $	80% refi. = $ 75% refi. = $ 70% refi. = $
Investment property (3)	$	1st = $: 2nd = $: Total = $	1st = _____% 2nd = _____%	$	80% = $ 75% = $ 70% = $	80% refi. = $ 75% refi. = $ 70% refi. = $
Investment property (4)	$	1st = $: 2nd = $: Total = $	1st = _____% 2nd = _____%	$	80% = $ 75% = $ 70% = $	80% refi. = $ 75% refi. = $ 70% refi. = $
Investment property (5)	$	1st = $: 2nd = $: Total = $	1st = _____% 2nd = _____%	$	80% = $ 75% = $ 70% = $	80% refi. = $ 75% refi. = $ 70% refi. = $
Investment property (6)	$	1st = $: 2nd = $: Total = $	1st = _____% 2nd = _____%	$	80% = $ 75% = $ 70% = $	80% refi. = $ 75% refi. = $ 70% refi. = $
Subtotals	$			$	80% = $ 75% = $ 70% = $	80% refi. = $ 75% refi. = $ 70% refi. = $

Don't skip this page. It is critical you use it over and over. This page shows the investor how to strategically get money out of their real estate through refinancing.

Zero-down financing can and will work for both beginner and sophisticated investors. Just make sure that you are aware of what can happen when the real estate market tightens up and you face increased vacancy rates and decreased rental rates. Otherwise, you may be unprepared for the increased negative cash flows when the real estate market takes a downward turn.

Take this example one step further. In addition to having no property to leverage and no equity, let's say that you've got bad credit, too. I'll admit, the situation is not ideal, but it's not impossible. In this case, you may need to go to a hard money lender to obtain financing.

Just remember that because of your bad credit, you will be a credit risk, and any lender will want to be compensated for taking a risk on you. This means that you will not be able to get the best rates. Accept this and move on. Sometimes, this is the cost of doing business.

> **DEFINITION**
>
> A *hard money lender* is a person or institution that will loan you money with no credit and no collateral. Because they understand that you are a higher credit risk and need their assistance, they will usually charge you high interest rates and high points. This might be the only way you will be able to get started.

INHERITED MONEY

Everybody likes it when they suddenly come into some unexpected money. Over the next 20 years, Americans will be experiencing the greatest intergenerational transfer of wealth that has ever occurred. Some reports indicate that over $13 trillion will be transferred between generations. It will be transferred from the baby boomer generation to the Generation Xers who may or may not be prepared to receive this inherited windfall. It is not uncommon for me to work with clients who have inherited substantial wealth from their parents or relatives who have been frugal and dedicated investors throughout the years. This newly acquired money sometimes falls into the hands of adult children who have not been taught the fundamentals of financial management and investment theory. They are often excited about their new wealth, but are also frightened and confused about what to do with it.

It is critical for people who know they will be inheriting wealth to get sufficient training and guidance so they can learn to sustain, maintain, and grow their money. Inherited money can often be a down payment on a new investment property as well as help to secure a more favorable interest rate loan. It is such a shame when people inherit great amounts of wealth and whittle it away due to ignorance, by refusing to pay for good financial advice, or by not knowing how to protect the money they have just inherited.

Getting good financial advice for these windfalls is worth every dollar you pay for it. It is becoming more common for people to begin planning their investment strategies before they receive the money, based on the idea that they will be getting a large sum of money in the near future. Also sometimes their families make the yearly tax-free gift contributions allowed by the IRS. This preplanning makes all the difference in the world for long-term wealth development. Investors who know they will be inheriting money and know little to nothing about investment real estate do themselves a huge financial favor by going to workshops on the subject and reading books about investment strategies.

FAMILY MONEY

It is not unusual for families to invest together. Oftentimes, a member of the older generation who has been working with money and investments for years will be willing to go into partnerships with younger family members. That is what happened with me. If it weren't for my mother Carol's and grandmother Gracey's generosity, I may not have ever begun investing in real estate. A benefit of multigenerational investing is the opportunity for the younger generation to learn about financial and money management from those who have already made mistakes and learned from them.

Family investment ventures generally entail the older generation funding the down payment and taking a percentage of the equity and the younger family member finding the investment opportunity and then living in or managing the property. The younger family member is usually the working partner and is responsible for making most, if not all, of the monthly payments and decisions on the investment. The older family member, who contributed the down payment, may want the tax benefits of depreciation or need a place to invest her money. As you can see, investing this way can benefit both parties.

When approaching family members for down payment contributions, you must make sure that you sign legal papers for the partnership agreement. Just because you are "family" is no reason not to treat this like the business arrangement that it is. They say that blood is thicker than water, but it is amazing how the rules suddenly change when money is involved. If your investment suddenly goes downhill, you don't want to create family tension just because you did not have the terms of your agreement clearly defined in writing. These legal documents are essential and are the beginning steps to learning how to be a sophisticated investor. Eventually, because you have managed to grow your money wisely over time, you will be the financing partner, and beginner investors will be looking to you to provide the down payment. You will need to learn these fundamental steps no matter what phase of real estate investing you are in.

CONVERTING 401K MONEY

Given the state of the economy, more and more investors have recently become frustrated with the returns they receive on their stock portfolios and want to convert their retirement holdings into real estate. Fortunately, the federal government and the IRS have begun changing their rules about investors using 401K money for this purpose. It is not a simple and easy process, however, so you should be sure that you get good professional advice before you liquidate or transfer 401K funds into a real estate transaction. Most importantly, it is critical that you follow the many specific regulations and rules in order to fulfill the specific IRS codes of using 401K money. If you do it incorrectly, you will be paying some stiff IRS penalties for taking the proceeds out of a 401K program before it is mature.

Before you make any moves, be sure that you discuss this conversion with a competent accountant. But be aware, many accountants are still telling their clients that this is not allowed by the IRS. *This is incorrect information.* If your accountant continues to refuse to help you with this, go to another accountant. These kinds of transactions are being performed both safely and legally.

PARTNERSHIP MONEY

So, what happens if you have no saved money of your own (401K or otherwise), own no real estate, have bad credit, and don't have any family members with money? Is there still hope? Heck, yes! The answer can be found in one simple word: partnerships. When searching out a partner, beginner investors should look for people who have the assets and skills they are lacking. This could be as simple as extra cash to invest or as desirable as good credit. In the partnership, the beginner investor will be the working partner in the deal. This is not much different than the situation discussed in the family money section. The only real difference is that these partnerships are usually done with someone who is not related to you. The downside to this kind of arrangement is that your partner's only vested interest is financial. No amount of sad puppy dog eyes or pathetic excuses will work here. These investors want to be paid handsomely for their willingness to risk their money with you because you have nothing tangible (money or credit) in the deal.

To make this kind of arrangement work, you will need to provide your partner with good documentation and with sound real estate deals. I would suggest that you target discounted properties. This will give you a buffer to account for market adjustments and increase your odds of making this first investment a success for you. This is not the time to be stingy or selfish. Make sure that you create a good deal for these partners who are willing to get you started in the game of real estate investing. These investors have proven themselves in the past; that is why they have money to give to you. You are coming to them with nothing but a dream, a willingness to invest, and hopefully good investment properties for them to partner with you.

Ideally, partnerships should only be a stepping stone to investing on your own. Once you have enough money to invest on your own, start getting out of your partnerships. As a rule of thumb, it is always better to invest on your own than to be troubled with a partnership. Investors usually get involved in partnerships when they can not do the deal on their own or if they are taking on a new level of sophistication that they don't want to accomplish on their own. There is nothing wrong with this, and you almost always learn something new about investing when you have a partner. Just be aware that partnerships can be laden with troubles because you are essentially starting a business with another person who has different investment strategies, intentions, and philosophies. Oftentimes, one partner will want to sell the investment whereas the other wants to keep it, and they'll subsequently be forced to dissolve the partnership or battle it out. It is hard to maintain long-term real estate partnerships without tensions of one sort or another occurring. This is why it is critical to know who your partners are before you get involved with them and make sure you have exit strategies clearly defined in the partnership agreements. I'll talk more about partnerships in Chapter 14.

DEFINING YOUR ASSETS

Earlier in the chapter, I discussed getting money from many different areas. Now it is time to define what other assets you may have that can also be used for investing in real estate. The worksheet in Figure 5.2 will make that easier.

Once you've listed your assets, you are finally ready to decide which money you will use and when. The worksheet in Figure 5.3 walks you through this process. When filling in this worksheet, make sure you put a month and year to invest the money and an amount to invest. This is really important to getting you in to action.

• • •

Well done! Now that you have defined where to get the money to invest and how much you want to use, you can start acquiring or freeing up that money so that you can reinvest it. The trick though is to make sure you're reinvesting it wisely. Smart investments lead to smart results. In the next chapter, I'll show you the four key components you need to consider in order to make the best (and most profitable!) real estate decisions.

FIGURE 5.2: **What Other Assets Do You Have to Use?**

Type of Asset	Value of Asset	Currently Available?	How Much Will You Use?
Business ventures	$	❏ Yes ❏ No	$
Cash reserves	$	❏ Yes ❏ No	$
Family assets	$	❏ Yes ❏ No	$
Mutual funds	$	❏ Yes ❏ No	$
Stocks	$	❏ Yes ❏ No	$
Bonds & CDs	$	❏ Yes ❏ No	$
Retirement plan (401K)	$	❏ Yes ❏ No	$
Insurance buildup	$	❏ Yes ❏ No	$
Subtotals	$		$

FIGURE 5.3: **The Money You'll Use for Investing**

Make a committment and decision now! State how much money you are going to use.

Type of Asset* (Mortgage, Refinance, Stocks, 401K, Cash, etc.)	Current Value of the Asset	Amount Used for Investing	When to Invest Month and Year**
	$	$	
	$	$	
	$	$	
Grand total	$	$	

* Get the money you committed from Figure 5.1 on page 58.

** Make sure you fill in this form and put a date on it to get into action.

$$

From Rags to Riches

I thought my situation was impossible. I didn't have a lot of education, I barely made enough money to pay the bills, I had an IRS tax lien, and I couldn't see myself out of the hole I was in. Yet deep down inside there was a voice that kept telling me not to give up, to ask for help, to believe, and to keep moving forward. More than anything, I wanted a home of my own and financial security for my family. I decided that I wasn't going to give up until I found hope and a way to own a house.

I realized that I needed to shift my thinking from *if* I buy a home to *how* to buy a home. I got the name of a good lender and discovered some loan programs where I did not have to have a lot of money for the down payment to get started. We structured the purchase contract so that the seller paid most of the closing costs, and I scraped together the down payment with the help of family and friends. Amazingly, within 30 days I was sitting in "my" new living room astonished that I was actually a homeowner at last. My dreams were finally fulfilled. I had thought it was out of reach for me, but in reality it was right there all along.

The excitement and benefits of homeowner ship did not stop with the thrill of owning my own home; it came throughout the next several years with my ability to pull equity out of the house through refinancing several times. We have put my husband through college, helped my brother out in a bad financial situation, and are now having fun expanding our investment portfolio through buying more properties. I've learned how to safely and strategically leverage so that I can keep and sustain the property in all circumstances. It is amazing that a little while ago I was wondering how to pay all of my bills and now I know how to make fortunes for the future.

The next learning curve I have taken on is learning how to pass this knowledge along to my children. My kids are excited by what they have seen, and we are beginning to invest as a family. Now that is really exciting and worthwhile for me. I now know that dreams are possible; I just needed to swing out beyond my comfort zone and trust myself.

—PATTY B., SENIOR SALES MANAGER

Four Real Benefits to Smart Investing

"All of our dreams can come true if we have the courage to pursue them."
—Walt Disney

I t's fair to say that people who get involved with investment real estate want to achieve the biggest bang for their bucks or, in more technical terms, a large return on their investments. That's the whole point of your real estate plan, after all. But how do you know whether or not you are investing your money wisely? To determine this, there are four key components you need to consider: cash flow, appreciation, loan reduction, and tax benefits. These four factors, when combined, form the rate of return on equity (ROE) and help determine the value of any property you might be buying or evaluate property you already have in your real estate portfolio.

Many investors are tempted to look at only one or two factors (usually cash flow and appreciation) and try to establish the true value of their property based on limited information from only these two items. To me, that's like trying to bake a cake, leaving out some of the ingredients, and then wondering why it doesn't look or taste right. Leaving an ingredient out of a cake will not give you the results you desire, and investment real estate works the same way. Consider the four factors, the ingredients, you need in your recipe for real estate success, and take all of them into account when you evaluate real estate.

Decisions on whether to buy a property, hold onto it, or sell it should be based on the overall rate of return on equity, so it is critical that you know how to accurately calculate it. Throughout this chapter, I will be using a property located at 1234 Sunshine Lane as my example. In this example, you'll learn how to calculate the overall rate of return on equity for the time that you are purchasing your investment property. The example will include all four benefits of owning investment real estate: (cash flow, appreciation, loan reduction, and tax benefits. But before you attempt the math, it's important to know what I'm talking about, so come with me to 1234 Sunshine Lane:

Property address:	1234 Sunshine Lane
Purchase price:	$350,000
Down payment (20% of purchase price)	$70,000
Loan amount (7% @ 30 years):	$280,000
Number of units:	Two: A duplex
Unit description:	One: 3-bedroom/1-bath
	One: 2-bedroom/1-bath
Gross scheduled income (GSI): monthly $2,900	$34,800 per year
Expenses 20% (of GSI): monthly $580	$6,906 per year
Vacancy rate 5% (of GSI): monthly $145	$1,740 per year
Loan payments	
(principal and interest): monthly $1,863	$22,354 per year

Now that you've seen the property, it's time to learn how to calculate the value of the real estate using methods of evaluation that will help you determine the real value. As I said, it's important to use all four factors (appreciation, cash flow, loan reduction and tax benefits), and to combine them to calculate the overall rate of return on equity. Decisions on whether to buy a property, hold onto it, or sell it should be based on the rate of ROE, so it is critical that you know how to determine it. The examples that follow demonstrate how to calculate the overall rate of ROE for the first year of ownership.

THE POWER OF CASH FLOW

Cash flow is the income you've generated from your rental property after the expenses for holding the property and management fees have been taken out. Cash flow is calculated by using a simple formula:

Gross scheduled income − Operating expenses − Loan payments = Expected annual cash flow

Your gross scheduled income is the income you expect to collect for the year based on the rental rates for all of the units in the property. From this, you subtract your operating expenses—all of the expenses required to maintain the property. You can use the acronym TUMMI, which stands for Taxes, Utilities, Maintenance, Management, and Insurance, to help you remember. There will be other fees that don't fit with this acronym very well such as homeowner fees, vacancy rates, and reserves that need to be included, but this acronym is a place to start. Finally, you subtract the loan payments, which includes the principal and interest payments on the loan. What's left after making all the payments, if anything, is your expected cash flow.

In this example, determine the annual cash flow as follows:

Gross scheduled income	$34,800
Less annual operating expenses (TUMMI + Vacancy rates)	−$8,700
Less annual loan payments	−$22,354
Expected annual cash flow	$3,746

As you can see, the expected annual cash flow for this property is $3,746. You will next want to determine the rate of ROE, or how valuable it is as it relates to the amount of equity you have in the property. To do this, the amount of expected annual cash flow is divided by the amount of equity in the property.

Note: when you are first deciding whether to purchase a property, the equity you have will be the down payment. Once you've purchased the property, and in future years of ownership, you should use all of the accumulated equity in the property for determining its cash flow benefits. Equity is calculated by taking the current estimated value of the property and subtracting all of the equity built up for the property, such as cash flow appreciation, loan reduction, and tax benefits each year.

CASH FLOW RATE OF RETURN AT TIME OF PURCHASE

$$\frac{\text{Annual cash flow}}{\text{Amount of down payment}} = \text{\% rate of return for cash flow at time of purchase}$$

CASH FLOW RATE OF RETURN EVERY YEAR AFTER FIRST YEAR

$$\frac{\text{Annual cash flow}}{\text{Amount of all equity in property}} = \text{\% rate of return for cash flow after first year}$$

In this example, the rate of return on cash flow at time of purchase is:

$$\frac{\text{Annual cash flow}}{\text{Down payment (purchase calculation only)}} = \frac{\$3,746}{\$70,000} = 5.35\%$$

The rate of return on equity for cash flow, at time of purchase, is 5.4 percent (rounded up) using estimated income and expense numbers. It's important to note that there is no specific amount that you want for each of the four components. You only need to look at the *overall* rate of ROE. Each individual part will contribute to the overall ROE. In each of these examples, you will estimate the property's income and expenses for the first year; for the following years, you will use the actual numbers based on the income and expenses generated on the property. The numbers you use as estimates should be conservative and based on information obtained from the seller, agents, and others during the purchase period.

> **Hot Tip**
>
> What if I told you that sometimes your greatest investment opportunities might be properties that have a negative cash flow in the beginning of your real estate plan? This does not mean that I am promoting going out and filling up your real estate portfolio with all negative cash flow properties. You would not last long as an investor with that scenario! But sometimes you may find great properties that initially have negative cash flow. Be prepared to investigate these possibilities to see if they can make you millions in the long run. Be smart, and be prepared!

SAYING NO TO CASH FLOW IN THE EARLY PHASES OF THE REAL ESTATE PLAN

There will be times in your investment career when you are presented with real estate opportunities that have a negative cash flow. Do not throw all of these deals away just because they do not have positive cash flow initially. They may not be as bad as they appear. Remember: your wealth development is not all about appreciation and cash flow; you must run your numbers and calculate the overall rate of ROE. You can only determine if a deal is a good one when you look at all four factors.

When you evaluate a property from this vantage point, you may be pleasantly surprised when that ugly duckling property with a negative cash flow becomes a beautiful swan and one of your greatest assets from a rate of return standpoint. Sometimes, you might have a small negative cash flow, but the overall rate of return may be very inviting. It might even get better when you investigate it a bit further and discover that the rents are undervalued (and so you can raise the rent to increase monthly income), the property can be fixed up, and it adds to your diversified portfolio. Or perhaps you may find that you want to keep the property in a hot or appreciating market even when it has a monthly negative cash flow because the gains in appreciation far outsurpass your monthly negative cash outlay. Don't be foolish and throw away all of those negative cash flow properties until you dig a little deeper and find out how they really can perform for you and your goals within a diversified real estate portfolio.

It's worth noting that it is considered normal for investors in other financial markets to put money into their investments on a monthly or annual basis. Lots of people have money automatically withdrawn from their paychecks or checking accounts to be deposited in their 401Ks, pension funds, matching funds, or other investment avenues. Isn't that the same thing as having a negative cash flow on your investments? And strangely enough, most people feel excited about having this option. They understand that they have to put money away each month to create financial stability and freedom for their futures. It's time to fix the misconception that buying or holding onto a real estate investment with a negative cash flow is a bad idea when the same concept is esteemed and revered in other investment arenas.

> **Hot Tip**
>
> In the early phases of your real estate plan, don't use the cash flow or passive income from your real estate investments if you don't need to. It is better to keep your properties leveraged, which diminishes the monthly cash flow so that you can produce higher rates of return on your investments. If you are getting a lot of positive cash flow in the beginning of your real estate portfolio, you may not be using your money or your leverage very wisely. Your money may be lazy and not working hard enough for you. Live within your means—live off your active income until your real estate portfolio is better established.

If you intend to purchase a negative cash flow property, it is important to consider the sustainability of making financial contributions to that property. Ask yourself: How long can I afford the negative cash flow, and what methods or techniques can I use that will protect me when I can't contribute to the monthly negative cash flow situation? Now you might ask, how do I make payments on a negative cash flow property if I have no disposable income? Good question. Not all investors can buy negative cash flow properties. You may need to buy some properties that have a positive cash flow to help sustain those that are not producing an income yet, and you may need to look at your different loan programs that are designed to keep monthly payments low. There are ways to help alleviate the hit every month. Just be open to looking at it from a different vantage point.

Some properties are actually better performers overall and may be slightly negative, but beginner investors will not even look at the opportunity because of the fear of negative cash flow and the belief that all real estate should have cash flow. Please eliminate that concept. Real estate is like any other investment vehicle. You need to put money in to get money out, and time is your greatest asset for creating long-term sustainable wealth.

THE POWER OF APPRECIATION

Appreciation, or how much your property increases in value over time, is one of the most powerful tools for wealth building. It helps your equity *grow* every year, and when you multiply this by 10 to 20 years, the incredible power of compound interest is brought into play. Let me assure you, compound interest will become your new best friend. With compound interest, the growth from your investment works together with your original down payment to continually create more equity. As a result, your money grows at an exponential rate.

Appreciation rates vary each year and depend on the location of the property. Some years there will be declining rates of appreciation or no appreciation growth at all. However, over the long haul (remember: You're investing for the long-term), the increase in value through appreciation is where you'll get those exponential rates of ROE. Appreciation produces amazing growth rates that can't be found in many other investments because of the ability to use leverage (that is, using other peoples' money).

To determine the appreciation rate of return of a property at the time of purchase, use this formula:

APPRECIATION RATE OF RETURN AT TIME OF PURCHASE

$$\frac{\text{Amount of appreciation rate expected (using conservative estimations)}}{\text{Amount of down payment}}$$

APPRECIATION RATE OF RETURN EVERY YEAR AFTER THE FIRST YEAR

$$\frac{\text{Amount of appreciation rate expected (actual rates)}}{\text{Amount of all equity}}$$

The Appreciation Rate of Return (first year only) for our example at 1234 Sunshine Lane is:

$$\frac{\text{Property appreciation (2\% of \$350,000)}}{\text{Down payment}} = \frac{\$7,000}{\$70,000} = 10\%$$

For the purpose of this example, say that over the next five years the appreciation rate is consistently 2 percent. (This rate is used to show how appreciation works, but appreciation rates usually fluctuate each year.) Because the property is valued at $350,000 when you first buy it, the appreciation for the next five years will be:

Year 1: **$350,000 x 2% appreciation = $7,000 in equity = $357,000 value**

Year 2: **$357,000 x 2% appreciation = $7,140 in equity = $364,140 value**

Year 3: **$364,140 x 2% appreciation = $7,283 in equity = $371,423 value**

Year 4: **$371,423 x 2% appreciation = $7,428 in equity = $378,851 value**

Year 5: **$378,851 x 2% appreciation = $7,577 in equity = $386,428 value**

Notice that the appreciation gained each year is automatically rolled into the previous year's property value. Then, the following year's property value is calculated based on the new increased value. Over a five-year period, you can see how compounded appreciation can be very powerful and can make investors wealthy fairly quickly. This investor gained over $36,428 in equity over this five-year period.

I chose to use 2 percent, a conservative appreciation rate, which is below the national average of 7.5 percent per year appreciation when calculated over a ten-year period. However, in most central states across the country, the appreciation rate is around 3 to 5 percent per year (over a ten year period) when accompanied by a healthy stable economy. Other states, such as the coastal regions and regions with warmer climates, have much higher appreciation rates, sometimes into the double digits. Even knowing these high appreciation rates along the coast and in warmer regions, I still recommend that investors use conservative numbers of 2 to 4 percent when calculating the expected performance for the coming year. This more conservative method of calculation demonstrates how appreciation can be extremely powerful, even when conservatively used. It is also important to use conservative appreciation rates so that the overall ROE is statistically significant. When investors use appreciation rates that are high and too aggressive, they set themselves up for unrealistic expectations of how their property "should" perform.

The benefits of appreciation are so powerful that if higher numbers are used, investors will have too high expectations of how their real estate portfolios will perform. These investors tend to get disappointed when real estate goes through its normal cycles of real estate value declines. Your best results come when you can keep your expectations

WARNING

Do not expect to use double digit appreciation when calculating the ROE. You must account for the cycles of real estate, when appreciation is not in your favor. Therefore, 2 to 4 percent appreciation rates are conservative and stable for analysis when making assumptions about how the market is going to perform.

Because the national average for appreciation is 7.5 percent per year when looking over a ten year period, using 2 to 4 percent appreciation rates are safe and conservative numbers with which to work. It is more important to use conservative numbers that are more likely to work than aggressive numbers that are sure to disappoint the investor.

of appreciation realistic so that you can manage the years when real estate does not perform as well as you would like.

Can you now see how investing in real estate can truly make you wealthy? And we're only half way through our benefits! You can expect to enjoy rates of return between 15 percent and 30 percent each year when using the four components of real estate return, so let's move on to the benefits of the other real estate returns.

THE POWER OF LOAN REDUCTION

The third benefit of real estate investing is the loan reduction. The power of loan reduction occurs as the loan matures and larger portions of the principal are paid down each month. Loans are amortized (paid off over a period of time) by having a larger portion of the interest paid in the early years. Banks benefit when they lend money by getting their rewards in the early phases of the loan process. The majority of the principal gets paid down in the later years of the loan. As you pay down your loan, you build up your equity. In simpler terms, let's pretend that David loaned Bill $20 to buy a CD that he really wanted. Technically, David owns the CD since it was his money that was used to buy it. But, with each portion of the $20 that Bill pays David back, Bill "owns" more and more of the CD. It works the same way with real estate. Every bit of equity counts in determining the value of the property. The loan reduction adds to the equity build up each month and every year and needs to be calculated as one of the benefits.

The equity growth from loan reduction is relatively small in the early years of a loan's repayment schedule. Over time, as you gain more equity in your property, the rewards are greater. To determine your equity from loan reduction, you would use the following formula:

Total loan payments – Interest payments = Loan reduction

For the example, loan reduction is:

Annual loan payments	**$22,354**
Less interest paid on mortgage	**−$19,510***
Principal reduction: (for that year)	**$2,844**

*Note: This number can be found in your mortgage payment statement book or will be given to you at the end of the year by your lender.

Now that you've determined that your loan reduction for that year is $2,844, you'll want to see how well that money is working for you (with the rate of ROE). To find this, use the following formula:

RATE OF RETURN ON LOAN REDUCTION AT THE TIME OF PURCHASE

$$\frac{\text{Principal loan reduction for the year}}{\text{Amount of down payment}} = \text{\% rate of return on loan reduction}$$

RATE OF RETURN ON LOAN REDUCTION EVERY YEAR AFTER FIRST YEAR

$$\frac{\text{Principal loan reduction}}{\text{Amount of equity}} = \text{\% rate of return on loan reduction at first year}$$

The rate of return on loan reduction at the time of purchase for this example is:

$$\frac{\text{Principal loan reduction}}{\text{Down payment}} = \frac{\$2{,}844}{\$70{,}000} = 4.06\%$$

The rate of return on loan reduction (at time of purchase) for this example is 4.06 percent. The following years will have calculations based on actual loan reduction rates generated on the property divided by the amount of equity in the property.

THE POWER OF TAX SAVINGS AND BENEFITS

The final component to consider is tax benefits. This area of real estate investing is the least understood and one of the most powerful and silent benefits for investors who own real estate. It is not unusual for investors who own several properties or who have owned investment property for years still to have a vague and unclear idea of how their investment portfolio profits from these amazing tax savings. The tax savings of investment real estate can make or break a deal and help investors slowly build their wealth each and every year. Some of these tax benefits can be used for the current year, and some will need to be rolled forward for use in future years.

There is one major tax benefit investors should know about, and that is how to use depreciation to calculate tax write-offs. Investors should not overlook the power of these

Hot Tip

Your tenants are your best partners in reducing your mortgage loan balance (debt) and producing long-term wealth. Their rent payments pay most, if not all of your loan payment. As an added benefit, the government allows you to take a tax write-off on your loan. (I'll discuss this in greater detail in the next section.) You get two perks, a loan reduction and tax write-off, all for the price of one—getting a real estate loan!

Understanding depreciation can be complex and frustrating for some investors. If you get lost in these numbers, DO NOT PANIC. You can still be a great real estate investor. I have a real equity calculator that does the figuring for you. You can purchase this calculator at my web site at www.pacblue investments.com.

incredible tax benefits. They are the hidden, sleeping giants of long-term investment real estate.

HOW TO USE DEPRECIATION

The IRS gives owners of investment real estate a tax break for the deterioration of their buildings every year over a specific period (27.5 years for residential properties and 39 years for commercial properties). According to the IRS, the building and physical structure of real estate is called the improvement value. It allows investors to have a benefit for the deterioration of their building over time. So, even though your building will probably not crumble to the ground during this time, the government lets you act as if it will and gives you tax benefits for this deterioration. The good news is this tax break applies to properties you own as an investment, and the bad news is it does not apply to your personal home or residence.

Owners of investment real estate are only allowed to depreciate the physical building, not the land it sits on. The government rightly assumes that the land isn't going anywhere, so unless you happen to live in California and can somehow convince them of those "falling off the coast" rumors, you're out of luck. To determine the value of the building improvement, you can use either of two methods: looking at tax records, which already split the total property value between the land value and the improvement value, or using the standard percentage method. The most popular method is the standard percentage method.

Tax Record Improvement Value

On many property tax records across the country, the total assessed value of a property is divided into two sections: One line contains the value of the land, and another line gives the value of the improvement.

The value of the property using tax records can be calculated using the following formulas:

Land value + Improvement value = Total assessed property value

In my example, remember that the duplex purchase price is $350,000. Say that the property tax records show:

Land value	$105,000
Improvement value	+ $245,000
Total property value	$350,000

$$\frac{\text{Improvement value}}{\text{Total propery value}} = \text{Percentage improvement value}$$

For my example, the ratio would be:

$$\frac{\$245,000 \text{ (improvement value)}}{\$350,000 \text{ (total property value)}} = 70\% \text{ improvement value}$$

Percent value of improvement x Value of property = Improvement value

From the example above, according to the tax records:

70% Total property value x $350,000 = $245,000 (improvement only)

Now you have the improvement value figured out according to the tax records. One hint though, don't take the values on the property tax records at face value. In some states, these assessed values can be very inaccurate, and the tax assessor's ratios (what I just calculated) may be outdated and inaccurate for determining the tax benefits you are able to receive on the property. So why would you use these ratios if they can be inaccurate? Some people use them when they are in their favor (such as 90 percent improvement value) and they are advised by their accountants to use these figures. Most people don't use the tax record ratio value unless they are in an area that is not in a common subdivision and, therefore, it is hard to come up with a ratio between improvement and land.

Standard Percentage Improvement Value

This formula is the method most commonly used by accountants and investors. It assumes a standard improvement value rate of 75 to 90 percent of the value of the property at the time of purchase. There are no set IRS rulings that dictate how to calculate the ratio between the improvement and land values, so you should discuss using this method with your tax advisor and accountant to make sure that you are comfortable using these numbers for investment property tax benefits. The 70 to 90 percent improvement value applies when there are no outstanding features, that make the property significantly more valuable than neighboring properties, such as being right on the ocean, on a lake front, or having lots of land in a ranch or farm.

DON'T FORGET

Rule of thumb: The percentage of improvement value for a property in a subdivision that is not on a lake or ocean front, in the inner city, on an extra large lot, or on lots of land will be approximately 70 to 90 percent of the total assessed value. (But I usually use 75 percent.)

If a property is in a condominium complex, then sometimes you can use the 85 to 90 percent improvement ratio. If the property is on the ocean or on a lake, then the value of the land is greater than homes that do not have this special feature, so you may only be able to use 50 to 60 percent. This is also true if the property is located in a rural area and has lots of extra land. The improvement ratio would be lower for the improvement because of the extra land. It is critical that you check with your tax accountant before you decide which method to use.

It's important to state here that the examples and formulas used in this book are very basic. The tax laws can change frequently, and there are many exceptions to the rule of taking depreciation benefits each year. You will need to run your specific numbers with your tax accountant and attorney to ensure the most accurate calculations for your real estate portfolio.

Now that you have calculated what the improvement value is, you need to start determining how much tax benefit you get to take each year with that improvement value. There are several different ways to claim your property depreciation. Some accountants and tax advisors are aggressive, and some are more conservative. The examples given are for the average investor. The method most widely used by investors is *straight line depreciation*. In straight line depreciation, the IRS allows investors to take the value of the improvement and divide it by a given number of years:

27.5 years for residential properties = (one to four rental units)

39 years for commercial properties = (15 + residential units, commercial, retail, and industrial)

With the following calculations, you can determine the annual depreciation allowance for your taxes. For example, use my example of an investment property purchased for $350,000, where the percentage of improvement value was 70 percent. As you'll recall, the improvement value is calculated with the following formula:

Percent value of improvement x Value of property = Improvement value

or

70% Total property value x $350,000 = $245,000 (Improvement only)

Then divide the property improvement value by the number of years the government allows for depreciation:

$$\frac{\text{Improvement value}}{\text{Number of years of depreciation}} = \text{Depreciation allowance}$$

In this case, because it is a duplex, you divide the improvement value by 27.5 years:

$$\frac{\$245,000 \text{ (Improvement value)}}{27.5 \text{ years (Straight line calculation)}} = \$8,910 \text{ Annual depreciation allowance}$$

You're not completely done yet! You still have a couple of more steps to consider before you will have accurately calculated all of the taxable benefits. Next, you'll want to determine what the total tax benefits are for owning this investment. You use the following formula:

Depreciation benefits − Cash flow − Loan reduction = Tax benefits

In the original example, the duplex has $8,910 in depreciation benefits, $3,746 in cash flow, and $2,844 of loan reduction equity. Applying the formula you get:

$8,910 − $3,746 − $2,844 = $2,320 Tax benefits

These tax benefits then need to be multiplied by the investor's tax rate, usually ranging anywhere from 15 to 50 percent. This number should come from your accountant or tax advisor to ensure accuracy. For this example, you'll assume a tax rate of 33 percent.

Tax benefits x Tax rate = Tax savings

Applying the formula, the tax savings for investing in the duplex are:

$2,320 Tax benefits x 33% = $765 Tax savings for real estate investing

Finally, because you always want to know how your money is working for you, you'll determine your tax savings rate of ROE with the following formula:

$$\frac{\text{Tax savings benefit}}{\text{Amount of down payment}} = \text{Tax savings rate of ROE}$$

In the example, the tax savings rate is:

$$\frac{\$765 \text{ tax savings benefit}}{\$70,000 \text{ down payment}} = 1.09\% \text{ tax savings ROE}$$

Tired yet? I hope not. Here are a couple more things to know about tax benefits and the IRS.

As in all things regarding the IRS, it is never quite this simple. The IRS makes it a little more complicated, but it is still not too hard to understand. The IRS limits the use of the depreciation tax benefit for investors who have an adjusted gross income that exceeds $100,000 per year. A graduated allowance scale is given when adjusted gross incomes range from $100,000 to $150,000. After adjusted gross incomes exceed $150,000 per year for active income, the use of depreciation can only be applied to passive income generated from your real estate investments. In other words, when you make a lot of money, the IRS does not allow you to use the tax benefits for that year against the active income that you get at your current job. But do not fear, the tax benefit is not lost all together if you are one of the lucky few who make more than $150,000 adjusted gross income per year. It is carried forward into future years to be used against future passive income or against active income if your adjusted gross income drops below $100,000 or $150,000 per year.

Why is that important to the long-term investor? It's important because the whole point of a long-term real estate investment plan is to create enough passive income to have a great life that you really love, right? The use of depreciation becomes exceptionally beneficial when investors convert their leveraged real estate holdings to passive income generators in the latter phases of their real estate plans. The depreciation tax benefit that was not used when the active income exceeded $150,000 can now be used to reduce the tax on the income generated from passive income at the end of your real estate plan. This is a powerful tax savings plan for established real estate portfolios that will be generating substantial income in the twilight of the investor's real estate portfolio. Phew. You finished calculating the maze of tax benefits. Congratulations.

CALCULATING OVERALL RATE OF RETURN ON EQUITY (ROE)

Now comes the fun part, being able to calculate the overall rate of ROE. The ROE from all four components of return, including appreciation, cash flow, loan reduction, tax savings, are divided by all of the equity in the property. In this case, because you've just bought the property, it is the down payment.

Cash flow return	$ 3,746 = 5.35%	Rate of return on cash flow
Appreciation growth	$ 7,000 = 10%	Rate of return on appreciation
Loan reduction	$ 2,844 = 4.06%	Rate of return on debt reduction
Tax savings	$ 765 = 1.09%	Rate of return on tax savings
Total ROE	$ 14,355 = 20.51%	Overall rate of ROE

$$\frac{\text{Return of all four returns}}{\text{Amount of down payment}} = \text{Overall rate of ROE}$$

Wasn't that a lot of numbers and calculations! That is the extent of calculations you need to do. Now you will accurately know what rate of ROE you are getting on the properties you want to buy and the properties you already have in your portfolio.

• • •

Congratulations! You've done it! It might feel like a lot of work, but determining the true value of your property and the return on your investment form the foundation of your real estate plan. Together they are the primary factors necessary for making millions through real estate investing. With practice (and with the help of some good advisors), calculating each of these four benefits will become second nature for you. Not only will you then be able to get the most out of your investments by having all of the necessary and relevant information, but you will also be certain to make the decisions that will put you on the path to long-term wealth.

Hot Tip Check out the "Real Equity Calculator." This calculator runs the numbers, including return on equity for prospective real estate purchases and properties currently owned. For more information visit www.pacblueinvestments.com.

$$$

Real Estate Agent Learns for Personal and Professional Reasons

We got into real estate back in 1981, when I was first married. Originally, my husband was more willing to invest in real estate than I was. I was too scared and frightened. Back then, he wanted to buy a four-plex that had a negative cash flow, and I refused to look at it. I did not understand how to evaluate the true value of real estate, and the idea of putting more money into a property than I was getting out of it just didn't make sense to me. I didn't realize that there were three other factors I should have been considering, not just whether the property cash flowed or not. I know now that had we bought that property, we would have a lot more equity today and be in a terrific financial position.

Because of that and other missed opportunities throughout the years, I am wiser and able to help my clients avoid some of these mistakes. My clients continue to come back to me because I give them the important investment information they want. I am building clients for life, and they have someone cheering them on. So everyone benefits.

—BETSY M., REALTOR, SAN DIEGO

How Much Money Do I Really Need?

"Don't let the fear of striking out hold you back."
—Babe Ruth

I've already established that making money can be fun. Everybody likes to see the numbers in bankbooks increase, and because of the wonders of compound interest and leverage, the numbers can often increase even faster with real estate. But how do you know when you've made enough money or that you have arrived at the goals that you have been working towards? The first time I asked myself these questions, I was amazed to discover that I had absolutely no idea how much money I really needed to live the life that I dreamed of and wanted. A giant light-bulb went off in my head. I realized that I needed a financial goal, an actual dollar amount that I could work toward that would let me afford everything I really needed and desired for my retirement years.

This chapter is going to help you figure out your own magic number. With this number, you'll have a concrete goal to work and plan toward. If it turns out that you want to live like a rock star, well, you may have to work a little harder to get there. On the other hand, you just might realize that you won't have to work as hard as you think in order to get a better life than you could have imagined. Whatever your result, you'll now be able to adjust your plan accordingly. Start out with a fun exercise (Figure 7.1) that will help you figure out how much money you *really* need.

USING THE WORKSHEET

There are three exercises you are going to do to arrive at your net equity goals and to discover how much passive income you will be working to generate from your real estate plan.

The first exercise, called "basic," is to define how much money you need to survive right now. The second exercise is called "stretch," because this is how much income you would like to have to create or live a great lifestyle. This second exercise usually stretches people in how they spend money. The third exercise is called the "dream" phase. This is where investors really begin to dream big. Don't hold back. See how much money you want to spend in order to have a great life. This last phase is where dreams really happen.

Once you have finished all three exercises (basic, stretch, and dream), you are able to go to the next part and determine if you have enough money to begin your investment plan, the amount of time you'll need to be a real estate investor until you reach your goals, and the overall rate of return on equity (ROE) that you need to target in order to obtain your dream.

Basic Lifestyle

The first line asks for your current monthly personal expenses. Take a look back at the budget worksheet (Figure 4.1) you completed in Chapter 4 for this number. Make sure that your number does not include any business expenses you have. On the second line, list the amount of money you are currently putting away monthly for retirement or investment planning. Be honest with yourself. If you haven't started saving yet, that's okay. Just fill the line in with a zero. Then, on the third line put the amount of money you are spending per month on vacations or dreams. When you have completed all the lines, add them all up. This monthly total is the passive income goal you need in order to have the same lifestyle you have now. Then multiply by 12 to get a yearly total income needed to fund the lifestyle that you currently have.

FIGURE 7.1: **How Much Money Do I Need for My Real Estate Plan?**

This form will help you define an estimated amount of money you need to live a lifestyle that you will enjoy. It is the beginning step in estimating the amount of net equities needed in your real estate plan.

It is important that you check with your accountant, tax attorney, or financial planner to confirm that your real estate plan aligns with your other financial objectives.

1. **Basic Living Expenses.** (monthly amount currently needed)

$ _____ + $ _____ = $ _____ X 12 = $ _____ ÷ 0.06 = _____
Personal expenses   Retirement   Dreams   Monthly total   Annual amount   Net equity needed at
                                                needed   end of R.E. plan

(Passive income goal)

2. **Stretch Living Expenses.** (monthly amount for stretch)

$ _____ + $ _____ = $ _____ X 12 = $ _____ ÷ 0.06 = _____
Personal expenses   Retirement   Dreams   Monthly total   Annual amount   Net equity needed at
                                                needed   end of R.E. plan

(Passive income goal)

3. **Dream Living Expenses.** (monthly amount for dream fulfillment)

$ _____ + $ _____ = $ _____ X 12 = $ _____ ÷ 0.06 = _____
Personal expenses   Retirement   Dreams   Monthly total   Annual amount   Net equity needed at
                                                needed   end of R.E. plan

(Passive income goal)

This formula assumes a 6 percent estimated annual rate of return on the net equity generated from the real estate plan. Many investment counselors feel this is a conservative figure. The monthly total needed is the amount of passive income you want generated from your real estate portfolio.

A quick way to see if you have accurate numbers is to look at whether your monthly expenses on this worksheet equal your income. Most people spend all of the money they make. The monthly income and the monthly expenses should be fairly equal for most people in the early phases of the real estate plan. If they are not, go back and find out where the numbers are off. Finally, take this number and divide it by 6 percent (0.06). The 6 percent represents a conservative annual rate of return you might expect to get on investments such as bonds, certificates of deposit, or secure money markets. This means that at the end of your real estate plan, if you liquidate your real estate and put the net equity into one of these conservative investments that are providing approximately a 6 percent return, this passive income is enough to sustain the monthly income lifestyle you want.

This first net equity number is usually not very satisfying for most investors who read this book or take my workshops. Most people don't want to maintain their current lifestyle for the rest of their lives. Oftentimes, they are living paycheck to paycheck or just getting by. Instead, they want to have more money to play with and be able to spend freely on vacations, hobbies, or time with their friends and families. Does this sound like you? I thought so. That's why there is another exercise that lets you stretch yourself and dream a bit larger.

Stretch Lifestyle

Now that you have determined how much money you need to live with your current lifestyle, push it a bit. When you start to dream a little, how much money would you spend on expenses? To get this number, think about what kinds of things you would spend your money on. What lifestyle would you like to create for yourself? A bigger house? A fancier car? Nicer clothes? A dinner out every once in a while? Loosen up and have fun with this! You're not committing yourself to anything. Just state what you would like, and see what happens.

Next, remember to think a little bigger when you decide how much money you would like to put away each month for retirement and investments. Most investors want to put money away in a retirement account, but they have either never been disciplined enough to do it or haven't had the extra money to begin. Take this time to add the amount you would like to put away for retirement or investment purposes that would make you rest at night and bring you peace. Then, fill out how much you want to spend for vacations and dreams. Again, it is here that many investors have been sacrificing and holding back on vacations and enjoying themselves. This is where you want to add the extra expenses so that you can get out there and play like you haven't been able to in the past.

Once you have filled out these three areas, add them together, again, to get a monthly passive income goal with your new stretch goals. Then multiply by 12 to get the annual income you need in order to live a new and improved kind of lifestyle. How does that feel? Do you like the numbers you are working with now? Did you resist writing down a larger number, and ask yourself, "Why do I need to do this crazy exercise?" Or did you tell yourself that you could not put down a number unless you knew that it was realistic, that you would be able to create it for sure? Often people resist writing what they really want because they are afraid. Let yourself have fun creating whatever you want. I hope you stretched yourself creating an income that excited you and got you motivated to go forward. Once you've got an annual income figure, do the same thing you did above and divide it by 6 percent (0.06). This new number will be the amount of net equity from real estate investing you will be targeting to get the lifestyle you just created. Do you like the amount that you just created for yourself? Is it enough to match your lifestyle dreams and plans? Well, you are not done yet. One more step.

Dream Lifestyle

Now is when you can really get excited. If you thought the stretch lifestyle sounded good, wait until you *really* start dreaming! Ask yourself: How much money would I want if money were no object? How much money could I spend to really have an amazing life, doing exactly what I want with whomever I want? Write that new monthly amount in the expense line. Next, write in the amount that you want for retirement or investments for each month. Finally, finish it off with how much money you want to spend on hobbies and vacations per month. Don't forget that you're a dreaming person! Now's the chance to plan that vacation to Europe you've always wanted (and pay for your family to go with you), take up deep-sea fishing, or donate money to your favorite charitable organization. Once you have all of these numbers, add them together, and once again get a monthly passive income goal. Multiply the total by 12. This now needs to be divided by 6 percent (0.06) to get you the net equity you would be targeting. Is that number too large for you? Or maybe it isn't as big as you thought it would be. Have you thought about having that much in real estate equity before? Well, now is the time to start thinking about your life in that regard. With this one small exercise, your vision has given you a concrete goal to work toward to achieve your dream life.

I am frequently asked why I separated the three numbers (expenses, retirement, and dreams), and I say that is because most people have these three things on their mind all the time. They are concerned with paying their bills and keeping up with their expenses. They are worried about their retirement. And they either play a lot with hobbies and dreams (and the higher number will reflect that), or they are frustrated because they do not get to play enough and really want to have more balance and fun. When I separated these numbers, people had a physical demonstration of what they wanted. They began to see how they naturally focused their energy and how they wanted to spend their money. This helped people respect and pay attention to what they were already concerned with and to create a plan around what they are already focusing on.

For example,

Basic	$5,000/month +	$300/month +	$200/month
	Expenses	Retirement	Dreams
Stretch	$10,000/month +	$1,000/month +	$500/month
	Expenses	Retirement	Dreams
Dreams	$15,000/month +	$3,000/month +	$3,000/month
	Expenses	Retirement	Dreams

What you would know from this is that the person currently (basic) is not putting much per month in retirement and dreams. When that person stretches a little, you see he wants more monthly income (doubled expenses) and a three time increase in retirement spending. This person is serious about retirement and investing. It should not be hard to get him to invest. The energy and desire are already there. Dreams did not increase too much, so it is not as important now as the retirement. But at the dream phase, the expenses increase by $5,000 per month. The contribution to retirement triples again, which indicates this person is a serious investor. The dream line expense jumps up dramatically to balance out the equation.

I would assess that this person wants a better lifestyle as indicated through the consistently increasing expenses. The immediate increase in retirement spending shows that this person is eager and willing to invest. This also indicates that once security and retirement have been developed, spending on vacations and hobbies is an option. This is one way to see what part of your life you are focusing on. If you increased dreams and hobbies first, it may be that you have not played enough. It is important to pay attention to this indication and make sure you have play integrated into your real estate plan.

It's important to remember that the net equity numbers you just created are merely a place to begin your real estate plan. You will be determining later on in the book if you will actually be able to get to that net equity amount, but for right now you have identified an amount that would bring you a lot of joy and happiness. So, let's see if you can make this work. Start with your dream, and work backwards from there. Create a plan based on what you really want and what would make you really happy.

This exercise gave you two things: a monthly passive income goal to work toward and a net equity amount to focus on when growing your diverse real estate portfolio. Having these two things will make a tremendous difference as you are growing your real estate fortune.

ZEROS ARE YOUR FRIENDS

It is not unusual for investors who do this exercise for the first time to be afraid to put down such large numbers. It felt a little weird, didn't it? Most people just aren't used to writing down so many zeros when they think about what they want. And how about that grand total you will be targeting? It can all be a bit overwhelming, especially for beginner investors. But instead of getting overwhelmed, consider this: I'm giving you permission to escape the reality of your current life and truly imagine what it *could* be like. Why not get shocked, frightened, motivated, or excited by those big numbers? The more you work with numbers with lots of zeros, the more familiar you will be with accumulating and writing offers that will create lots of zeros in your bank account. Have fun getting used to zeros. They will soon become your friends.

HAVE A NET EQUITY GOAL IN MIND

In this chapter, you've learned how to calculate the net equity you'll need to have in order to live in your current lifestyle, a better one, and the lifestyle of your dreams. This is what you will be working towards in your real estate plan. Try to imagine which one will be right for you. Is the number you've picked worth the amount of work and effort needed to create it? Now that you've selected a net equity goal, you will be using this for the remainder of your real estate plan. You can decide to increase or decrease the amount you've chosen, but first let's see if you really can create what you truly want. Let your dream last for a little while before you shut it down or say it is not possible for you. OK?

DON'T FORGET

Remember that what you are trying to create using the real estate plan is an ability to produce a lifestyle you love that really excites you. That is the intention of the entire book. I want you to be able to look at your life and determine if you can change how you are experiencing it. If you can work strategically, make improvements, and take some directive actions, you have a better chance of being able to have the life you really want. This is within your reach! But nothing comes without work and some adjustment to your lifestyle. You must be willing to plan and be a bit uncomfortable. Anytime you take yourself into areas that are unfamiliar or uncharted, you will experience a little discomfort and anxiety. This is normal and expected. Keep moving on despite the uncomfortable feelings. The other chapters will help you understand why I want you to take the time planning for your future before you jump in and start buying investment real estate. Having a plan and knowing where you are going first will help you arrive where you want to go with more success.

• • •

In the next chapter, you will begin to look at how reasonable it is for you to get to those numbers and what you need to do to get there. Have fun planning and dreaming. Those who plan and create ways to get there are more likely to arrive at their destinations than those who sit back and never accomplish their goals. Remember: you are in charge of your own financial destiny!

$$\$$$

Contractor/Builder Takes It to the Next Level

Ever since I was little, I dreamed of building homes, but it wasn't until five years ago that I started learning about investment real estate. I knew that I wanted to retire early, but just didn't know how much money I would need to make in order to achieve that dream lifestyle. With one easy formula, I was able to figure out my net equity goal and set up a real estate plan to work towards reaching that goal. Since then, I have made over $4.3 million in equity, and amazingly, in a couple of years I will be able to retire and do whatever I want. I've got the financial security I was seeking, and I don't have to worry about working all of the time to pay my bills.

Looking back, I've often wondered why it took me so long to start investing. Real estate fits my personality. I like architecture and enjoy taking old, run-down buildings and cleaning them up to make them beautiful. It doesn't hurt that I can also make a lot of money. I now have so many properties and assets that it is especially important that I stay alert and protect the equity I have created. It's been hard knowing exactly what decisions to make because I have so many choices, but aiming for a specific financial target has made it easier. It has helped a lot that I know how much money I need to live the life of my dreams. Fortunately, these aren't such bad problems to have. I would rather worry about what to do with all the money I have made than worry about not having enough money to do the things I want. The quality of my problems today is pretty amazing because of real estate investing.

All I can say to people now is make sure you know where you are going and what you really want. Listen to your dreams, and follow through with them. And before you know it, you will have gotten there . . . look where I am today. You can have it, too.

—CHRIS CRUZ, CONTRACTOR AND BUILDER

How Long to Invest and Goal Declaration

"Every shot not taken is a goal not scored."
—Wayne Gretzky, who holds the National Hockey League record for goals scored

In the last chapter, you figured out your basic, stretch, and dream net equity goals. While it's fun to see all of those zeros and start fantasizing about how you'll spend your future riches, you're probably wondering how long it will take to get there, right? That's an excellent question. The answer can be found by looking at three factors: the amount of money you invest, your net equity goal, and the rate of return on equity you are getting. Once you've determined these three factors, it is simple to calculate how long it will take to invest. But first, you need to make sure that you have the right numbers to work with.

Remember in Chapter 5 when you calculated how much money you had to invest and when you would be investing it? That number comes into play now. If you've forgotten what it is, please refer back to Figure 5.3 and write the number down here:

I will invest $_____, and I will get this money from the following places: _____.

The money will either come from refinancing a piece of real estate, savings, a stock account, family, partnership, or 100 percent financing. Which place did you get the money?

Next, you'll need to know your net equity goals. These numbers represent where you want to be at the end of your real estate plan and what lifestyle you will have. They should be fresh in your brain because you just calculated them in Figure 7.1. Write those numbers down here:

Basic net equity goal: _____ Monthly passive income goal: _____

Stretch net equity goal: _____ Monthly passive income goal: _____

Dream net equity goal: _____ Monthly passive income goal: _____

Finally, your rate of return on equity (ROE) is going to be one of the most important numbers throughout the years of your investing career. You will be making investment decisions based on this number, so it's important to become very familiar with what rate of ROE you should be targeting to get the results you desire. I try to advise my clients not to set ROE goals that are over 30 percent. That is too aggressive. I prefer that clients invest where they have a greater likelihood of succeeding and winning as well as being able to weather the various real estate cycle storms. Psst. When investing, if you get ROE's over 30 percent, that's a bonus. My wealthiest clients play to win over and over again. I want that for you as well. (Slow and steady really wins in the end.)

So, try to set ROE goals that are closer to the 20 to 29 percent marks. If you are below a goal of 20 percent, your money may not be working hard enough. Exceptions to this rule are investors who have time (in their 20s and early 30s) and those who are further along in their investment plans and have money or equity behind them. If you don't fall into either of those categories, you need to have a more aggressive rate of return on equity goal that is usually 20 to 29 percent.

So, now that you know how much you'll invest, what your net equity goal is, and your monthly income goal, and a rate of return on equity that is realistic for your situation, you can use Figure 8.1 on present/future value to calculate how long it should take to reach your goal. You may need to adjust one or more of the numbers to get the results you desire. For example, you might want to retire in five years and realize you will need ten years to reach your goals. Or perhaps your plans are to use all of the equity in your home, and now you discover you can decrease the amount of money you need to invest. Others may realize that getting to their net equity goals is easier than they thought.

I never promised you that this would be easy, and some of you may have an unrealistic idea of how long it should take you to reach your goals. Remember how I keep talking about patience? It counts here as well. It might take you 20 years to reach your goal. But look at it this way: in 20 years, you'll *still* be 20 years older, you might as well be rich, too.

THE PRESENT VALUE/FUTURE VALUE TABLE

To use Figure 8.1, look at the column on the left-hand side, and follow it down to the amount of money you will be investing. Next, look at the column to the right, and locate the row that corresponds with the number of years you plan to invest. After looking above at your targeted rate of return, find the intersecting point of the row for number of years you want to invest and column for the expected ROE. That number is the total amount of money (net equity) you can have at the end of your plan based upon those initial numbers. For example, if you have $40,000 to invest and it will work for you for 15 years at an average rate of return on equity of 25 percent, the total dollar amount earned will be $1,136,868. Another example is to invest $300,000 for 15 years at an average rate of return on equity 25 percent of the total dollar amount earned will be $8,526,510. Now that is a fun number to target, isn't it? And it is very doable with strategic real estate investing.

DON'T FORGET

When you increase your ROE goals, you produce larger net equity amounts, but you also increase the level of risk you need to take in order to produce these results consistently. Getting higher ROEs requires continuing to leverage your property over and over again. As a result, your monthly loan payments increase and your monthly cash flow decreases. Some of these refinances might even mean that you are creating a negative cash flow on your properties. When you increase the numbers over 30 percent, your ability to sustain the properties sometimes becomes unrealistic. You want to be sure that you are able to make these increased loan payments and hold onto these properties in all real estate cycles. Thus, in order to reach the goal you have in mind, it is important that you come up with reasonable and realistic numbers for your ROE.

Was that fun for you? Or perhaps it was a little frustrating to discover that I didn't provide a miracle way of making a zillion dollars in five years. Sorry about that. What I did give you, however, was a formula that has worked time and time again for creating long-term sustainable wealth. These numbers and the goals you set for yourself should be evaluated, and adjustments made to your plan every year. The most important thing to remember is that time is in your favor. The sooner you get started, the better off you will be.

FIGURE 8.1: **Present Value/Future Value Table**

Circle the amount of money you're investing in the first column. Then circle the number of years you have to invest and identify the amount of net equity you are targeting. Then circle the column that matches your goals and dreams.

Money to Invest	Number of Years	ROE = 20%	ROE = 25%	ROE = 30%
$10,000	10	$ 61,917	$ 93,132	$ 137,858
	15	$ 154,070	$ 284,217	$ 511,858
	20	$ 383,376	$ 867,361	$ 1,900,496
$20,000	10	$ 123,835	$ 186,264	$ 275,716
	15	$ 308,140	$ 568,434	$ 1,023,717
	20	$ 766,752	$ 1,734,723	$ 3,800,992
$30,000	10	$ 185,752	$ 279,396	$ 413,575
	15	$ 462,211	$ 852,651	$ 1,535,576
	20	$ 1,150,128	$ 2,602,085	$ 5,701,489
$40,000	10	$ 247,669	$ 372,529	$ 551,434
	15	$ 616,281	$ 1,136,868	$ 2,047,435
	20	$ 1,533,504	$ 3,469,446	$ 7,601,985
$50,000	10	$ 309,587	$ 465,661	$ 689,292
	15	$ 770,351	$ 1,421,085	$ 2,559,294
	20	$ 1,916,880	$ 4,336,808	$ 9,502,481
$60,000	10	$ 371,504	$ 558,793	$ 827,150
	15	$ 924,421	$ 1,705,302	$ 3,071,153
	20	$ 2,300,256	$ 5,204,170	$11,402,978
$70,000	10	$ 433,421	$ 651,925	$ 965,009
	15	$ 1,078,492	$ 1,989,519	$ 3,583,012
	20	$ 2,683,632	$ 6,071,523	$13,303,424
$80,000	10	$ 495,338	$ 745,058	$ 1,102,867
	15	$ 1,232,562	$ 2,273,736	$ 4,094,871
	20	$ 3,067,008	$ 6,938,893	$15,203,971
$90,000	10	$ 557,256	$ 838,190	$ 1,240,726
	15	$ 1,386,632	$ 2,557,953	$ 4,606,730
	20	$ 3,450,384	$ 7,806,255	$17,104,467

FIGURE 8.1: **Present Value/Future Value Table**

Money to Invest	Number of Years	ROE = 20%	ROE = 25%	ROE = 30%
$100,000	10	$ 619,170	$ 931,320	$ 1,378,580
	15	$ 1,154,070	$ 2,842,170	$ 5,110,858
	20	$ 3,833,760	$ 8,673,610	$19,004,960
$150,000	10	$ 928,760	$ 1,396,984	$ 2,067,877
	15	$ 2,311,053	$ 4,263,256	$ 7,677,884
	20	$ 5,750,640	$13,010,426	$28,507,446
$200,000	10	$ 1,238,350	$ 1,862,640	$ 2,757,160
	15	$ 3,081,400	$ 5,684,340	$10,237,170
	20	$ 7,667,520	$17,347,230	$38,009,920
$250,000	10	$ 1,547,934	$ 2,328,306	$ 3,446,462
	15	$ 3,851,755	$ 7,105,427	$12,796,473
	30	$ 9,584,400	$21,684,043	$47,512,409
$300,000	10	$ 1,857,520	$ 2,793,960	$ 4,135,750
	15	$ 4,622,110	$ 8,526,510	$15,355,760
	20	$11,501,280	$26,020,850	
$350,000	10	$ 2,167,108	$ 3,259,629	$ 4,825,047
	15	$ 5,392,458	$ 9,947,598	$17,915,063
	20	$13,418,160	$30,357,661	
$400,000	10	$ 2,476,690	$ 3,725,290	$ 5,514,340
	15	$ 6,162,810	$11,368,680	$20,474,350
	20	$15,335,040	$34,694,460	
$450,000	10	$ 2,786,281	$ 4,190,952	$ 6,203,632
	15	$ 6,933,160	$12,789,769	$23,033,652
	20	$17,251,920	$39,031,278	
$500,000	10	$ 3,095,870	$ 4,656,610	$ 6,892,920
	15	$ 7,703,510	$14,210,850	$25,592,940
	20	$19,168,800	$43,368,080	

Note: The compounded interest formula is $FV = (PV)(1 + ROE)^{nth}$. FV = Future value of investment; PV = Present value of money invested; ROE = rate of return on equity you expect to earn on investment as a decimal; nth = number of years money is invested as an exponent.

So, to summarize what you have decided to do. You have just determined:

1. **How much money are you going to initially invest?** $_____
2. **How many years are you going to work the real estate plan?** _____
3. **What is the targeted rate of return on equity (ROE) each year?** _____%
4. **What's the net equity goal of the real estate plan?** $_____
5. **Monthly passive income target.** $_____

Congratulations! You have just created your real estate plan! That was much less painful than you thought it would be, wasn't it? The key to your success is going to be sticking to the plan and having fun when you are doing it. I've found that a plan is much easier to stick to if it's actually written down.

Hot Tip

ROE goals should range between 20 to 29 percent annually.

I've provided a Statement of Purpose (Figure 8.2) for you to complete for that very reason. Research has shown over and over again that people who write down their specific goals and work toward them are more likely to accomplish them. This document is for your own records. Put it somewhere you pass by often (the refrigerator always works for me!) to remind yourself of your commitment to getting rich through investment real estate with a plan and goal in mind.

When you fill out your Statement of Purpose, you will be asked to provide the date when you will begin investing. Maybe it's today, maybe it's next Thursday. The important thing is that there is an actual date when you will start investing. This is what separates the people who get into action from those who will just talk about getting into action. Put a date down on paper, and start taking action steps to make this a reality.

Committing to investing is more than just setting a start date, however. You will also need to define when and where you will be getting the money to invest. It will be important for you to stick with these commitments. If you said that you were going to refinance, you need to set an appointment with a lender. Now, not later, not sometime in the future. The longer you wait with investment real estate, the more you will lose in compounded interest and wealth for your future. Use the equity in your home to get started creating the life you really want. Stay involved in the process. You are the only one who can ever determine your destiny. Now it is your chance to prove (and improve) it.

Pretty empowering stuff, isn't it? Are you feeling motivated? If that is the case, then do one more really empowering thing. Statistics show that if you want to really produce results, it is not enough just to write your goals down (which I assume all of you

Tell other people about your goals, and you increase your odds of really making a change in your life.

FIGURE 8.2: **Your Personalized Real Estate Plan Statement of Purpose**

Your Name: _____   Today's date: __/_____/____

Original Contribution: I am going to invest $_____ on ____/_____/_____ for _____ years in real estate investments at a sustained rate of return of _____% and have a net worth from this investment of $_____ at the end of the plan term.* I will get the initial $_____ from the following sources:

A. $_____ @ _____% rate from what source _____.
                                       (Interest rate to obtain the money)   (Refinance, cash, inheritance)

B. $_____ @ _____% rate from what source _____.
                                       (Interest rate to obtain the money)   (Refinance, cash, inheritance)

C. $_____ @ _____% rate from what source _____.
                                       (Interest rate to obtain the money)   (Refinance, cash, inheritance)

Second Contribution: I am going to invest $_____ on ____/_____/_____ for _____ years in real estate investments at a sustained rate of return of _____% and have a net worth from this investment of $_____ at the end of the plan term. I will get the initial $_____ from the following sources:

A. $_____ @ _____% rate from what source _____.
                                       (Interest rate to obtain the money)   (Refinance, cash, inheritance)

B. $_____ @ _____% rate from what source _____.
                                       (Interest rate to obtain the money)   (Refinance, cash, inheritance)

C. $_____ @ _____% rate from what source _____.
                                       (Interest rate to obtain the money)   (Refinance, cash, inheritance)

* ROE goal should range between 20 to 29 percent annually.

have done). It is just as important to let other people know what your goals are. The more you tell others what you are working on, the more they will ask you about it. This has the amazing result of pushing you to work harder and to actually produce the results you desire. It becomes a self-fulfilling prophecy!

I wrote this book because I told people I would do it and they kept asking how it was going. I had to stick to my word and do what I told them I would do, no matter how long it took or how many bumps were in the way of getting it accomplished.

· · ·

Now it's time to figure out what strategies you will use to meet the goals you have just set up for yourself. In the next chapter, I'll show you how you can build your own team of motivators. The success of your plan is often determined by the people that you have advising and assisting you. It's up to you to find the best!

Married Couple Learn About Investing Together

When Carl hit his middle fifties and I was following close behind him, we started to get worried and concerned that we had missed the boat on owning property and would not have financial security for our future. We had been renters for almost 40 years in New York City where rent control was very common. We had a nice apartment at a good rate, so we never thought about moving or buying real estate until we decided it was time to take a chance and uproot our lives by moving to California. We couldn't believe that we were going to buy our first home! We moved to a new city and found the house of our dreams. It was unbelievable how good it felt to finally *own* something. Soon the house began to gain lots of equity and the prices kept going up.

Real estate represents hope to us. We created a Statement of Purpose that has given us a sense of self-direction so we can be proactive in our own lives. Because we got started later in life, we know we are on a tight time constraint, but we are glad that we have a way to make our dreams come true. We figured out how long we needed to invest and then simply got into action to make it all happen. We are now able to make decisions for ourselves and are gaining back a sense of control over our future. That is really empowering and feels great.

—Noemi B., PhD., Clinical Psychologist and Karl W., Doctoral Candidate/Teacher

Gathering Your Winning Team

"Great discoveries and achievements invariably involve the cooperation of many minds."
—Alexander Graham Bell

How many times have you heard the statement, "No man is an island?" It's an undeniable truth that no one can do everything by himself. The most successful people surround themselves with teams of people who advise and counsel them on producing success over and over again. In this chapter, you'll learn how to put together your own powerful team of professionals to support, guide, and direct you toward accomplishing your real estate plans and goals.

CREATING POWERFUL PARTNERSHIPS AND PROFESSIONAL ALLIANCES

It is a common misconception that the wealthiest people are also the smartest people. How else would they have gotten rich? While I have known my share of brilliant millionaires, for the most part the only extra knowledge a wealthy person has that a poor person doesn't is the value of a good team. Rich people are smart enough to have realized that they can't accomplish their goals without surrounding themselves with people who know more than they do. The hallmark of business brilliance is not determined by being able to do it all on your own, but by being able to orchestrate and select the associates and affiliates who will do an excellent job for you.

If you fail to put the structures of success into your real estate plan before you start building your real estate portfolio, you are setting yourself up to fail. You wouldn't build a house without first consulting an architect, engineer, and contractor would you? Of course not. Just because you know how much lumber to buy doesn't mean you know how to construct a house. That's why it's crucial that you choose people for your team who are competent and, just as importantly, willing to help you meet your goals and fulfill your dreams.

STRUCTURES THAT CREATE SUCCESS IN REAL ESTATE PLANNING

To begin building a steady foundation for your wealth development plan, there are several steps you should follow. First, make a list of the professionals and supportive friends or family you want to interview. Yes, I said interview. Remember: This is a business you're getting into. Don't forget to treat it like one. You want to choose team members who will increase your chance of success. Here's a sample list of potential advisors:

- Real estate agent
- Banker/lender
- Property manager
- Escrow/1031 accommodator
- Financial planner
- Stock broker
- Insurance agent
- Bookkeeper
- Accountant
- Attorney
- Contractor
- Success coach
- Friends/family members
- Colleagues

SELECTING YOUR TEAM

Building your team of players is just as important as building your real estate portfolio. The people you select are fundamental to helping you obtain your goals. You may find that there are areas where you don't already have candidates in mind. If this is the case, ask your friends, family, colleagues, and clients for referrals of professionals. Remember: it takes time to develop your team.

The following is a short list of important criteria for building a successful team:

- *Choose the best in the industry.* The team players you select should have excellent reputations in their industries. Request a list of satisfied clients you can call for references. All team players should have proven track records of creating success for others.
- *Interview three people in each category.* Before making your final selection in any category, take the time to interview or go to lunch with three different candidates. Sometimes, the best choice isn't the most obvious one.
- *Select someone you can talk to openly.* You need be able to discuss things openly and honestly with your team players. Choose someone with whom you are comfortable sharing your financial situation.
- *Select someone who has skills you are lacking.* Your team players should be aware of both your strengths and your weaknesses and be able to complement them accordingly. If you already know that you aren't a financial whiz, finding someone who is good with numbers should be a top priority. Self-awareness can save tremendous amounts of time, money, and lost energy.
- *Select someone who will tell you things you might not want to hear.* Contrary to what you might think, you are not always right. You must be willing to listen to new ideas and thoughts that are different from your own. Strong teams have players with differing viewpoints. A diverse team approach has a better chance of withstanding changing market conditions because the different perspectives will balance each other out. Include players who are conservative as well as risk-takers, those who are detail-oriented and those who are conceptual. Create a well-balanced team.
- *Select someone willing to teach.* Learn from your team; they are your most valuable resource. This is a perfect opportunity for you to gain priceless knowledge about several industries. Treat this like a Ph.D. in all things real estate!

How to Interview People for Your Team

People ask me all the time how to interview different professionals when they are trying to build their teams, so I've developed a little cheat sheet for that very purpose. When setting up the interview appointment, ask them for a free 15- to 20-minute consultation or ask them out to lunch (your treat). Let them know what you are attempting to do. There are several questions that you should ask of any professional you interview. You will want to know how long they have been working in their field, what types of clients they have, what their long- and short-term goals are, and what are the most important things an investor should know about their particular field. In the next section, I've outlined some specific field-related questions for you to ask. By the end of the interview, they should be able to tell you why they think they are best choice for your team. If you like them, tell them that you are trying to select the right mix for your team and ask if they would be willing to meet with other members of your team to discuss your plan. Thank them for taking the time to meet with you, and let them know when you'll be getting back to them. Do not decide on your team players until you have completed all of the interviews. Then, fill in Figure 9.1, listing members of your team.

This process should be fun and enjoyable. I have learned so much from interviewing professionals over the years! It's important to remember that none of your decisions is permanent. You will be changing some of the players on your team throughout the years as your real estate portfolio becomes more sophisticated and complex. For example, when you are just starting out, you need team players who will teach you the fundamentals of investment real estate. In time, as your portfolio becomes more complex, you will need players who know how to deal with tax and protection information. You will need advisors with different skill levels as you mature with your real estate portfolio.

Specific Questions to Ask When Interviewing Professionals for Your Team

Different industries obviously require different questions. You may think of additional questions during your interview, but below I've outlined some specific questions you should ask, depending on which professional you are interviewing. These questions are only the beginning. Have an appetite for learning and ask lots of questions.

Real estate agents

- How long have you been selling real estate?
- What areas or specialties do you have?
- What part of town do you sell in or have the most knowledge about?
- Do you sell investment real estate?
- How many transactions have you completed with investment clients?

FIGURE 9.1: **Who Are the Players on Your Team?**

Select your team carefully. Be sure to have fun and take time to develop your team. The interviews are over and it's time to choose your team. List the players you have chosen for your team in the following areas:

- Real estate agent(s): _____

- Banker/lender: _____

- Property manager: _____

- Escrow/1031 accommodator: _____

- Financial planner: _____

- Stockbroker: _____

- Insurance agent: _____

- Bookkeeper: _____

- Accountant: _____

- Attorney: _____

- Contractor: _____

- Success coach: _____

- Friends/family: _____

- Colleagues: _____

Choosing the right team members is key to your success.

Banker/lender

- What states are you able to generate loans in?
- Do you broker all of your loans out, or do you work for a company that will port-folio their loans?
- Do you have underwriters in the office?
- Do you generate loans to investors who intend on refinancing frequently and want to keep their expenses and costs down?
- What loan programs are best for an investor like me?

Property manager

- How long have you been managing property in this area?
- What are the vacancy rate fluctuations in a ten-year cycle?
- What are the typical drops in rent when the market softens up?
- Are you willing to provide monthly statements for the property to include all income sources, itemized expenses, and receipts for repairs?
- Are you willing to send digital pictures of the property every six months that include the interior and exterior of the building?

Financial planner

- What types of licenses or certifications do you have?
- How are you paid? Do you need to sell product or are you fee-for-service for generating a financial plan?
- How much do you know about real estate? Are you allowed to give advice about real estate investing? Are you restricted on what advice you are able to give?
- What percentage of a retirement plan should be in real estate?
- What other clients have you worked with who have had most of their assets held in real estate?
- How familiar are you with asset protection and estate distribution?

Escrow/1031 accommodator

- Do you specialize in investor transactions?
- Are you a licensed 1031 accommodator?
- How are you bonded for the monies that are held in your escrow accounts?
- Can you easily explain the 1031 exchange process?

Stock broker

- What designations or credentials do you have?
- What types of stocks and portfolios do you usually recommend?

- Do you specialize in any particular theory or strategy for wealth development?
- How are you paid?

Insurance agent
- What types of insurance do you sell?
- Do you sell home, auto, health, and life insurance?
- Do you suggest any kind of special insurance for property owners?

Bookkeeper
- What accounting software do you use?
- Are you familiar with investment real estate?
- How much do you charge per hour?

Accountant
- What types of clients do you usually work with?
- Are you a conservative accountant, or do you take liberty with interpreting the IRS rulings?
- How much do you charge per hour?
- As an investor, what is important to know when selecting an accountant?

Attorney
- What are your areas of specialty?
- What types of clients do you work for?
- What should an investor look for in an attorney?
- Do you specialize in real estate law or estate planning? What should I be aware of when selecting an attorney?

Contractor
- What types of construction have you done? Ask for references.
- Can I speak with three references about your work, rates, and service?
- How much do you charge for managing the construction site?

Success coach
- How can you help me accomplish my goals?
- What is your model of coaching?
- What training or education have you received?
- How much do you charge for coaching clients to their goals?

Friends/family members
- Do you want to invest in real estate together?

- Are you ready to take the necessary steps to invest in real estate?
- Do you want to be business partners, equity partners, etc.?

Colleagues

- What have you discovered when you look at investment real estate?
- What are your strategies and plans for keeping your wealth?
- What has worked? What hasn't worked?
- Who do you know that has been great to have on your real estate investment team?

GETTING STARTED

Now that you have selected the most competent professionals in each field for your team, it's time to meet with them collectively. If some members of your team live out of town, set up a conference call so that everyone can participate. The purpose of this meeting is to let each member of your team defend his or her financial recommendations to you in the presence of your other team members. Each person needs to articulate how he or she will best direct and advise you so that nothing is unclear or left out. This way, you'll have each component of your plan accounted for and double-checked by other competent professionals who have only your best interest in mind. Plus, your entire team will be aligned with the goals you have established.

• • •

Feel like you're ready to begin investing? I know that by now you're probably chomping at the bit to get out there and buy some property. It may be frustrating, but rushing might be the biggest mistake you could ever make when you are considering making a long-term investment. In the next chapter, you'll start to hit the pavement. You'll discover what options you have regarding types of property to purchase as well as learn how to locate the best property for you.

$$

I Can't Believe I Did It!!!

For a long time I wanted to invest in real estate, but I could never make it happen. I would investigate, research, look at some more properties, and still end up year after year with no investment real estate in my portfolio. It became the running joke with some of my friends and co-workers. Eventually, since I knew I had to do something, I refinanced my house and took out $80,000. Even though I was scared, I saw that I could make this work for my family as long as I took it one step at a time and knew what I was doing. With the help of a buddy, I finally bought my first investment property.

The most difficult part about real estate investing has been my need to have all the answers. I have found that the most beneficial part of the real estate plan is that it encourages me to set up teams of people who will guide me to succeed throughout the years. As long as I have the right people around me, I actually *will* have all of the answers.

—DANNY GLESSNER, FIREFIGHTER

PART THREE

Real Economic and Financial Environments

How to Buy Different Kinds of Real Estate

"Buy land. They've stopped making it."
—Mark Twain

Mark Twain knew what he was talking about when he pointed out the value of land ownership. As he so cleverly wrote: "They won't be making any more of it, so you'd better buy it now." Since the beginning of time, wars have been waged over property ownership, and it is always the rich and powerful who end up controlling the land in the end. Now is your chance to start creating your own little kingdom. But how do you know which is the right property for you to buy?

SELECTING PROPERTIES

It is really important to realize that when you begin to choose properties, you must not only look at the return on equity (ROE) goals that you have set, but also pay attention to who you are and what you like to do. It won't do you much good to purchase property that you can't stand and will ignore. Instead, you'll want to match your personal investor profile with the types of properties you want to buy. For instance, if you hate to tinker, it is probably not a great idea to buy a property in need of repair. In contrast, if a fixer-upper makes your heart skip a beat, then it is better to find properties where you can add a little elbow grease to improve your profits. Figure 10.1 has some questions to ask when looking at investment real estate.

FIGURE 10.1: **Who Are You?**

Have fun respecting who you are while you are building your real estate empire.

1. How do you enjoy spending your time? _____

   A. What are your hobbies? _____

   B. Do you like gardening, sports, exercise, reading, TV, or music? _____

   C. Do you like tinkering around the house? _____

   D. Do you like spending time with friends and family? _____

2. How do you view your home?

   A. Is it your personal oasis and an island of tranquility? _____

   B. Is it a place to park your body to rejuvenate after a hard day's work? _____

3. What are your investment strategies when purchasing real estate?

   A. Are they based on sound financial decisions? _____

   B. Are you a bargain shopper, need the best resale value, or want a good view with the best location? _____

   C. Do you prefer fixer-uppers or a combination of the attributes listed above? _____

   D. Please list values in order of importance to you. _____

   _____

   _____

REAL ESTATE OPTIONS

Now that you've figured out what type of investor you want to be, it's time to look at different types of property. Smart investors understand that investment real estate is about more than picking the cutest house in the neighborhood and slapping some paint on or putting new curtains in the kitchen. Real estate is a serious business. The more you understand the various benefits of owning different kinds of real estate in your portfolio, the more you will be able to take precise and specific actions to improve the returns on your overall portfolio for greater profits and versatility. There are several different kinds of real estate that investors can own, and each has its own unique characteristics.

Condominiums

More commonly referred to as condos, these are residential attached housing units that are owned in cooperation with other property owners. The exterior space is owned as an undivided share or interest with other owners in the same location. The interior space is owned individually by each property owner. Monthly, quarterly, or annual maintenance and homeowner fees are typically assessed on condominium developments, and owners must follow common bylaws and homeowner regulations called codes, covenants, and restrictions (CC&Rs). The sales price of condos tends to be lower than single-family residences, so they are more affordable for first-time buyers or empty nesters.

Although condominiums have not always been good investments due to the high cost of monthly homeowner fees, higher vacancy rates, and management costs,this appears to be changing. More people are moving into condos these days, attracted by the ease of maintenance and features like pools and workout rooms. You may have noticed the recent trend of older apartment buildings being converted into condominiums to increase the profits of the property owner. Because apartment buildings can cost as little as half as much as condominiums do (when calculated on price per door), property owners can make great returns on their investments by buying an old apartment building at a lower per door cost and then converting it into single units with their own assessor parcel number (APN). So do the math; buy an apartment building for $50,000 a

> **DEFINITION**
> *Price per door* means the amount the buyer/owner paid for each of the units in the building. For example, if the owner bought a fourplex for $200,000, the price per door was $50,000 per unit or $50,000 per door.

door, convert the units to condominiums, and sell them or reassess the value at $100,000 per door. Not a bad investment, wouldn't you say? But this process can sometimes take years to complete, with government regulations, property improvements, etc. Still, many investors are makeing lots of money doing "condo conversions."

Investors who are really wealth oriented and have their eyes on the ROE prize would not immediately sell off each of these individual condominiums, but would keep them in their real estate portfolios after the conversion work is complete. They would then sell or exchange them at a later date when the ROEs have dropped below their targeted rate or when the property has at least doubled or tripled in value. Many investors are making tremendous income from these condo conversions, but don't be fooled. There are many regulations and details that need to be followed, and the time frames for converting existing apartment buildings into condominiums varies from state to state and county to county. Make sure you do your research before you venture into converting an apartment into a condo.

Single-Family Residences

These properties are detached homes and are not owned in partnership with other properties. Single-family residences are the most common piece of real estate and are great for both personal homes and investment purposes. They are easily bought and sold and appreciate at very solid rates across the country, making them a fairly liquid asset in real estate terms. They are the most expensive type of real estate to have based on the income and expenses produced. Do not fill up your portfolio with only single-family residences. It can be costly.

Multiple-Unit Apartments

This type of property has in the past been predominantly owned by more advanced investors, but this has been changing in the last several years as more beginner investors get involved in real estate. A popular choice in this category for a beginner investor is a duplex (two individual housing units on the same property that often share a common wall). Duplexes cannot be subdivided and only have one property APN. Oftentimes, the investor will choose to live on one side and rent out the other side. This is a smart way to get into the multiple-unit rental market without feeling too overwhelmed.

In the past, more sophisticated and seasoned investors have typically owned properties consisting of five or more units. Some of the largest profits in real estate are generated by multiple-unit rental properties because the more units a complex has, the lower the price per door, which increases the returns for the investor. Because these complexes tend to be larger, the overall cost is prohibitive to the general population. Investors who buy multiple-unit properties need to know how to efficiently manage the expenses and incomes on these properties. There are also specific federal and state regulations that go into effect once you get into larger units. For example, you must have on-site managers when there are over 16-units in a complex, and certain states require the use of union labor for repairs and capital improvements. These increased mandatory costs increase the expenses on these larger units, but the profits are still consistently better than smaller units or single-family residences or condos.

Land

Land ownership is usually reserved for people who have financial staying power to pay monthly payments on a nonincome-producing piece of real estate. Land owners must use larger down payments and don't get the benefits of depreciation or income unless there are agricultural or other income producing activities on the raw land. Investors who own land are speculating that the area of their parcel will appreciate over time. Be aware that land can go through many phases, and the governing offices may change the zoning and the usage on the land. So although land can be really lucrative, it can also have its problems and setbacks.

> **Hot Tip**
>
> Passive income tip: Some smart land owners look at producing income on their land by renting parking space if the property is near a city or downtown area.

Land has its own specific real estate cycle that is every 15 to 20 years, depending on where the land is located. For this reason, land is for longer term investing or for eventually converting to land development. Land can be very profitable when the market is hot and can be very costly when the market is flat or dropping.

Commercial Property

This type of property is best for the advanced investor or business owner. Larger commercial buildings are generally owned by the very wealthy and by major financial institutions, such as insurance companies and Fortune 500 companies. The contracts and calculations are more sophisticated and require special knowledge and understanding. For this reason, real estate agents either specialize in residential or commercial real estate. Investors who are interested in commercial property need to work with commercial real estate agents and investigate the different types of leases, terminology, and conditions of renting or leasing this real estate. For example, commercial properties in nicer areas and locations require triple net leases (NNN). This means that the tenants are required to pay all of the taxes and other expenses and utilities on the property. On some properties with NNN, the owners pay only the debt service, a "sweet" deal for the owners.

There are four ways to categorize the condition of a commercial property: A, B, C, or D. "A" buildings are the most professional and best-kept properties in commercial real estate. They have nice entrances, good furniture, expensive carpeting, flooring, and materials. "B" buildings are older "A" buildings that do not have the luster and appeal that they had when new, but are in nice areas and are good places for conducting business. "C" buildings are usually older "A" and "B" buildings. They are where most of the profit is made for investors. Investors can take a "C" building, convert it into a "B" building, and increase the rents and profit. "D" buildings are very run-down, are almost out of service, and may soon be functionally obsolete, which means the property is better torn down than redesigned.

Most commercial investors are very happy with the results of their investments because the tenant leases are typically for longer periods of time and at higher rates that are incrementally increased according to the lease. Business owners also make steady clients because they are often reluctant to move their businesses. In addition, the rental price per square foot is higher than in residential real estate. Investors also do not have to deal with the hassles and costs of residential rentals because there are fewer kitchens and bathrooms, and people are not in residence all the time. The downside to commercial real estate is that when vacancies occur, they tend to last longer. Vacancies can last from six months to a year or two, and maybe longer depending on the job market and the size of the commercial property.

Timeshare Property

This property is designed for the vacationer. People choose timeshares when they want to own a small portion of a vacation home that can be traded or exchanged for other properties and to avoid paying hotel fees. The rates of return are very low (if not nonexistent) for investors, but it's important to realize that not all real estate has to be strictly for investment purposes. Some of the best money you spend may be for your family and friends to relax on vacation. Timeshare units may have personal value and be worth the money if you want to travel. But keep in mind, reselling timeshares is not very profitable and their resale market is not very good.

Vacation Homes

These properties can be costly for the beginner investor. Often, the additional home is in an area some distance from your personal residence. Vacation homes can be made profitable if rents are consistently generated during the busy vacation seasons, but expenses are usually greater for these homes because of additional costs such as advertising, marketing, furniture, higher management fees, and maid service. They are generally managed by a vacation rental company in the area the property is located. The property management fees for vacation homes can run from 25 to 60 percent. Investors need to make sure they run their numbers for these kinds of properties. Vacancies also tend to be higher. Sometimes, you will only fill the units for four to nine months out of the year, but the rental rates while it is filled can sometimes outweigh these other costs. Vacation homes are also projected to appreciate at very high levels in the next 20 years as people retire and want to have alternative places to live. Appreciation is higher in mountain, ski resort, lake-front, and beach areas. Some economists say that vacation homes will be the highest appreciating asset over the next 15 to 20 years. Who knows, we'll see.

REAL ESTATE PLANS AND DREAMS

Now that you know the types of real estate you can purchase, use Figure 10.2 to help identify what kinds of real estate you currently own and what you want to own in the future. Don't worry about being reasonable. Instead, allow yourself to have fun dreaming about the number and types of real estate you want to own someday.

FIGURE 10.2: **Property Holdings/Goals**

Property Address and Number of Units	Number of Current Properties (Owned)	Number of Future Properties (Desired)
Condominium		
A.		
B.		
C.		
Single-Family Dwellings		
A.		
B.		
C.		
Multiple Properties		
A. # of units _____		
B. # of units _____		
C. # of units _____		

FIGURE 10.2: **Property Holdings/Goals**

Property Address and Number of Units	Number of Current Properties (Owned)	Number of Future Properties (Desired)
Land		
A.		
B.		
C.		
Commercial		
A.		
B.		
C.		
Vacation Homes		
A.		
B.		
C.		
Timeshare Homes		
A.		
B.		
C.		
Total Number of Buildings:	Current Number of Buildings:	Future Number of Buildings:
Total Number of Units:	Current Number of Units:	Future Number of Units:

Make certain you fill in the bottom so you know how many properties you want to end up with. Don't limit yourself. This is the place to dream big.

INVESTING MADE EASY WITH INTENTION AND FOCUS

Understanding the types of real estate you own is like knowing how to skillfully play a good game of cards. As Kenny Rogers once famously sang, "You've got to know when to hold 'em and know when to fold 'em." I might add that it helps to know how each card works with all of the other cards, so you can stay in the game and win. The more knowledge you have about how real estate works and interacts with other kinds of real estate and the various market conditions, the better your decisions will be to grow a balanced and diversified real estate portfolio that will persist through good times and bad.

Don't let your only goal be to buy the cheapest or best-priced homes on the block. Instead, be more concerned with making sure you can afford the payments

> Sustainability is the key to long-term wealth.

and that you have accurately evaluated how the property will hold itself when the market is not good. If you keep one eye on the cash flow and the other eye on the rate of ROE, you should be able to do very well making millions through real estate investing.

Remember to keep your real estate plan in front of you when you buy so that you don't make spur-of-the-moment decisions. By using the real equity calculator, you will be able to determine the ROE with ease. (See my web site www.pacblueinvestments.com.) I know that it's easy to get carried away, but try not to let the excitement of the sale distract you. Don't forget to ask yourself if the property you are buying or selling fits in with your real estate plan. Of course, none of this is an absolute science. If the property you are looking at doesn't match your goals, you can still choose to buy it. It just means that you may have to contribute more money to your plan sometime in the future, or you may have less money (remember that net equity thing?) at the end of your plan. All of this adds up to taking more risks than you might be comfortable with. The decision is yours. Just remember: you set your own goals, and they are to be used as measuring sticks to keep you on track to obtain the things that really inspire you.

BUYING DISCOUNTED PROPERTY

As an investor, it probably seems pretty obvious that you might want to consider buying property that has been discounted. Who doesn't like a good bargain? Be cautious though, it's easy to be shortsighted and consider buying discounted properties the most valuable buying strategy. Sometimes waiting to find the "best deal," keeps the investor from moving forward and getting involved in real estate. Please don't miss the opportunity to have your money work efficiently for you now while waiting for that perfect deal to come along. It is much more important to get into the game than to wait only for discounted properties.

With all of that in mind, there are definitely benefits to buying property at a discount, including the fact that you can immediately reap the rewards of your purchase and are able to capitalize on instant equity. You might also have opportunities available to you now that were once out of reach, due to the reduced price. Here are some of the ways to purchase discounted properties:

- *Foreclosures.* Properties that are in foreclosure are either in the process or have already been taken back by the bank. Often a property might seem like a good bargain until the numbers are thoroughly calculated, so it is crucial that you do sufficient research to ensure that the property is actually being bought at a discount. Most foreclosures must be bought in an as-is condition, which means that repairs and fix-ups are sometimes needed before the property is useful.

- *Home owners association litigation (HOA).* There are many HOA properties that have lawsuits pending. As a result, obtaining financing on the property becomes difficult, and buyers are required to put more money down because fewer people can pay the higher down payments required, and values will artificially drop during the litigation and repair phases. Provided you have the down payment and the patience to wait for the litigation to be over, these purchases can be real winners. Litigation usually takes no more than five years, but the restricted financing on the property will be in place for only a couple of years. Get in while you can because these are sleepy little gems to put in your real estate portfolio. Immediately after the homeowner association has completed the repairs, the prices will rebound causing an inflated appreciation as the property goes back to market values because financing is restored and more people can buy into these complexes again.

> **Hot Tip** Don't be fooled into thinking that just because it is a foreclosure that it is a discount. I once read a report from a reputable title company that said foreclosures usually sell for around 95 percent of their market value. Pay attention to repair costs.

- *Domestic reorganization.* Couples who are splitting up often want to sell their homes to get out of uncomfortable situations. Look for these properties because they are often in excellent condition and can be bought at reduced rates and have lots of added value.

- *Probate sales:* Properties go into probate when the owner dies without a will or trust. In this case, the courts determine the price and negotiate the sale. The heirs are generally interested in a quick sale and just want their money out of the home, so a good deal can often be negotiated.

- *Lower market rents.* Look for properties where the current rents are lower than market rents in the area. Then, immediately after purchase, raise the rents. This will increase the cash flow and the operating value of the asset. This is an easy way to pick up thousands of equity dollars that can help speed up the refinance process. It can take from three to nine months to increase the rents, especially on large multiple unit complexes. Be patient and consistent. The rewards are tremendous.

- *Fixer uppers.* Buying property in need of repairs can be easily converted to your monetary gain through sweat equity (otherwise known as your own labor) or where physically improving the condition of the property will bring it up to the standards of the rest of the neighborhood. Be careful though to keep your eye on the number of repairs the property needs. Too many necessary repairs can gobble you up before long, and the property will no longer be a good deal.
- *Job transfers.* New jobs often require a quick relocation. When this happens, owners need to quickly sell their property and will be more likely to accept a lower offer. This is an excellent opportunity for you if you can act quickly.
- *Inheritances.* Families are often distraught after the death of a family member and want to sell the property quickly to settle the estate and disperse the proceeds. Unless it was a childhood home, they are generally not attached to the property and bargains can be found.

BUYING PROPERTIES THE EASY WAY AT MARKET VALUE

Don't get discouraged if you are unable to find a discounted property. Many of my clients would actually prefer to buy according to their ROE goals and pay the asking price rather than take the time to search for a discounted property. This way, they are able to save time and easily select properties so they can simply get on with owning real estate. There is nothing wrong with this method of investing. In fact, I often think it is more beneficial because you are able to quickly get your money working for you. You can still become very wealthy when you buy properties at market value as long as you hold the investment for a long period of time. I've said it once, I'll say it again: time is the most important factor for the long-term investor. Get it working in your favor!

> **DON'T FORGET**
> Most investors can become wealthy by buying properties at retail prices, as long as they manage the physical and fiscal condition of the property and watch their equity growth.

PLAYING THE GAME TO WIN OVER AND OVER AGAIN

Once you start investing, you'll want to keep investing. There are many steps you can take to put yourself in a better position to win repeatedly at the game of real estate. The following ideas are just a beginning for how to successfully be prepared for normal market fluctuations that are inherent to a long-term real estate plan.

- *Be a verb! Stay in action with your real estate portfolio.* Master the distinctions of various investment theories, stay in touch with current market trends, and annually evaluate the intentions and goals of your real estate plan. The more you know, the better decisions you'll make.

- *See yourself as an investor.* Tell people that you are an investor and have teams of successful people around you. Join investment clubs and have investor friends. Seeing is believing.

- *Protect what you have.* Make sure that you have the necessary protection on the equity that you have built up over time. It is crucial that you have proper title and that you are not exposed to unnecessary risk. At the end of the day, it's *your* responsibility to protect your own investments.

- *Diversify your portfolio.* Diversity creates internal strength, flexibility, and durability for long-term wealth development during shifting market conditions. As Mom always said, don't put all of your eggs in one basket!

- *Seize golden opportunities when they come along.* Informed investors know how to act on good opportunities when they present themselves because they are knowledgeable and are prepared to make the next move. Don't be afraid to make it!

- *Keep sustainability in the forefront.* Your real estate plan is not a get-rich-quick program. Long-term investors have their money in real estate for at least 10 to 20 years and need to focus on sustaining it through all the real estate cycles. Remember to think long-term.

- *Set up to win all the time.* Set up equity lines and/or second trust deeds on all of your properties when the market is strong and in good condition. Use credit when jobs are plentiful. Think ahead, and be prepared for when the market conditions shift.

- *Consider cash cows.* Properties that generate good "cash flow" and have high rates of returns are usually not in the best parts of town. Having several of these kinds of properties can be valuable because they can sustain the lower performing properties in your portfolio—personal residences, retirement homes, vacation homes, and some single-family residences and condos. Balance your portfolio.

> **Hot Tip** When you are confused about what to do . . . remember one very simple thing . . . go back to the real estate plan. That is where all the answers will be for you.

• • •

Have you decided what types of property you'd like to purchase? And are they the right ones for you? Excellent.

Hopefully, you've learned some great techniques for finding discounted properties as well as discovered the benefits to buying at market value. Plus, you've got some new tips for achieving success over and over with your real estate investing. In the next chapter, you'll learn how to evaluate the market and discover six easy steps to buying property in any real estate market. You're well on your way to putting those dreams and ideas into action!

$$

Ever Expanding Real Estate Possibilities

I started investing in real estate with a small condominium when I was 26 years old. I was excited to get into the market at a relatively young age. Within a couple of years, I was able to move into a single-family residence that needed a lot of fixing up and got right to work improving that property. Soon, I got what they call the "real estate bug" and started buying one property after the other. I love buying and fixing up properties. It's a thrill for me to find the house that everyone hates because it is the eyesore on the block. I fix it up, and it becomes one of the nicest homes and the envy of the neighborhood.

The smartest decision I've made along the way is that I did not sell any of these properties after I finished fixing them up. I decided to keep them, refinance, and buy another property. Within a short period of time, I made over $2.3 million fixing up properties and still owned all of them. I am now buying commercial property to house my business, and within six months I will be adding residential multiple units to my portfolio. I have learned to diversify and add a variety of real estate to my portfolio so that I have a stable investment future.

—CRAIG W. YOUNG, UNMARRIED INVESTOR/SMALL BUSINESS OWNER/ENTREPRENEUR

How to Buy in Any Real Estate Market

"There are no secrets to success. It is the result of preparation, hard work, and learning from failure."
—Colin L. Powell

Knowing what type of property interests you is important, but it is just as important to know how to properly evaluate the market where you're thinking of buying that property. In the last chapter, you figured out your "what;" now it's time to figure out your "where." Have you ever heard the parable, "give a person a fish, feed him for a day; teach a person to fish, feed him for a lifetime?" That is what this chapter is about, teaching you how to find real estate that works for you over your lifetime.

Hot Tip

Use the Computer: Let your fingers do the walking!

1. Research a market on the internet first: check out prices, seasonal markets, appreciation rates, how long property is on the market, demographics, and attractions.

2. Research local real estate companies which are the most active in the area and who know about investment real estate. There are many companies (including mine) which can help you find local agents who will assist you greatly.

3. Check out the chamber of commerce web sites, and see what they are advertising.

4. Go to the AARP web site (www.aarp.org), and find out what the projected moving patterns are for the upcoming seniors and baby boomers.

5. Look at weather patterns, and check out local weather conditions. People are moving to warmer climates.

THE WONDERS OF COMPUTERS

The modern age of computers and information technology has arrived, and it's not going away. The internet can be your best friend, especially when looking at evaluating real estate. By using your computer to expedite your real estate research, you can do a lot of your work right from the comfort of your home or office. The more information you gather and read the better. Of course, you already know this because you're reading this book! Remember: you are going to be an investor for many years; you have a lot to learn. The time you spend on researching and reading about different areas and markets is never lost time. You will be surprised at how that learning is going to pay off down the road. You may not use it all right away, but it will come in handy in the 10 to 20 years you have to be an investor.

SIX SIMPLE STEPS TO EVALUATING ANY AREA

What if I told you that you could learn how to go into any market and in six simple steps evaluate whether the real estate in that market is good for your specific goals? You would no longer need to be completely dependent on having the real estate gurus tell you where to go. Sounds too good to be true, doesn't it? Don't worry, I'm not suggesting that you take me out of the picture or eliminate any of the other trusted advisors you have selected to be a part of your team in Chapter 9. You won't have to do it alone. Instead, consider how much fun you could have discovering and developing information and skills of your very own that you can share when you meet with other investors.

By applying just six steps, you'll take the guesswork and anxiety out of finding the hottest, most perfect real estate markets. Remember: your primary goal is to find properties that will work for your real estate plan. Fortunately for you, you will be able to buy in many markets across the country—you just need to know how to look. I hope that excites you because it is a lot of fun finding real estate and learning how to fit each property into a long-term strategic plan for your life. It really works over and over again. I'll show you how.

Step 1: Determine Why You Are Investing in Another Area

When you are thinking of diversifying your real estate portfolio into a market away from where you live, you want to first determine why you have decided to go outside your neighborhood. Here are several reasons why you may consider buying real estate away from your own back door:

Appreciation rates are better in other areas. Many people buy real estate outside of their area when properties appear to be increasing in value more rapidly than where they live. In other words, they buy in a market that has a lot of potential for value increases and higher rates of appreciation in a shorter period of time. This is known as buying at the bottom of the market. It is easy to make a lot of money when you buy in a real estate market when it is near the bottom. You win just for being in the market at the right time. Buying property in an appreciating market is a good idea. Try to do this as many times as possible in your real estate investment career.

Cash flows and rates of ROE are higher. There are many places in the country where appreciation is not the name of the game. For example, properties in the Midwest are usually better known for their cash flow and slow and steady growth than for their appreciation rates. Properties in this part of the country can be good to have in your real estate portfolio because they produce a positive cash flow and have high ROEs.

Entrance fees are more reasonable in lower priced areas. There are some markets that are cheaper to get into than others. The down payments required are lower because the overall value of the property is less. This is ideal for investors who need to start their real estate investment careers in lower priced areas because they do not have much cash on hand.

You want to diversify your real estate portfolio to include other markets in other areas. Having a variety of real estate in different markets protects investors from having all of their investments depreciate because they are all in one market or economy. Real estate cycles are very different across the country. Some areas of the country will be hot for several years whereas others are going down. It is important to keep a mixture of types of real estate in different markets to balance out these market cycles. You want your overall portfolio to maintain a certain level of performance. Diversification will help make that happen.

You have a personal interest in an area through family, business, or vacations. Many investors like to buy real estate in areas they know. They may have family or friends in an area they visit frequently and have been looking for a good opportunity to buy property nearby. Others buy in an area because they have a business relationship or interest in that market. Some people choose to buy real estate in a new market because they love a particular resort area and want to plan ahead for a family vacation home. So, they buy their dream vacation home and convert it to a seasonal rental property until they are able to afford to use it themselves.

Step 2: Evaluate Regional Trends and Investment Patterns

Real estate growth and values are affected by regional trends. This means that a region of the country will typically experience real estate booms and busts at the same time. More specifically, when one city has layoffs or increased unemployment, then the surrounding cities in that region will be impacted by a corresponding decrease in real estate values. Make sure you take a look at the local economy of the area you are considering.

In addition, different regions have different rates of appreciation. Real estate markets along the coast or in warmer climates have recently been experiencing higher rates of appreciation than areas with depressed economies and in the central United States. As you saw in step 1, this is an important factor to consider when purchasing property.

People's migratory patterns also affect regions. Parts of the northwestern United States have had great population increases due to industrial growth, affordable housing, safe communities, and employment opportunities. Areas like the coastal Northwest (Washington and Oregon) have recently experienced lower appreciation due to wet weather and economic downturns. This is also true of the rust belt areas of the Northeast where there has been a decline in market values due to lack of industry and cold climates. As a rule, people don't want to move to a place where they won't be able to find a job or where the weather is less desirable. There are always pocketed areas that do well, and heck, some people love weather. But you want to look at overall trends in a region. Many reports state that these colder areas and economies will not be rebounding any time soon, except for the inner cities where money has been put into redevelopment. All of these trends should be taken into consideration if you are looking to purchase property in a particular region. I define the current trends across the country in greater detail in Appendix A.

> Regional trends are very time sensitive. You must reevaluate a region every 6 to 12 months to be able to accurately read the economic forces.

Step 3: Investigate Municipalities

When investigating a new area, it is important to speak with local governments and municipalities to discover what growth patterns are expected and if there are any building restrictions in place that might impact future growth, business development, and investment. Municipalities hold the keys to growth and long-term wealth of an area, and it is worth spending the extra time to investigate them. It is very fascinating when you get to see how our government regulates the growth of an area. It can even be a really fun field trip. Treat this as an opportunity to ask lots of questions of the people you elected. I've provided some questions for you to ask in Appendix B that should help you in investigating a new market.

Step 4: Investigate Real Estate Markets

This next step is where using the internet really comes into play. Before you physically go into a real estate market, you can start your research online. You'll want to find out if there is a lot of standing inventory on the market, what the vacancy rates are, and whether prices are going up or going down. You'll also want to identify what part of the cycle the market is in. I discuss how to time the market in Chapter 13.

Contact both a residential and a commercial real estate agent in the areas you are considering. Make sure that you are getting good advice from professionals who have been in the business for a while and who are interested in giving you accurate and time-tested information. Ask if there are many foreclosures in the area. Find out if the building developers are putting in a lot of new housing as well as new commercial anchor tenants like Home Depot, Kmart, Wal-Mart, and larger restaurant chains. These larger companies spend lots of money on market research to determine the viability of a market before they move their businesses to a new area, and their research can save you a lot of time. If you notice these

Hot Tip

Take the time to go into the city planning department and ask to see the zoning maps. Look at how the city is mapping out the growth and development in that area. Notice the different ways the city and municipalities are dividing up the land. See if what they are planning makes sense to you. Are they planning properly for schools, freeways, open park space, and public transportation? What about commercial and light industrial spaces? You want to have a good mix of zoning so that the economy can grow and flourish in an area, especially when you have a vested interest in the area growing and being vibrant for the next 10 to 20 years. Do the zoning of the residential housing and commercial properties make sense?

Notice all of the different types of zoning and regulations faced by city planners and developers. Find out where they are promoting growth and development. These maps are usually very colorful and will tell you a lot about what the city is planning for future growth.

larger chains coming into an area, you can be pretty confident that the area is expected to grow and expand.

Get printouts from the real estate agents of what kinds of properties are available and what the going rents are. Find out if there are any special financing issues about which you should be aware or any special tax situations or incentives from local government authorities that make it difficult or easier for investors. Once you get these numbers, you will be able to evaluate the ROE (see Chapter 6 for a refresher on how to do this) and determine if you can get your targeted ROE rates in this area. You may discover that the rents are too low and the prices are too high. On the other hand, you may discover that the rental prices are great, the prices are low, and you can get in with a lot less money. Yahoo, bingo, now that is strategic buying! If this is the case, congratulations, you have met your real estate investment goals, so go ahead get started buying some real estate.

You may be surprised to learn that there are many places where you will be able to make your real estate goals work. It is really important that you use conservative numbers when calculating your ROE. I can't stress this enough. Optimism is good, but you don't want to stick your head in the sand and assume that appreciation on your property will always be over 7 percent a year. As I've already mentioned, I advise my clients to use appreciation rates of 2 to 4 percent per year. This way, if the market outperforms that year, you will be pleasantly surprised. In contrast, by using numbers that are unrealistic or too aggressive, you will be disappointed when your expectations are not met, and you might be tempted to jump out of the market too soon.

> **Hot Tip**
>
> As long as you are meeting your targeted ROE goals with the money you have set aside to invest, and determine that you can sustain the property by looking at the cash flow, you are on your way to making millions with real estate investing.

I've found that managing investor expectations is one of the most difficult obstacles to overcome. Unfulfilled expectations can be much more troublesome than what happens in a declining market. Declining markets can be easily managed if the investor is prepared and sets realizable goals. When you set your sights on more realistic numbers and work slowly and steadily, you are more likely to be prepared and stay in the game, which, if you remember, is where wealth is made. This does not mean you can't make some risky decisions. Just be sure you spread them around and have some sure bets in your portfolio to balance out those riskier ventures. I discuss more about diversifying your real estate portfolio in the next chapter.

Step 5: Do Area Research

After you have done all your research, you get to go visit these new places. When you arrive in an area, have several appointments set up with key people who can help explain the growth of the area. Spend some of your time with these scheduled appointments, but make sure you give yourself some time to freely roam around in the area to investigate on your own. You never know what you will stumble upon. Feel free to talk to everyone you run into, including store clerks, fast food servers, waitresses, etc. Ask them why they live there, if it is affordable for them, what job opportunities they have, and what draws people to the area. I've often found that I learn the most valuable information in the most unusual places. Don't be shy! People love to talk about themselves, and if they don't like where they live, you'll want to know why. When driving around, look at the following:

- *Retail strip centers.* Look at what large companies and chain stores are coming into the area. If there are lots of "for lease" or "for rent" signs, pay attention to whether the economy looks like it is growing and vibrant or is in need of revitalization.

- *Building developers.* Check out what the local building developers are offering. See what kinds of housing products they are building, and note what is selling and what is not. Ask the sales reps how long the properties take to sell. Ask them who is coming to look at the properties. You are not looking for any particular answer from the developers' sales offices. You simply want to get an understanding of who is coming into the area or is on the lookout for housing. Seniors take time to research an area before they buy because they have the time. Ask the sales person where people are coming from. This gives you a better understanding of how people are moving around in the United States.

- *Resale homes.* Drive around in local neighborhoods. See if there are many "for sale" or "for rent" signs. See if the yards are kept up and if roofs are in good shape. What kinds of cars are in the neighborhood or area?

- *Community colleges or educational facilities.* Pay attention to whether or not there are community colleges and advanced educational institutions in an area because they help with job diversification. In addition, seniors like to take classes when they move into new areas. They have the time and want to keep themselves busy in their retirement days. Community colleges can also be beneficial for educating the population when larger corporations come into an area. In general, educational institutions are very valuable to have in any market. This also includes good elementary, secondary, and high schools.

> **Hot Tip**
>
> Do not follow what developers are doing! They are short-term investors. Gather information to answer supply and demand questions as well as demographic information of who is coming into the area. Don't blindly assume that if developers are busy selling properties, it is a good long-term investment for you.

- *City parks and recreational facilities.* When driving around, notice if the city has enough parks and recreational facilities to keep people interested in the area. Having enough ballparks, picnic areas, playgrounds, and open spaces is vital to attracting families and creating a sense of well-being in an area.

Step 6: Investigate Property Managers

This last step is the most crucial part of your long-term real estate investment plan: finding and selecting a good property management company. It is important that you make sure you investigate the market by speaking with several local property managers. They should be familiar with the area and have been managing properties locally for at least ten years. Make sure they are willing to work with you and provide you with all the necessary paperwork to keep you informed about how your asset is performing. I talk property management in much greater detail in Chapter 15.

That is all the research you need to do to determine whether an area is valuable for you. That wasn't so bad, was it? The first couple of cities or towns you look at might frighten or overwhelm you, but trust me, after you interview several of these people or places you will get into the swing of it. Practice does make perfect. You will soon discover that it is much easier than you think.

Real estate can be fun for everyone involved. It is a great way for families to work together. Your kids might think of questions to ask that wouldn't even occur to you or discover some retail business or retail need that is not being met, such as no ice cream parlors in the area. Check out where the hospitals are and how many medical facilities are available for the aging population. You can even make these trips a mini-vacation for you and your family. Just make sure you give yourself some time to play and have fun. And remember: as an investor, all of these mini-vacations can be write-offs for your taxes. That's just one of the many benefits of investment real estate!

• • •

In the next chapter, you'll start bringing some of the information you've learned in the last couple of chapters together. You'll learn about the benefits of having a diversified portfolio and discover some alternative real estate investment opportunities. I'll also show you what important factors you should consider when evaluating the investments within your portfolio.

$$$

I Learned How to Ask the Right Questions

For years I had heard about people going into different markets and learning how to gather the facts and talk to the right people, but I never felt confident that I would say the right thing. I felt like a fish out of water until I learned about the six simple steps to take when evaluating any real estate market. I finally had the right kinds of questions to ask. Most importantly, I quickly was able to evaluate a real estate market and decide for myself whether it was a good investment or not.

I find that I have to look at quite a number of properties and make a lot of offers before I buy the right one. Sometimes this can be frustrating, but it is better to do the homework, investigate the property thoroughly, and then move forward confidently to purchase it than to rashly rush in and buy properties that are not right for my portfolio. Having these skills has made me feel confident and steady because I now know that I can go into any city by myself, look at a variety of properties, and know whether this property or area would blend well in my diverse real estate portfolio.

—PETER BLACK, ENGINEER AND REAL ESTATE AGENT

It's All About Diversity

> "Money is like manure. If you spread it around it does a lot of good,
> but if you pile it up in one place, it stinks like hell."
> —Clint W. Murchison, Texas Oil Millionaire

Financial advisors have been promoting how important it is to diversify your stock portfolio for years, but for some reason, the significance of diversifying your real estate portfolio tends to get overlooked. The fact is, having a diversified real estate portfolio can be very profitable for you as an investor and can produce many long-term benefits such as stability and flexibility. In this chapter, you'll see that the rationale for a diverse portfolio holds true in real estate investing just as it does in the stock market. But first I should define my terms.

WHAT IS A DIVERSE REAL ESTATE PORTFOLIO?

A diverse real estate portfolio combines four factors. They are:

1. Different types of real estate (condominiums, single-family residences, multiple units, land, etc.)
2. Different risk levels as they relate to leverage (high, medium, and low risk)
3. Different rates of return on equity (high, medium, and low)
4. Different regions of the country for properties

By diversifying your real estate portfolio, you'll have the greatest likelihood of success in all market conditions. This is especially true for the investor who owns more than three or four properties because now she has the ability to make a wide variety of choices. You'll find that the longer you are a real estate investor, the more equity you have and the more you need to refinance and purchase additional properties to make your real estate plan work. This means that you will need to continue growing and hopefully diversifying your real estate portfolio to keep and meet your ROE goals. Preplanning for this diverse portfolio can save you big money in the long run.

DON'T BE AFRAID TO LOOK AT DIFFERENT KINDS OF REAL ESTATE

Diversity sometimes means that you'll need to consider buying types of property you know nothing about. I've seen many investors immediately reject a certain type of property as an investment possibility because they've got a "gut instinct" about it. Usually this response is not based on any sort of information about that specific kind of property, but is more fear based. People are generally afraid of the unknown. Don't let this be you. Instead of avoiding a particular type of property, it is really important to educate yourself by talking with people who own these kinds of properties before you make your assessments. You may be pleasantly surprised by the information you get. Listen intently with an open mind, and pay extra attention to what they say worked and what did not. The trick is to be sure not take all their words as the "all knowing truth." After getting new information, talk to several people and verify that the information you've received. You'll quickly see that the more open you are to investigating and evaluating different kinds of properties, the more able you'll be to create wealth for yourself through diversifying your real estate portfolio.

DON'T BE AFRAID TO TAKE A RISK

You probably noticed that I mentioned you should have some high-risk properties in your diverse portfolio. The important thing to remember with these properties is that although high risk can equal high rewards, you also need to be prepared to experience some loss along the way. If you are too risk averse, you will prevent yourself from actively investing to get the returns that you are capable of having. On the other hand, if you are too aggressive, you may find that you have such high peaks and valleys that your stress levels won't be able to keep up with the roller coaster ride. When you begin to diversify your real estate holdings, some of the properties will be low risk and stable whereas others will be more risky and more speculative. The key is balance.

ALTERNATIVE INVESTMENTS:
Local, National, and International Markets

As you are becoming more familiar with the types of real estate in which you can invest, you will start to hear a lot about investing in different areas or regions around the country and world. In the last chapter, I discussed how you could go into any market and evaluate whether it is a good market or not. When diversifying your portfolio, you will now look at what is called the "asset mix" of your properties. This includes the different types of real estate and the regions where you want to own property.

For example, you may own property in the Midwest, which produces positive cash flow and has reasonable entrance costs, but the appreciation rates tend to be lower than other parts of the country. If you keep all your real estate investing in that regional market, you might find that your portfolio does not have enough growth through appreciation to get you the net equity that you are targeting. The solution is *not* to sell your property in the Midwest that produces a solid cash flow. Instead, you can diversify some of your equity out of the Midwest and place it into a more appreciative market that will not get you cash flow, but will get you equity growth. This will help diversify your overall portfolio gains while keeping your portfolio stable.

Remember though: when entering an appreciative market, you want to be able to accurately determine which part of the real estate cycle you're in for each property. Determine whether the market is at the top and going down or at the bottom and going up. You definitely do not want to be caught behind the eight ball and start investing in a declining market if you bought in that market for appreciation purposes only, unless you intend to hold onto that property for at least five to six years. Unfortunately, sometimes investors buy into an appreciating market, and the market turns on them when they are not prepared. As I've said before, the key to making millions in real estate investing is to be prepared and make sure that you are able to sustain your property during the down times if the market turns for the worse.

Being able to sustain your property can become more difficult if you have purchased property along the U.S. coasts. These properties have historically produced greater

DON'T FORGET

Real estate provides the flexibility, freedom, and diversity that allow investors to experiment with different types of real estate opportunities that they may not have tried before. A balanced real estate portfolio is going to include a variety of real estate investments—condominiums, single-family residences, land, and commercial units.

appreciative returns throughout the years, but they are harder to maintain due to the high cost of entry and the lower market rents in comparison to purchase prices. Being able to keep, hold onto, and preserve these properties is more difficult when market conditions adjust. I'll talk more about timing the market in the next chapter.

Purchasing property outside of the country has become a hot concept recently. Mexico, South America, and New Zealand are just a few areas that have become popular. It is important to understand the impact of government regulations and funding sources for these foreign markets. I highly recommend that you invest in your own country until you fully understand the fundamentals of investing. If you are still interested in going across borders, go for it and know that you will be learning something new. It is typically considered more risky and even more speculative, so you need to be prepared for both the upside of that decision and the downside.

INVESTOR OBJECTIVES FOR DIVERSITY

Knowing the objectives for each property helps determine how to move your real estate equity around with precision and strategy. Becoming familiar with all the options and moves you can take will greatly increase the rewards and benefits of owning investment real estate. When you take the time to think through why you own each piece of real estate, and what some of the factors are that influence your decisions and strategies, you can realize the benefits of long-term investing much more quickly and with freedom and selection. The following are some items to consider when evaluating the investments within your portfolio.

Financing

Examine the different types of loans available, including the number of years for the loan and whether it is a fixed, adjustable interest rate loan, or a negative amortization loan.

You should also know the terms of the loan so that you know how much the loan payment might fluctuate during the time you have it. The terms and details of the loan should be thoroughly discussed with your loan officer. Ask him what will happen in one, two, three, and more years as the market conditions change. Find out how much your payment could potentially adjust per month or per year. I'll discuss loan terms in more detail in Chapter 14.

Remember: you are a long-term investor. The monthly payments and your ability to sustain, not just acquire, the property are your intentions. Knowing this will help you determine how long you intend to hold onto the property and if you will be refinancing it soon. For example, if you are at the top of the market and have decided that you are going to hold onto a property instead of sell it, then the type of loan that you have on the property will be specific for holding and sustaining, not for refinancing. If instead you are buying at the bottom of the market and the indicators are that the market is going to improve, then you will get financing that may be adjustable with no prepayment penalties. You won't even mind if it is a negative amortization loan because you will be in an appreciating market and you will recapture all the principal buildup through appreciation

Leverage

The degree of leverage you take out on each property will depend on a number of things. First, it is important to determine what phase of your real estate plan you are in. If you are a beginning investor, you are more likely to want to leverage more aggressively just to get started in the program. If instead you have been investing for several years and have gained some net equity, then you do not have to be as aggressive and may choose less risky levels of leverage. The amount of leverage you choose should always be based on your ability to sustain the property and the rate of return on equity you get. Always remember that the more leverage, the higher the rates of return on equity, but the more risky and vulnerable you are to shifting market conditions. Properties that are being used for personal use, such as personal residences, vacation homes, or timeshares, will generally be less leveraged. In contrast, properties that are held for investment purposes are more likely to be highly leveraged. The trick is that lenders will not let investors refinance their investment properties to the same degree they will let personal residences be leveraged. Investors can sometimes only leverage their investments up to 65 percent whereas personal residences can be leveraged up to 80 or 90 percent. And the cost and rates are always cheaper on the

DON'T FORGET

A *negative amortization loan* is a loan that is not paying the interest and loan reduction each month, like a fully amortized loan would do but is, in fact, adding to the principal balance each month. Many investors in appreciative markets take out negative amortized loans because they speculate that the gains in appreciation will outperform the increase in principal. Negative amortization loans also take properties that are experiencing negative cash flows and turn them into positive cash flow properties. This way, investors can buy properties for their portfolios that are either too expensive or will not work. Just make sure you read through the loan papers, and there are not any hidden clauses that will put you in jeopardy.

personal residence. Investors who understand the rate of return on their overall portfolio will strategically decide to leverage their personal residence at higher degrees because it is the cheapest money to use and keeps their equity working for them for investment purposes. Though it is cheaper to get money out of your personal residence, my experience is that most investors still won't look at it this way and underleverage their homes for personal reasons. Either way is fine. The beauty about real estate is that you get to choose which way works best for you.

Location

Where you decide to buy or sell makes a big difference in the overall performance of your portfolio. The old adage "location, location, location" doesn't mean what it used to. Now, I say it is important to have "lots of locations, lots of locations, lots of locations." A minor shift in the wording of this simple phrase can make all the difference in your wealth development.

Capital Improvements

The amount of capital that is put into the property is determined by how much the rents will be increased (or vacancies decreased), which directly affects the overall value of the property. Keeping properties in good condition also helps you maintain high levels of liquidity for that asset. It's important to remember that the more you keep up with the physical condition of the property, the more likely you will be able to quickly sell the investment when needed. This in turn can immediately provide extra access to available cash through refinancing, which increases the rates of return on the capital invested into the property. When investors know how long they plan on owning a piece of real estate, they are more likely to strategically spend money on capital improvements and will pace the improvements of the property based on market conditions. If the investment is intended to be a short-term venture (bought, fixed up and sold for a quick profit), then the capital improvements need to be watched carefully, and the funds must be available immediately after purchase.

Purchase Price

The price that long-term investors are willing to pay is definitely different than the price that short-term investors are willing to pay. Each investor has a different goal or intention and will need to price the property according to the objectives that she has set for herself. The purchase price is not as important for investors who plan on holding a property for a full real estate cycle. In contrast, in properties bought for a shorter time, price and timing of the market is very crucial. This is not to say that long-term investors do not have to be careful about purchase price. They should always know how much they are paying and how it fits in with market values, but price is not the only way the investor is going to create wealth in the long run.

Exit Strategies

Having a specific plan for what to do with each property at the end of your real estate plan helps you determine when to lighten up on leveraging, especially as you approach the exit strategy phase of your plan. Investors with enough equity in their real estate portfolios can stop leveraging particular pieces of real estate and begin to generate passive income from their real estate holdings. If the intention is known for each property (for example, purchasing a retirement home, giving it to charities, or passing it to heirs), investors can preselect properties for these purposes 10 to 15 years ahead of time. How fun is that? Knowing what you will be doing at the end is so critical to knowing what to do in the beginning. This is not such a foreign concept. Many places around the globe teach long-term planning and passing on legacies to their families. Americans are just not that used to thinking long-term. They are more familiar with fast food, quick fixes, and short-term rewards. Take the time to think about what you plan on doing with each of the properties you own, and you may see some phenomenal results. I'll discuss this idea in more detail in Part Five.

THE REAL MAID FORMULA

When evaluating your real estate portfolio for diversity, it is also important to determine which of the "MAID" formula objectives apply to each piece of real estate you own. MAID is a simple acronym that stands for: **M**oney, **A**ppreciation, **I**ncome, and **D**epreciation. Here is how each of these objectives is defined:

> *M (money).* The property is used primarily for refinance purposes to get money out now. Investors continue to refinance and leverage to pull money out of the asset.
>
> *A (appreciation).* Growth in value over time with the intention to grow and maintain equity in the property, not necessarily for getting money out of the property. These properties will not be refinanced frequently. Examples are personal residences and homes for retirement.
>
> *I (income).* The major benefit is cash flow from rents and other income from the property. The property is maintained in the portfolio because of the passive income it is generating.
>
> *D (depreciation).* Tax benefits and savings that are determined by the IRS and accountants. Oftentimes, these are properties that do not produce great cash flow

and are in flat or stable real estate market. In this case, one of the strongest benefits is the ability to depreciate the investment for the tax benefits.

Every asset has several of the MAID formula distinctions, but each property differs in the degree of significance of each one. You'll find that for some properties, the primary benefit of owning it is that it produces tremendous income. Other properties are in good locations (like vacant lots on the edge of a growing area) and are appreciating at tremendous rates. Others still have low mortgages that can be refinanced for immediate cash. See Figure 12.1 for an example using MAID.

Unfortunately, not all of the benefits of owning real estate are equal. Usually, when one objective is attained, it will hinder the results of another factor. For example, you may want to own a property in the midwestern region of the United States, which as you may recall produce good cash flows but will not necessarily produce tremendous appreciation rates. In this case, you will sacrifice appreciation (A) for cash flow (I); the reverse is true if you are buying properties in heavily populated areas such as the northeastern coast and the Southern California coastal areas where appreciation has been tremendous but cash flow is tight. Knowing this helps investors understand the intention of each parcel in their portfolio, so later on when they are determining which properties to sell, exchange, or hold onto, they are clear what benefits and intentions each property is adding to the overall rate of return on equity and the investment portfolio. They can also determine if they are stacking the deck or creating a real estate portfolio that is too heavily weighted in appreciation and not very stable in producing income to sustain the overall portfolio. Don't forget the importance of balance in your portfolio!

The more informed you become on how to diversify your asset mix through the MAID formula and the ideas discussed above, the more likely you will match your objectives more closely to your needs and desired outcomes for your portfolio. Now that I have defined the MAID formula, write down how each is prioritized for each of your properties in Figure 12.2. Knowing the intended purpose of each property you own will help you understand what actions and moves to make next.

· · ·

Now that you have spent some time thinking about how to diversify your real estate portfolio, I think you are really getting ready to buy some real estate and make a difference in your life. In the next chapter, you'll learn how to accurately time the real estate market. You'll learn what to do when you're at the top and what to do at the bottom. Hopefully you are beginning to see real estate investing as a lifelong project. Are you getting warmed up to the idea of making millions?

FIGURE 12.1: **Sample Real Estate Portfolio Evaluation**

Below is an example of how to evaluate a real estate portfolio through the objectives established in the real estate plan. Each property is assessed by several factors that include: the annual ROE generated, the investor objectives using the MAID formula, strategically altering the type of financing, the amount of leverage, location, capital improvements, purchase price, exit strategies, and calculating the next adjustment necessary to continually increase the return on equity in the overall portfolio.

Step 1: Assessing ROE. It is important to know what ROE is being generated for each parcel.

ROE 25%	ROE 15%	ROE 30%	ROE 40%	ROE 20%	ROE 40%	ROE 30%	ROE 15%	ROE 45%	ROE 20%
Condo	Primary Family Residence	Single-Family Residence	4-Units	Condo	8-Units	Single-Family Residence	Land	Comm. Real Estate	Vacation Home

Step 2: Know the MAID formula. Determine what's most important and the intention of each property within the real estate plan.

Condo	Primary Family Residence	Single-Family Residence	4-Units	Condo	8-Units	Single-Family Residence	Land	Comm. Real Estate	Vacation Home
M	M	A	I	A	I	A	A	I	A
A	A	D	D	D	D	D	M	D	M
D		M	M	M	A	M		M	I
I		I	A	I	M	I		A	

Step 3: Evaluating the investor's objectives. Deliberately adjusting factors such as finance, leverage, location, and purchase price to produce a diverse and well-balanced real estate portfolio is critical to producing the goals established in the real estate plan.

FIGURE 12.2: **Priorities for your Properties**

1st priority _____

2nd priority _____

3rd priority _____

4th priority _____

50-Year-Old Single Mother Begins Investing with Vigor

I had failed to save and invest throughout my life. Instead, I had focused on running a business and raising kids. When I got into my early 50s, many of my friends were talking about when they would be retiring. Listening to them, I was quietly dying inside. I felt scared, embarrassed, and hopeless. I knew that I needed to get started with my investment plan if I was going to have anything for myself in retirement.

By coincidence, I met Lisa on the beach, and she told me what she was doing. I loved her investment strategies, and they seemed like something even I could apply. I am proud to say that since first meeting Lisa, I have bought a condominium, taken money out of that investment, bought a multiple-unit property in Austin, Texas, and am looking at buying more properties out of state that I can hold onto and create a healthy retirement for myself. I discovered how important it was to diversify my investments to get the most out of my portfolio and have security and stability during any market changes. I never thought that I could have my hope restored, but I can tell you that I do, and I have lots of joy and possibility in my life today. The strategies I learned have given me the courage to go out and buy real estate according to my personal real estate plan. I can tell you that I could not be happier in my life because I feel like I have control again over my own future.

—IRIS W., BEVERLY HILLS LITERARY AGENT AND SINGLE MOM

Timing the Real Estate Market Accurately

"To win you have to risk loss."
—Jean-Claude Killy, three-time Olympic champion

One of the most frequently asked questions I hear is, "What is happening in the real estate market today?" Investors want to know the best way to prepare to invest so that they can survive and thrive in the coming months and years. It's such an important question that many real estate advisors spend countless hours defining and interpreting when to get into the market and when to sell.

Learning to time the market can be a valuable skill. This information is crucial for short- and long-term investors alike, but it is especially important for short-term investors who have the intention of making the most of their profits in six months to five years.

When investors need their money out in a short time, accurate timing of the market is imperative. One false step in interpreting the real estate market can cost an investor all of the expected gains and profits.

As was mentioned in the last chapter, long-term investors should be aware of where the market is so that they can make the best decisions regarding whether to hold, liquidate, sell, or exchange their properties into different markets when conditions are changing. Contrary to what you might think, you should not aim to buy *only* at the bottom of the market and sell *only* at the top of the market. Investors benefit by holding onto property until they meet their investment goals, regardless of when the property was purchased. This may mean selling a property anytime in the market cycle. For example, many investors have recently been selling their properties in Southern California, speculating that they are at the top of the market. They are parking their money in safe accounts generating really low rates of returns. This is not very wise business. As a long-term investor, you can still receive the benefits of owning real estate, even when the price drops, so it is important to remember that although timing the market can be helpful, it is not the only factor you need to consider as a long-term investor. Don't feel pressured to time the market perfectly.

THE FIVE STAGES OF ALL REAL ESTATE MARKETS

As you can see from Figure 13.1, there are five stages to every real estate market. What goes up, must eventually come down—and then go back up again! It's real estate's own circle of life. Over the past 90 years, real estate values have doubled almost every ten years in healthy and diverse economies. Be prepared for these real estate cycles to occur because they are normal. I wish that I had a crystal ball and could promise you that these cycles would occur exactly every ten years. Unfortunately, real estate is not an exact science. Some cycles will last longer than others. What you can do, however, is plan for these cycles by using past information to inform you of patterns that have occurred. This way, you will be prepared for the cycles and can make some assumptions about the future. The key is determining the stage that any market is currently in.

Stage 1: Top of the Market

This stage is represented by *A* on the chart. You know that you are near the top of the market when the asking prices are so high that most of the population can't afford to purchase the average priced home in the area. It has been demonstrated historically that when affordability indices drop below 14 percent, it is a sign that the market is likely to be correcting soon.

The top of the market is characterized by sellers asking ridiculous prices and by buyers becoming more and more reluctant to pay those prices. Investment properties no

FIGURE 13.1: **Timing the Real Estate Market**

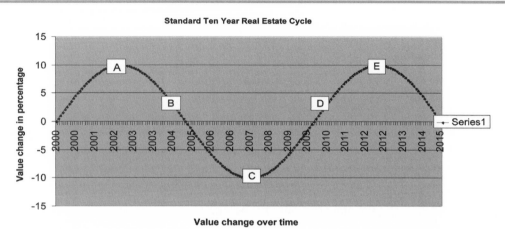

Fact: Real Estate Values Fluctuate. They Go Up And They Come Down!

A = Top of market, novice investors focus on appreciation, concerned with value and constraints on cash flow, low returns on equity.

B = Declining market, novice investors fear value drops, most want to sell, high rates of return on equity generated during this time.

C = Bottom of market, novice investors want to buy, but fear continued market drops, depressed attitudes, highest returns on equity.

D = Inclining market, novice investors become "geniuses" by market increases, lost returns by focusing on value, not rate of return.

E = Top of market, novice investors focus on mistakes by their noninvolvement during last RE cycle, skeptical of market data.

Actions to Take in the Different Market Cycles

A –C Declining Market
- Improve the physical condition of the property
- Keep vacancy rates low
- Slowly reduce rental prices
- Use the cheap labor

C – E Appreciating Market
- Be very active moving around properties in your portfolio
- Exchange, sell, refinance
- Set up a home equity line of credit
- Don't get loans with prepayment penalties

Stay focused on sustainability, not real estate values!

Top of the market steps to watch out for:

1. Property list prices begin to drop
2. An increase in market time
3. An increase in the amount of inventory
4. Sold prices begin to decline

longer make financial sense, and investors begin pulling their money out of the market. Unfortunately, novice and beginner investors don't always recognize the top of the market when they see it. Never having experienced an adjusting market correction, they are excited about the recent gains and wealth made in the market and still believe that the market will continue to climb for a long time to come. There are some specific things for you to focus on to avoid those rookie mistakes.

Pay attention to lulls in the market. It is important that when property values are at their peak and there is excitement everywhere, you pay attention to what is happening with prices. If you notice a lull in the market or a slowing down in the rapid increase in prices for a period of more than six months, it is likely that a dip in pricing is about to take place. It is important to pay attention to because when property prices begin to shift downward, they usually continue to decline for a long period, sometimes as long as five to six years. Keeping a watchful eye will help you decide when to liquidate some of the properties in your portfolio that you do not want to keep in a particular declining market.

Refinance property and get fully leveraged. The top of the market is the perfect time for you to refinance and get all of your properties securely financed. Leverage your properties to the maximum level that you are able to sustain and that produces rates of returns on equity that match your overall plans and goals. Whenever possible, this is the time to get home equity lines of credit (HELOC) or second trust deeds established on the property, but don't use the HELOC for buying lifestyle items. Keep the HELOC in place so that when market conditions shift and you are unable to pay the mortgage or other expenses, you are protected and able to use this money safely.

HELOCs should be established to protect the investor in order to retain the property in case of a job loss, rent decrease, or mortage or variance rates increase. HELOCs can be used in the same manner as reserves and savings accounts.

Sell the property now. If you are thinking about selling or exchanging a property because you do not want to wait out the adjustment in the cycle, plan on selling the property right when the market begins to level out or early in the declining market. Otherwise, you might need to wait for the entire cycle to readjust itself to get the same favorable conditions. Be aggressive in selling your property so that you get your gains now when the market is just beginning to turn. You don't want to chase the market on its way down. When you sell, make sure that you buy another property that is producing a better rate of return than you were getting on the property you just sold. Don't sell out of panic. Be strategic. Know why you are selling and what your intentions are for the replacement property.

If you do not find replacement property that has higher ROEs than the property you are selling or does not improve the asset mix of your real estate portfolio, maybe you should wait until you find a suitable opportunity to buy. Keeping your real estate equity (from the sale of a property) in a low yielding savings or mutual fund account is a costly investment decision. Make sure you are strategically selling the property and not reacting to what everyone is telling you. Be strategic and thoughtful about the decisions you are making.

Take your money to another market. It can be beneficial to place the money you get out of a declining market into a market that is at the bottom of the curve and about to take off for a long period of appreciation. Doing thorough research to find such a market will not only improve the gains you make, but it will greatly assist you in protecting and growing your real estate portfolio.

Stage 2: Declining Real Estate Market

This stage is marked *B* on the chart. When the real estate market turns the corner and begins to decline, it is usually not going to correct itself for many years. Property owners can try to hold back the decline by staying firm with their prices and not budging too much when they are negotiating the sale of their properties, but when the tide of real estate declines has arrived, there is generally not much anyone can do about it. There are very specific actions investors should be taking during this downturn in the market.

Improve the physical condition of the property. When property values are declining, long-term investors will find that this is often a quiet time in the ownership. They will not be moving their equities around through refinancing or exchanging. This is the perfect time to work your way through your to-do list and make those physical improvements on your investments you've been putting off. New paint, carpet, and landscaping should be done during this slow time. These improvements mean a lot to tenants, and if they feel like they are treated fairly, they will be less likely to move. It is also important to attend to repair items immediately. Doing this decreases tenant complaints, increases their willingness to stay, and encourages others to move into the property.

This is the time in the market when the property owner is looking to increase the efficiency of running her properties to create the greatest profits from the physical and fiscal management. Focusing on decreasing vacancy rates through improving the property condition is one way to increase efficiency by decreasing expenses and increasing income. You may choose to use some of the money you have in your home equity line or from the second trust deed to make these necessary repairs. Luckily for you, a downturn in the market is often when labor costs are the cheapest because many people are out of work.

Keep tenants happy by reducing rental rates. The last thing you need during a market downturn is vacancies. While vacancies will naturally occur in residential rental ownership, you'll want to do anything you can to make your tenants happy so that they will stay in your property. This sometimes includes dropping the rents slightly (but not too dramatically) to stay competitive with the going market rates. If you keep the physical condition of the property in good shape, and your tenants are happy with how you manage the property, you should not have to drop the rental rates very much.

If you do have a vacancy, don't be stingy and wait for the highest priced rents. It is better to reduce the rates and fill the unit than to wait to get your price. Act swiftly to fill up the unit with good, qualified candidates. You may also need to offer other incentives such as bonuses for encouraging relatives or friends to move into vacant units.

Stage 3: Bottom of the Market

Represented on the chart as *C*, this is the time when there is the most despair in the marketplace. Everyone hopes that the market won't get any worse. Foreclosure rates will have begun to slow down, and the general atmosphere in the market is depressed. Beginner and novice investors are reluctant to invest because they have been witnessing nothing but bad news in real estate values. For informed investors who know how to read the signs and are strategically positioned to make decisive moves, the bottom of the market can be the best time to buy. Bargains and discounts are abundant in this depressed market. Keep your eyes peeled for the following:

Look for small commercial real estate spaces to fill up first. When the small commercial real estate spaces start to fill up, the economy is beginning to show signs of improvement, and the real estate prices are usually not far behind. Commercial real estate is one of the first indications that the economy is improving. People who were laid off or lost their jobs in the bad market have started their small businesses and can now afford to rent out an office space to expand their small but growing businesses.

Buy foreclosure and defaulted properties. When investors begin to come into the marketplace and are buying up the standing inventory, you know that the market is beginning to turn. You will notice that the amount of time a property is on the market will shorten and improve, and prices will stop declining and level out. This is a fantastic time to swoop in on those last foreclosures and defaulted properties. You will see a decrease or slowing up of the number of foreclosures in the market.

Buy rental properties. Investors are coming into the area because the properties will generate cash flow and sustain themselves. Rental properties are an excellent option when the prices are low. This is when prices will most closely match the rents that are generated on the property and cash flow is abundant.

Buy properties that are in good condition and/or in good neighborhoods. In a bad market, you've got the pick of the litter. You might as well go against what the masses are saying and buy under the best conditions. Now is the time to buy properties that are in good condition or in nice neighborhoods. It'll be a while before you see such bargains again, so definitely take advantage. Buy all of the property you can, but make sure they meet your goals and objectives. As long as you are informed on what is occurring in the marketplace, you are in the best position to capitalize on the seller's fear of continued market drops.

> *Hot Tip*
>
> There will also be a large surplus of properties on the market as depressed sellers finally feel they can sell their properties and get out from under them. This oversupply of inventory usually lasts no more than nine months.

A decrease in foreclosures and defaults. Most of the people who desperately needed to sell their homes will probably already have done so or will have lost their homes to the banks at the bottom of the market. Either way, you'll notice a significant decline in the number of foreclosures and defaults as the market improves.

Stage 4: The Inclining Market

We've made our way to *D* on the chart. In this phase, the real estate market will slowly show signs of price increases. Properties will sell faster, and people will finally experience financial relief after many years of real estate declines. This is often the time when sellers who have waited out the declining market put their homes on the market. You can get some really great deals as the market begins to pick up. The increasing market prices can last for many years, so hold on tight. The market can increase at tremendous rates. Watch for the following.

Big corporation or industry moves into the town or area. It is always a good sign when a large company plans on moving into a depressed area. Big corporations can really help the economy in a region, and if they will be bringing in lots of jobs and people, existing real estate prices will naturally jump.

Sellers begin to get their asking prices. Take note when the marketing and selling times decrease and sellers begin to get the prices they are asking. There is relief in the real estate market at last! Excitement is slow to come, however. People will still be reluctant to believe that their real estate will finally be worth more again. But you know better.

Pay attention to the equity in your properties. Now that the real estate market is improving again, this is one of the most active times to own real estate. You can't be lazy and fall asleep on your investments! It is crucial at this point in the cycle to keep your money working for you. This is not the time to be improving the physical condition of the property (remember, we already did that in step 2). Instead, pay closer attention to the appreciation you are getting. This is also a critical time to look at the rate of return on equity. Your ROE will begin to decline when you leave a lot of equity in each property. You need to be refinancing and deciding if you are going to be buying more real estate. Move your money around to ensure you get the best ROE from each property. This is the time in the market when investors need to know about 1031 exchanges and other more sophisticated real estate transactions that will help them capitalize on tax savings and tax deferred alternatives. I discuss those more in Chapter 18.

Stage 5: Back at the Top Again

The final stage is market *E* on the chart. This is a time in the market when owners who have weathered the storms of real estate investing are feeling pretty good. They may be a bit weather worn, but they are financially in a good position. Their overall portfolio should have doubled at least, and they should have some good equity built up. If they've paid attention to my advice, they have a substantial portfolio of real estate that is diverse and balanced.

Chances are, they own several properties that they really like and other properties that are more hassles than they are worth. Overall though, they are very satisfied with the results of their efforts and can comfortably look at being able to live off the passive income of their real estate portfolio in the near future. Some investors will decide to slow down the cycle, and others will want to continue investing. One advantage to having been in the real estate market for ten years or longer is that investors understand the maturity of the market and are not as starry eyed. They know how real estate can have its tough times and have not only discovered how to compensate for these challenges but also have learned from their mistakes. They are also more realistic about how to slowly grow their wealth and keep it. When you have a mature diversified portfolio for over ten years, you will have learned a lot and have plenty of options. Congratulations!

SUSTAINING YOUR REAL ESTATE OVER TIME

The number-one problem I see with investors today is their unrealistic expectation of how real estate really functions. They are unfamiliar with the real estate market, especially when it decreases in value or, worse yet, when it does not appreciate at the tremendous rates that have been seen recently in some parts of the country. It is natural for people to react to what they have most recently seen. An example of this would be the fact that for the past several years, Southern California, Florida, Arizona, and parts of the East Coast have experienced incredible market increases, sometimes 25 percent gains in property values in one year. It can't be emphasized enough how this is *not* standard and is not how long-term investors should be calculating their numbers.

Long-term investors need to be realistic and conservative in how they approach maintaining and sustaining their investment portfolios in the good times as well as the bad times. Because of the nature of the beast, real estate gains will be experienced for a time and then will immediately be followed by losses of up to 20 to 30 percent. When you are a long-time investor, you will experience some of the wins in the market and some of the losses. Fortunately, historically these gains have always outperformed the losses, so investors who keep and sustain their properties during these cycles will win in the long run. Smart investors want to be able to learn to sustain their property in both markets. Here a few tips to help investors stay in real estate during the changing markets.

Rental rates will drop. Be prepared to sustain your properties with a rental rate decrease of about 10 to 15 percent. Rates will typically not decrease by any more than that amount, but to be sure, ask a local property management company that has been working in the area for at least ten years what the historical trends have been when *that* market is depressed. It is worth noting that these numbers hold true for economies that are diversified. If the economy is too dependent on any one industry, it can be vulnerable to more severe drops. This is what happened in the Texas markets that have a lot of their economy dependent on large businesses and corporations. When they experience the normal flushing out of their companies, the whole economy goes into the tank and you see greater declines than those experienced in more diverse and dense economies which are made up of small- and mid-sized companies.

Prices and value drop. Most of the time, real estate values for single-family residences and condos will decrease no more than 20 to 25 percent in any market adjustment. Multiple unit properties and land have historically experienced greater drops in value, sometimes up to 40 to 50 percent decreases. Just remember that rents don't decrease that much, so you should only worry if you plan to sell during this downturn in the market.

Maintaining and keeping the property is more important than how much the price declines when you intend on holding onto the property through the market downturn.

Vacancy rates increase. When real estate decreases in value, usually the whole economy is going through a rough time. This means that unemployment rates increase. Because people without jobs don't often move, the unemployed are more likely to stay where they are or move in with family or relatives (i.e., leaving an existing rental unit vacant). In addition, children who might otherwise enter the rental market may feel the financial pinch and put off moving out of their parents' houses. Fortunately, vacancy rates do not typically increase to more than 10 to 15 percent, even in really bad markets.

Mortgage interest rates increase. Be prepared for interest rates to increase. When the mortgage interest rates go up, fewer people can afford to buy homes. Yet, sellers still want to sell their homes, so they drop their prices to keep the greatest number of buyers looking at their properties. Look at the terms of the note that you signed with the bank when you originated the loan. There you'll find some parameters that will tell you the maximum the loan can adjust and the amount per year it can increase your mortgage payment. These numbers are essential so that you know how to plan for the worst-case scenario when markets adjust.

MAKING WEALTH IN ANY REAL ESTATE MARKET

Hopefully, you've recognized from the examples above that investors can actually make very wise and strategic investment decisions by holding onto their real estate investments for the long haul in any given market cycle. Investors who react to the natural ebbs and flows of the real estate market are likely to make rash decisions based on fear and impulse. My goal is to give you the necessary strategy, planning, and understanding so that you make the best and smartest decisions. As you learned in Chapter 6, the key to deciding whether or not to hold onto an investment is to always keep the four components of smart investing in mind: cash flow, appreciation, loan reduction, and tax savings. These components, combined with targeting your ROE goals, will help you hold onto your properties in down-turning markets and lead you to long-term, sustainable wealth.

Investors who know what they intend to do and have a plan for each parcel of real estate they own can act slowly and cautiously when real estate does what it naturally will do, which is fluctuate. You may strategically decide to hold onto your real estate through the entire cycle because you like where it is located or want to keep it for personal or financial reasons. Understand that you may see a drop in the value of your investment during the down cycle, but this is normal. You must not forget to recognize the other rewards of owning real estate: tax benefits, rental income, and loan reduction. When you have a thorough understanding of all the benefits, it's easy to be more patient and wait out a market downturn. For more information about reading and understanding the economic conditions of any market, see Appendix C.

HOW TO BE PREPARED FOR MARKET DROPS

There are some key action steps investors can make to help sustain their investment real estate during all real estate market adjustments and conditions. First, take out an equity line on your primary residence to help augment mortgage payments when the rental income decreases during declining markets. Equity lines should be taken out when the market is healthy and you have a good paying job and good credit. Right now also happens to be a good time to establish low interest rates. Next, you'll want to review the Alternatives for Profitability Form in Figure 13.2. Fill out this form for each property you have in your portfolio. These alternatives for profit are crucial when you have either lost your job or you are experiencing a loss of rental income.

• • •

Now that you're prepared for any market condition, it's time to start thinking about financing. In the next chapter, you'll make sense of all of your options by looking at the various techniques available for obtaining financing through various loans. You'll also learn some valuable information about establishing partnerships and strategic alliances. Getting money suddenly got easier!

FIGURE 13.2: **Alternatives for Profitability: Creating Highest and Best Use**

Every property should have at least four different alternatives for profitability. Strategies need to be preplanned so they can fluctuate with market conditions. It is important that you define the top four priorities for each property so you are prepared. Here are some of your options:

- Raising rents
- Enhancing property condition
- Subdividing land
- Adding additional rooms or increasing square footage
- Refinancing to get money out
- Refinancing for lower interest rates
- Exchanging property
- Making charitable donations
- Making estate distribution to heirs
- Selling property and carrying paper
- Paying off debt, living on cash flow

Your Alternatives (do this for each property and review it every year)

First Alternative: _____

_____

_____

Second Alternative: _____

_____

_____

Third Alternative: _____

_____

_____

Fourth Alternative: _____

_____

_____

$$

I Sold My Expensive Home and Bought Investment Properties

I accidentally got involved in real estate back in 1978 when my family entered into a partnership where we owned a partial share of 58 units in Brooklyn, New York. We never really had to get actively involved with this investment, and over time I noticed how much equity and wealth we were acquiring with minimal effort. During the 1980s and 1990s, I was busy making a living in the stock market and financial planning world, and by the late 1990s I was tired of the rat race in the commodities market. So I decided to put a portion of my money into real estate and started investing full time in this market.

After evaluating my real estate portfolio, I realized that I had a lot of my money sitting in my personal home. I also had a young wife with a brand new child. I decided to put my values in alignment with my investments and sell my beautiful and expensive perfect house by the beach so that I could have extra money to invest. I thought that by living more modestly I could have a more secure financial future for my family. My wife and I had a difficult time deciding to sell our dream house, but made the leap anyway. We now live in a less expensive home in a great area, and I have increased my real estate portfolio by $600,000 in my first year. I could not be happier with our decision to put our money to better use for our lifestyle and dreams.

Today, the most satisfying part of my job is finding investment properties for my investor clients in areas that are appreciating around the country. I teach my clients how to time the market accurately and keep their investment dollars working for them, much like I saw my family's real estate investments pay off over time. I have turned my life around and am thankful that I have a solid strategy to make this happen as well as the tools to take control of our lifestyle while still respecting our values and personal needs. Real estate is one of the smartest investments on the planet. I love helping people realize this!

—JIM DUTKA, REAL ESTATE BROKER, INVESTOR, HAPPY HUSBAND, AND DAD

Securing Financing and Powerful Partnerships

"You have to think anyway, so why not think big?"
—Donald Trump

Obtaining and securing the right type of financing can be a daunting experience for *any* investor—new or seasoned. Some people have the desire to invest, but don't have the capital to get started and don't know where to get it. Others have the money, but get overwhelmed and frustrated when they try to make sense of all of the various loan programs and options available to them. Because all investors need access to money and a variety of lending sources if they are to grow and expand their real estate portfolios, it is important to be tenacious as you attempt to navigate the sometimes tricky waters of financing.

Do not be discouraged. The waters may be tricky, but I'm here to provide you with a strong and steady boat. The first place to start in securing your financing is with an attitude of confidence. Now is not the time to fall back on your favorite excuses. If you have some blemishes on your credit, don't let that stop you. If you have really great credit but are afraid to refinance your home and incur additional debt and monthly payments, relax. You have proven to yourself and to the world that you are worthy of having credit and being responsible. Now is the time to take your responsibility to the next level and grow your financial future. Don't stop looking for the money to make your real estate plan a reality until someone else puts the final nail into your financial coffin. More importantly, make sure you are not putting the nails into your own coffin and killing off all of the possibilities due to fear or anxiety. If you get overwhelmed, take it slowly, but make sure that you stay with it. Do whatever it takes to get started on the road to making your financial dreams come true.

CHOOSING A LENDER

It seems especially difficult to make informed decisions today because there are so many different choices. This is why selecting a lender you trust and who is knowledgeable about the field can be so crucial. Make sure you select someone who is interested in being a long-term business partner with you, someone who wants you to succeed today, tomorrow, and in ten years. Finding the right lender can greatly impact your profits in your real estate portfolio development.

DON'T FORGET
As you expand to different areas around the country, you will need different lenders who can secure loans in that particular state.

Once you've decided on a lender, it is critical that you share the details of your real estate plan with him. Your lender should know that you have different intentions for each property that you own. (Remember that from previous chapters?) That means that the financing that is selected should reflect where the property is located, its cash flow, how long you intend to own it, and the level of risk that you are willing to take. Be prepared to learn a lot about different loan programs that come available over the years. Lending is an ever evolving and changing world. Find someone who is competent and fully immersed in this world and who will give you good, solid advice about which loan programs will work best for you.

FINANCING INVESTMENT PROPERTIES

Financing is extremely important, especially as your real estate portfolio matures and you find yourself managing quite a bit of equity and cash flow. As you start investing, you'll discover that there are major differences between residential and commercial financing. The primary difference is that when evaluating your financing options, institutions lending on residential properties will always look at *your* household income while commercial lenders look at *the property's* income (cash flow). Residential multifamily complexes of up to four units are generally treated as residential properties. Multifamily complexes that are five units or more are classified as commercial loans, even if they are residential buildings. Look at some of the differences in how these properties are financed.

Residential Multifamily: Two to Four Units

Lenders want to know if the property will be owner occupied or nonowner occupied. This just means whether you live on the property or not. This is important to note because by living on the property, you are able to get

Nonowner-occupied interest rates can be half a percent to 1 percent higher than owner-occupied interest rates.

some of the best financing available. In most cases, the available interest rates and down payment requirements are lower for owner-occupied properties than they are for investment properties. In contrast, when you are seeking money for nonowner occupied properties, you will pay more to borrow the money and it will be at higher interest rates.

The loan amount will determine whether the loan is a conforming loan under the loan limits set by Fannie Mae (FMNA) or if it is a jumbo loan (where the loan amount exceeds conforming limits). The amount for jumbo loans changes frequently, and you will want to talk with your lender about the current jumbo loan limits. Conforming credit criteria set by FNMA and FHLMC (Freddie Mac) are standard nationwide and must be complied with if the lender wants to sell the loan after it has been originated. These criteria include a specific amount of down payment (usually 3 to 25 percent), income and debt ratios (which usually can not exceed 35 to 45 percent), and credit standards (good FICO scores).

One- and two-unit properties can generally be purchased with a zero down payment loan, while three- and four-unit properties could require

DEFINITION
Fannie Mae. The Federal National Mortgage Association, or Fannie Mae, is a privately owned corporation that buys loans from banks and loan brokers at a discounted rate in what is called the secondary market. Banks and loan brokers originate these loans for investors or homeowners and then sell them to Fannie Mae in mass quantities. Each of the loans must meet the specific lending criteria set by Fannie Mae or the lenders and banks can't sell them on the secondary market. This is why you will hear lenders and banks refer to underwriting criteria. This often refers to the Fannie Mae guidelines.

DEFINITION

Freddie Mac. The Federal Home Loan Mortgage Corporation, FHLMC or Freddie Mac, is a federally chartered corporation that is for the savings association industry. It has many of the same operations as Fannie Mae, but is run by the Department of Housing and Urban Development (HUD). It also buys loans in bulk and has loan criteria similar to Fannie Mae.

increased down payments from 5 to 10 percent and up to 20 to 25 percent. There are so many different loan programs that you will want to discover which ones work best for your given circumstance.

Jumbo loans usually require larger down payments. However, for many applicants, and especially applicants with good credit ratings (determined by a high FICO score) loans requiring lesser down payments are often available. These loans might come at the cost of a slightly higher interest rate or require private mortgage insurance (PMI), especially if the down payment is less than 20 percent. Check with an experienced mortgage banker or broker to determine the best options available for your particular situation.

Commercial Loans

Commercial properties are more than just the local mall or the 7-Eleven down the street. Properties that would be considered commercial include: five or more residential units, retail establishments, offices, industrial buildings, and hotels/resorts. Your choice of lenders to provide commercial financing will be different than for residential real estate. You can find financing at banks, savings and loans, insurance companies, private investors, and even the sellers of the property, who often have an interest in carrying paper or a note on the property. Regional, local, and community banks are typically very active in the commercial financing market-

DEFINITION

FICO score. The Fair Isaac Corporation (FICO) invented the three-digit formula that can dictate a lot about your financial future. A FICO score is a very important measure of your credit worthiness, i.e., your ability to pay back borrowed money. Your FICO score will determine the interest rate you will pay on credit cards, car loans, home mortgages, cell phones, and rent.

place. They typically offer loans ranging from $200,000 to $2,500,000. Other players in this market also have varying specialties and corresponding loan limits.

The property is the critical factor that is evaluated in commercial lending. Lenders often make exceptions for properties they particularly like (or dislike), especially local banks. For example, a local lender has a $2,500,000 maximum loan limit guideline for residential units. If a strong buyer wants to purchase a nice property that requires a loan larger than its limits, it is very possible (even probable) that the lender can obtain an exception from the guideline and make the loan. This is why many commercial investors have friendly professional relationships with local banks that keep the loans generated through their offices rather than sell them to the secondary market. This is called "portfolio money," or money that the bank will keep and use in its own bank portfolio. Banks are very cautious on their investments and want to see the credit worthiness of the investors and properties they keep in their own portfolios. They are also able to risk more if they like you and like what you are contributing to the community. Commercial lenders often specialize in certain types of property; therefore, it is important to make sure your lender is experienced with the type of property you are purchasing.

Now for the "million dollar" question: what determines whether you get a commercial loan? Commercial loan qualification is based primarily on the property's net operating income, value, debt service coverage ratio, and the strength and experience of the borrower. Lenders are not as interested in who you are as a borrower as they are in how the property's income will perform to support the new loan. It is important to consult with an experienced, knowledgeable commercial broker about loan qualifications and programs.

Land

Undeveloped land, often called "raw land," is financed differently than both residential and commercial property. Lenders generally require rather large down payments for buyers of raw land, sometimes more than 25 to 30 percent. In addition, because there are no improvements like a house or office building on the property, there is no possibility of the property generating any rent or cash flow, unless there is agriculture or parking that can generate income on the property. So why buy land? Raw land is purchased for one of two reasons: either to be held for a period of time in the expectation of price appreciation or to be improved soon after the purchase. If improvements are to be made to the property, the seller will often provide financing for the buyer during this time.

Lenders sometimes will also combine a construction loan with the loan needed to purchase the raw land. Once the improvements are made, a "take out" loan is completed, which results in the permanent financing for the project. Again, requirements differ by

> **DEFINITION**
> The *debt service coverage ratio* is the amount of debt (or loan) that is on the property compared to the amount of projected income (or gross scheduled income) that is coming in on the property. Most banks and lending institutions want to see a debt coverage ratio of at least 1.2. That number means that the amount of expected income for the property exceeds the amount of debt on the property by 20 percent. This ensures the lender that enough income is coming in to cover all of the bills, including unexpected expenses and vacancies that naturally occur with investment real estate. It is also important to know that most banks will run the expected income with a vacancy rate sometimes up to 25 percent. They run very conservative numbers to insure that they will get paid when there are troubles with the property or the overall rental market drops.

area and the desired use for the property. Seek a knowledgeable lender in your area for the specific details.

HARD MONEY LENDING

Hard money lenders get a bad rap in the world of business and finance, but they should not always be considered your enemy. In fact, they can sometimes be your best allies. There may be times in your investing career when you need short-term cash quickly, and it will be worth paying the higher points and interest in order to secure a deal. Paying a little extra money to get money quickly or to bridge two transactions can be a very profitable alternative for you. This does not mean that you should finance your long-standing real estate portfolio with hard money. However, in a pinch or for people with credit problems, locate good hard money lenders and keep them on your team. You'll be surprised how this can benefit you in the long run.

> **Hot Tip** If you are paying high interest rates of 18 percent—be careful. Try to find properties with seller financing who will work with you at more reasonable rates. Sellers are usually more understanding and will loan money to you at current interest rates or maybe a percentage higher than conventional rates.

If you don't have a proven track record of managing your money well, the bottom line is that it will cost you. You may look at paying anywhere from 5 to 10 points for the money and interest rates of up to 10 to 18 percent. Don't worry, it's not the end of the world. If you need the money to get into a deal and have run all the numbers to ensure that it is a wise business move, then it just might be the best money you spend. The longer you wait doing nothing, the more frustrated you will become because you have not built up the necessary net equity to keep you from relying on other people's money to get you into transactions. Don't be too resistant to having to spend a little extra money to make money. If you learn to stay safely in the game of real estate investing, you will not need to rely on this more expensive means of creating long-term wealth. You will be wealthy because you have stayed consistent and steady.

Repairing Your Credit

I discussed credit as it relates to reducing your debt in Chapter 4, but because we are talking about financing, it is worth mentioning again. Some minor credit repairs can be handled through your lender, but make sure that the lender knows what she is doing. It is also important that you don't attempt to figure out how to repair your credit without some outside assistance. Remember: your thinking got you into these credit problems, so don't rely on your thinking to get you out of them.

CREATIVE FINANCING

People love to see how they can get around the system with creative financing. Thinking outside of the box is a good part of what makes new companies succeed and flourish. Besides, if Columbus hadn't been curious about the unknown, he would have never discovered the Americas. The point is, in a world of round holes, there are plenty of square pegs. All it takes is a little creativity to find a way to make them fit.

Many people who buy real estate don't fit the conventional means of qualifying and must find other alternatives to make the deal work. These investors need to think creatively. You'd be amazed at how creative you can be when there is money on the line! Creative financing comes in the form of seller financing, hard money loans, federal grant or redevelopment money, plus many other ideas not thought of yet. I have used several of these methods in my real estate career and been very successful with them.

> **DEFINITION**
>
> *Insanity.* Doing the same thing over and over again and expecting different results. History has a way of repeating itself. Don't keep trying the same old thing and hope that somehow this time it will work out. Some problems just can't be solved on your own. Get help so that you stop your insane behavior, especially if it relates to spending habits and financial management.

When using creative financing, start using the words "how can I make this work?" and "what do I need to do to get this deal done?" Powerful statements like these and a positive can-do attitude are what make people wealthy in the game of real estate investing. Your real estate transactions won't complete themselves, no matter how much you want it, so you'd better start thinking about how to make your deals work. You are the most important ingredient in whether your real estate portfolio will grow and succeed. Be creative.

SMALL BUSINESS ADMINISTRATION (SBA) LOANS

Many investors will need to obtain SBA loans when they are looking at purchasing commercial real estate. These loans are not as easy to secure as conforming residential loans. The SBA was originally set up to help small business owners get the funding they need to start their companies. This many times includes commercial real estate that is housing the place where the business is being conducted. The SBA requires a sound business plan, solid tax returns, and an ability to pay the loan. They will allow the small business owner to borrow enough money to pay back the loan through monthly payments. For investors who have strong financial records, lots of collateral, and a good business plan, getting SBA financing is easy. For people who do not show strong credit scores, have low income tax records, and lack collateral, getting these loans can be much more difficult.

DEFINITION

Collateral. Using additional security such as real estate, coins, or jewelry as a pledge for the payment of a new loan. This means that if you default or are unable to pay the debt, the lender has a lien on another asset to recover the payments.

The SBA will tell you that there are no collateral requirements, yet I have seen very few loans go through that haven't been dependent on really good credit scores and an ability to collateralize some asset to secure the loan.

If this is you, don't give up. Keep going. If you are seeking an SBA loan for an office building and can't secure it through the SBA, ask the seller to finance the building for you on favorable terms. Many commercial transactions are put together this way due to tougher loan requirements in commercial lending.

CREATING POWERFUL PARTNERSHIPS

Partnerships can be a key part of the financing process and may even be necessary when beginning your real estate investment career. Investors use partnerships when they can't secure financing on their own or when the property they intend to purchase is going to produce a negative cash flow. Some investors do not have the necessary disposable income to incur the negative cash flow, so a good solution is to find one or more partners to minimize the monthly negative impact. Sharing the burden of investing with others will help you avoid feeling 100 percent exposed.

Once you have been investing for a while, have established a credit history, and have equity in your real estate portfolio, it is not uncommon for you to want to try new types of real estate or try larger investment projects. As I discussed in Chapter 5, this is typically another time when new partnerships are formed. They usually come about when investors feel they are not competent to manage a new project on their own.

Know What You Bring to the Table When Negotiating Partnerships

If you decide to create a partnership, take a serious look at who you are and what assets and liabilities both you and the other person(s) would bring to the partnership. Here are some types of partnerships:

- *Money partner.* Some of the partners with whom you will be involved will be strictly money partners. Most money partners are interested in what rate of return they will get on their money, the type of real estate they will be purchasing, and what risks will be involved with that purchase. They are less likely to be concerned with the day-to-day operations of the real estate portfolio. Money partners can be more mature investors who have already successfully invested and now have the proceeds to reinvest; they may have inherited their money or assets from their families; or they may simply have saved money from their careers.

- *Working or physical labor partner.* If you need to build up some equity and don't have a lot of money to invest, sometimes a good way to become a partner in a property is to become a working partner. They are the ones who manage the portfolio and have more hands-on experience relating to the growth and health of the investment. Often, the working partner locates the new properties, runs all of the numbers, puts together the partnership agreement, and does a lot of the management related to the investment. Working partners are not required to do the physical labor at the property or the property management, but would definitely be the contact person regarding the operations of the real estate investment. This type of partnership is an especially good option for a beginner investor.
- *Knowledgeable partner.* There are partners who don't want to put any money in the deal and don't want to give of their time, but come to the table with a lot of business acumen and experience. In exchange for this knowledge, they are willing to be advisors and get partnership shares. People who have put many properties together and have years of investing success are usually great partners to have on your team.
- *Credit partner.* Sometimes all you need is someone who is willing to let you use his credit for a portion of the equity in the real estate investment. Credit partners may not have much experience with investment real estate, they may not have cash, they may not have a lot of time to devote to the investment, but they have great credit and are willing to let you use it. This type of partner works well with beginner investors who have good jobs but bad credit.
- *Fee-for-service partner (contractors, realtors, attorneys, and architects).* There are many partners who will come into the transaction because they have specific skills and trades to offer to the partnership. Fee-for-service partners usually get paid their normal fee to conduct business for the partnership, but the fee for their service will be paid through a portion of partnership equity and liability.

Laying Down the Ground Rules for Your Partnership

Once you've determined what type of partnership you will have, there are many details you'll still need to plan when creating that partnership. These details, from cash requirements to partnership termination, need to be understood by everyone—and included in the partnership agreement.

Cash requirements. Every real estate transaction is going to require a certain amount of cash that needs to be put into the deal. You will want to know each and every cost of buying into the investment and decide in advance how you and your partner will split these costs. Specifically, make sure you know about all of the closing costs, the immediate capital improvements that are needed, and down payment requirements.

Expected rates of return. Make sure that all partners are aware of the positive and negative aspects of the real estate investment and have clear understandings of what the expected returns will be. It is especially important that you have all of the partners' expectations out in the open. Unmet expectations are where partnerships can get sidetracked or shipwrecked. Try to avoid these unnecessary headaches by discussing plainly what returns everyone is expecting out of the property.

Intention of partnership. Clearly define what each partner intends to do with the particular piece of real estate that is shared. Make sure that each investor is aware of the other's intentions. Again, the more time you take to address these items, the less likely you will run into problems later on in the partnership.

Length of partnership. Not all partnerships are alike. Some of them are short-term; some last for 10 to 20 years. Usually partnerships are formed over specific parcels of real estate. If you have a legal entity such as a limited liability corporation (LLC), you will need to clearly state what the length of the term is for the partnership. Even without a legal entity, it is a good idea to discuss how long each of you thinks the partnership will last.

Roles in partnership. There are many different roles that partners can play when coming together. Some of the partners may choose to be very actively involved in the real estate investment, whereas others will prefer to be more removed from the day-to-day activities of the property. It is important to define the specific roles for each person involved in the partnership.

Legal contract of the partnership agreement. It is crucial that you have a legally binding partnership agreement drafted before you establish a financial or real estate partnership, even if it with is a family member or your best friend whom you trust more than life itself. In fact, a legal contract is sometimes even more important in these situations because your judgement can be blurry when dealing with people you love. As I've said before, buying real estate is a business, and you need to treat it like one. Please don't skip this step. Make sure you address all of the necessary items that may seem unnecessary at the beginning, but are very important later on in the partnership term. Getting good legal advice is highly recommended.

Tax implications. Some partners need the depreciation or tax benefits, and other partners may not need it as much. It is really important to determine in the partnership agreement who is going to take the tax benefits and how they are going to be divided.

Sales and exchanges. When you decide to sell or exchange an investment that is held in partnership, you can choose to dissolve the partnership and have each go his separate way or you can choose to continue the partnership. When dissolving the partnership through a sale or exchange, the partners can decide either to sell outright or exchange their portion of the equity. For example, one partner may want all of the money immediately from the transaction, whereas the other partner may want to invest the money in another property through a 1031 tax deferred exchange. (I'll discuss this concept more in Chapter 18.) Each partner is able to independently decide what to do with the proceeds from the sale of the real estate investment. They do not have to take the same actions.

Credit reports, title issues. Many investors do not know how important it is to be selective when they are picking partners. One of the partners may go through a difficult divorce or bankruptcy and her financial problems could show up on the title for the property that is shared with you. Or perhaps you could be forced to sell or liquidate the property prematurely because of an IRS credit lien or an unforeseen problem your partner has. Be cautious about who you agree to partner with in real estate and protect yourself. The best way to do this is by having a good partnership agreement signed before entering into your partnership. You may also request a title search on your partner(s) before you enter into the agreement. Credit reports are one way to get a clear picture of your partner, but title searches are also credible because they will pick up on things that may not be on the credit report. Title searches can be purchased through title companies. They will run a personal search by using a person's social security number. Avoiding or disregarding some of these precautionary measures can be a very costly mistake.

Terminating partnerships. All partnerships will eventually end. Hopefully, in the process you both have made oodles of money and things have gone well. Unfortunately, sometimes partnerships do not end on good terms. Some partnerships are terminated because one of the partners wants to get out before the term of the agreement is complete. It is often an option in the partnership agreement for the remaining partners to buy out the partner who wants to get out of the deal early. Terminating partnerships can be touchy. To avoid the strain of a difficult ending, make sure you determine how your partnership will end before you even start.

• • •

Congratulations. You've already learned all you need to know to go out there and buy some property. Once you own the property, however, a whole new set of challenges will arise. Unless you intend to let your property waste away (and then what was the point?), you'll need to know the tricks of the trade for successful property management. In the next chapter, you'll learn how to become a property management expert. I'll covers topics such as selecting the right property manager, managing the managers, and keeping accurate records. You'll also discover ways to improve your property's value, appearance, and cash flow. With a few simple hints, you'll find that property management is much easier than you ever thought.

$$

Lender Helps Long-Term Investors Make Safe Decisions

I get so much joy from helping people buy their first homes or refinance properties so they can expand their real estate portfolios with more properties. It is important that I know how long they are going to own each property and understand their risk and comfort levels when refinancing to pull money out for new purchases. I ask my clients what their goals are and listen to what they want in the long run as well as provide them with a variety of loan options to help them avoid the most common mistakes made by investors today. Putting the right loan program together for investors provides them with the necessary tools they need to *keep and sustain* the property in all market conditions. At the end of the day, I know that I really made a difference for my clients' lives today and for their futures. That's a great feeling.

—GREG BROOKS, BRANCH MANAGER AND MORTGAGE BANKER

PART FOUR

The
Real
Approach
to Wealth

Property Management for Everyone

"You get the best out of others when you give the best of yourself."
—Harvey Firestone

The wonderful thing about property management is that it hasn't changed that much over the years. Sure, there are some new technologies and software programs that make managing all of the details easier, but the basics of owning and renting real estate have essentially stayed the same. Property management can be easy and profitable for the busy investor or it can be a nightmare and frustrating if you do not pay attention to it. Fortunately, it does not have to be a big headache. Just follow my eight simple property management rules, and you'll be on your way to happy real estate returns.

EFFECTIVE PROPERTY MANAGEMENT

Everyone is a born manager, but everyone can't learn to be one. And it may turn out to be easier than you thought. Here are eight steps to help you effectively and profitably deal with the challenges of managing real estate.

Step 1: Learn About Property Management

Unless you're one of those people who already knows everything about property management, the best way to increase your knowledge is to read what other people who are successful have to say on the topic. You're off to a good start with this book, but there are lots of other books in the marketplace with really good information in them as well. Make sure you consider all of the many different techniques and styles for producing a profit on your rental properties. The only way you'll be prepared for a situation is if you see it coming, so strive to continually update your knowledge. Put simply, *read a lot and read often.* It is important to build your real estate investment book library. You'll be doing this job for many years and will need some reference books. Go to the bookstore frequently and gather information about how to improve your properties and your real estate portfolio.

Step 2: Manage the Property Yourself

Remember the old saying "if you want something done right, do it yourself?" Sometimes the best way to learn about property management is to actually manage your own property. When starting out in your real estate plan, it can be very helpful to become familiar with the details of owning rental properties: collecting rents, fixing up the properties, finding and selecting tenants, and handling all the problems. There may certainly be reasons why you don't want to manage your property yourself (like you're too busy or it's too far from home; do any of these sound familiar?). If this is your situation and you would prefer to hire a competent management company, hire a good manager right away. The decision of whether to manage or not to manage is really up to you, but as my mother used to say, a little knowledge never hurt anyone, so make sure you do your research and learn before you leap.

Step 3: Manage the Managers

Over time, as your real estate portfolio increases in value, it is best to pull away from the day-to-day management of the property and begin the habit of practicing passive property management skills. It will be time to hire a property manager to oversee the property. When you hire him, make sure you communicate what documents you will need on a monthly basis and take the time to review these documents. Let the property managers handle the rest. One of the main reasons for hiring property managers is because they will reduce your stress levels and let you focus on things that are more enjoyable for you, right? Mastering the art of effective delegation will be one of the best skills you can learn. As long as you have communicated your expectations to your property managers, learn to feel comfortable giving up some of your control to others. Your goal should be to learn how to manage your property managers effectively so that you can spend your time on more profitable or pleasurable activities. Don't forget that when you hire property managers your expenses will increase because of those additional management fees. However, sometimes those property managers can give you tips or trade secrets that increase the performance of your property, which may help cover some of these extra expenses. As long as you are getting more free time and reduced stress, this added expense is well worth the money spent, especially as you accumulate more and more properties.

Step 4: Learn to Manage the Money, not the Property

Managing the money (or equity) in your property will increase your profits substantially. Don't forget that this is your main objective for your real estate plan. Learn how to manage the money and leave the lower-level tasks to a lower-wage earning person such as a property manager. Know how much you are worth, and spend your time on the more profitable tasks. Learn to use your brain, not your brawn. This is where the wealth is made.

Step 5: Get a Mentor

There are lots of people in this world who know more than you do. Start acting like a sponge, and hire or select a mentor who will teach you new skills to effectively and profitably manage property. It is best to find someone who has owned or currently owns investment real estate and who is willing to share stories of both triumphs and failures. Model your behavior after someone who has what you want, and do what they do. But add your own specific twist and flare to it.

Step 6: Join an Apartment Association

Becoming a member of an apartment association will keep you updated on changes in property laws and regulations as well as provide you with all of the necessary forms you need to create wealth through rental properties. They can also give you recommendations and referrals to attorneys or vendors you may need when managing your properties. These organizations are very helpful to property owners.

Step 7: Join Local Real Estate Investment Clubs

Investment clubs can provide you with tips and strategies to keep you current on creating a great profit center with your real estate. They can also be a great place to hear about good deals on properties to purchase and network for future members of your investment team. The friends and colleagues you meet at these events will continue to keep you on the right track for making millions through real estate investing.

Step 8: Keep the Right Attitude

A positive attitude can make all the difference in how you handle any situation. Keep confident, stay positive, and strive for a stress-free and balanced life. It is essential for gaining the maximum rewards from your real estate investments.

SELECTING THE RIGHT PROPERTY MANAGEMENT COMPANY

Some investors are too busy maintaining careers, raising children, and having hobbies to concern themselves with the physical labor to personally manage their real estate holdings. There is nothing wrong with hiring a property manager. If you value your time and can afford the expense, then it is probably a good idea for you to have someone else managing your property. Unfortunately, your job does not end with the decision to have a property manager handle the details of your investment. Dust off your interviewing skills because just as you learned how to gather your winning team in Chapter 9, it is now essential that you take the time to interview and select the right management company.

Hiring the right property manager is one of the most important jobs you will have while executing your real estate plan. Good property managers are essential, or you will lose lots of your equity, time, and energy from low performing real estate assets. Any company you hire should meet or exceed your expectations and goals for your long-term plans. Here are some suggestions for hiring a property manager or property management company:

- Interview at least three different property managers, and make sure they have some expertise and experience. Let them know what you expect, and ask what you can do to help maketheir jobs easier. Establishing good communication in the beginning will be worth it in the end. Most likely, the management company that you choose will manage several properties. Take the time to look at some of these properties to see if they are in good shape and managed well. Do this *before* you hire the company.

- Make sure the management company is willing and capable of managing the various pieces of real estate you own. Some management companies refuse to manage run-down real estate in low-income areas. Find this out early in your relationship with them. You may end up with two different management companies in the same area or find one company that works in all areas with all types of property. Don't assume that all management companies are the same. Just because they do a good job with one kind of property does not mean they will do a good job with all kinds of properties. Ask them in what areas they specialize and listen to their answers. Look at what kinds of properties they manage.
- Select property managers who will pay attention to the details of your property and report any problems to you immediately. Be sure that you clearly define to your manager both what you require and the response times for your requests and the tenants' requests. A little problem can snowball into a big problem if it isn't promptly attended to, so be sure that your manager is quick to respond to any situation.

REAL ESTATE IS LIKE OWNING A FRANCHISE

Throughout this book, I've talked a lot about treating your real estate investments like a business. Now it's time to start thinking of them like a franchise. Franchises have a higher rate of success because they use uniform systems that have been proven over time. For example, owners of fast food franchises don't usually go in and mop the floors or make deli sandwiches. Instead, they hire managers to hire the staff who make the sandwiches. This is how you should treat your real estate portfolio. As a franchise owner, it is important to take seriously the selection of the property managers who will be directly representing you to your tenants. Hiring and maintaining good staff are critical. Don't forget that those tenants are your ticket to great wealth, so you want to respect them and treat them well. Who you hire to take care of them will greatly affect your bottom line.

Many investors get excited about being able to manage the physical condition of their property themselves. It is great to be excited, but keep in mind that if you are doing the plumbing and the fixing up of the property, you consider yourself worth the wages of an electrician, plumber, or handyperson. If you want to be a millionaire, you need to think like a millionaire and start spending your time reading the reports and looking at more real estate rather than fixing the plumbing and collecting rents. Leave those tasks for others who are more willing to continue working for someone else. As your property wealth increases, your time becomes more valuable. Learn to work smarter, not harder.

MANAGING YOUR EXPECTATIONS

If you've hired a property manager, you'll want to be extra careful to manage your expectations of how the property will be managed and how it will perform for you. It's important to remember that your management company does not own the property. They are not going to be as concerned or as particular about the property as you are, so you must be prepared to accept a certain degree of waste and unmanageability in their management style. Investors who are highly organized and meticulous often have a difficult time turning over the details of their property management to someone else. Take the time to discover what your management style is and how involved you want to be, and then communicate that to your manager. It is important to let go of some of the control and let the property managers do their jobs.

I highly recommend that you be gentle and kind to your property managers. It is a tough job, and it does not always pay that well. The hours can be long and filled with thankless tasks. Buttering up your property managers and making sure they are well cared for will pay dividends to you. Treat people with respect, and they will respect you right back. Then you'll be able to relax, take a trip to the Bahamas, and buy some more real estate.

TENANT SELECTION

Selecting the right tenant is crucial to avoiding problems in the future. Take the extra time to find stable tenants that take pride in their homes. Examining both their credit reports and job histories are two ways to help you determine their stability. Be aware that when you interview the owners of the place the prospective tenant is leaving, these current landlords may have a vested interest in having the person move out. Current owners may paint a false picture of your potential tenant and say anything to ensure that their problem tenant becomes the problem tenant of someone else. Interview them, but just be aware of this potential hazard.

COLLECTING RENTS

Some property owners like the personal involvement of visiting their investments every month to collect the rents. Although this is not highly recommended, if you decide to have the rents sent to you directly (instead of to your management company), make sure the tenants send their checks to a post office box that you have set up. Do not have your tenants drop checks off at your home or visit your place of work. Your business life should always be kept separate from your home life.

One advantage of using a property management company to collect rents is that you won't personally need to worry about late or delinquent tenants. Train the managers to file the necessary paperwork and collect the late fees. Late fees must *always* be charged when tenants do not pay on time, and tenants who have developed the habit of paying their rent late should be evicted by the management company. Although this may seem harsh, remember that you're running a franchise. You wouldn't keep an employee on staff who regularly shows up late for work or not at all, would you? Collecting your rents on time will both increase your profits and the efficiency of your property.

RAISING RENT IMPROVES PROPERTY VALUES

In addition to collecting rents on time, make sure to increase the rent periodically to keep pace with the local market. To find out how high you can go with your rental increases, ask a local property management company what the rents for similar local units are. This information will give you a range on rental rates. In addition, knowing the price per square foot on similar properties will help you determine whether you are currently charging fair market rents on your units. For example, if local properties are renting from $.85 per square foot to $.95 per square foot and your rents are at $.75 per square foot at time of purchase, you know that you have the potential to increase the income of the property through rental increases.

Some investors purchase property when the rents are low and then immediately improve the condition of the property and raise the rents. This directly increases property value on the assets you own. It's important to remember, however, that although raising rents will improve your property value, property values will increase at a much faster rate than rental rates. Rents are more related to the job market than they are to property prices and can only increase at the level of the job market salary increase.

Don't forget: if you are relaxed about increasing the rents, you will not only lose monthly income but also will lose value in your property when you try to sell it. Part of the way real estate is valued is based on the income that it is producing monthly. If you have been too generous or lazy by not raising the rents, your profits will be lower than they could be on the property, and you might have to decrease the selling price.

KEEPING THE BOOKS

Clear, defined bookkeeping will make your job a lot easier as you mature into a seasoned property owner. Most property management companies will pay all of the bills for the property and directly deposit the proceeds into your business account. In addition, they will produce monthly and annual documentation of how the property is performing. You will receive a monthly profit and loss statement that includes all of the itemized expenses and income. They will also provide you with information on which tenants are not paying on time, the vacancy rates, and any necessary capital expenses and repairs. At the end of six months, review the overall performance of your property to see if you can improve some of the profits. Once you have done the analysis, make the necessary repairs and adjustments. This is money that can be taking you one step closer to being a millionaire. Don't leave it on the table.

It is important that you use your mind to think, plan, and strategize about how to create more profit and run your real estate portfolio more efficiently. If you are going to spend time creating more profit for yourself, then take the time to review the business reports that you get from your property managers and bookkeepers.

RUNNING EFFICIENCY MODELS TO INCREASE PROFITS

When you receive your monthly reports, look at how much money is being spent on expenses in relation to the income that is being generated by the property. A general rule of thumb for how much you should be spending on expenses is as follows:

> **1 to 4 unit properties: 20 to 25 percent of gross scheduled income**
> **5 to 14 unit properties: 25 to 35 percent of gross scheduled income**
> **15+ unit properties: 35 to 55 percent of gross scheduled income**

Larger apartment complexes require greater expenses due to increases in security, on-site managers, pools, gyms, and tennis courts. The larger the complex, the greater the management costs, but the rents are also typically higher because of the additional amenities that are offered. It all equals out in the end, and you'll find that larger unit buildings produce tremendous returns despite the increase in expenses.

INCREASING PROPERTY VALUES WITH REPAIRS AND IMPROVEMENTS

It's pretty much a given that at some point your property will need some repairs or improvments. Fortunately, those repairs and improvements will add to your property's value. When you are considering making repairs on one of your properties, take the time to strategically calculate how much money you will need to spend. The cost of repair should be measured against the value added from that expenditure. In other words, is it worth it? Being aware of the cost of repairs as they relate to the increase in either rental value or resale value can often guide investors in their decisions of what capital improvements are necessary. When investors make improvements and repairs to their properties they can see the following results:

- *Increased rental values.* The amount charged for rent will increase if the property condition is improved. Don't forget that there is a direct correlation between increasing the rental income (and therefore increasing your gross scheduled income) and the property value of investment real estate. You will want to get the neighborhood rental value from a local property management company or through reading the local newspaper to get current rental values. This will help you be sure that the money you are putting into any repairs will increase the rents received on your investment. If the rents you currently charge are already high for the local rental market, you might consider waiting to make the repairs because they will not allow you to increase the rents or profitability of your investment. An exception to this rule is if you are in a downward moving market in which labor is cheap and you want to maintain good tenants. In this situation, improvements can be a strategic move to retain tenants when vacancies are increasing.
- *Better tenants.* When properties are in good physical condition, you are able to demand a higher rent and get tenants who value well-maintained properties. Tenants who like nice properties will be more likely to keep them in good shape. They are also more likely to want their nice friends and family to live by them, something that keeps everything working in your favor.
- *Fewer vacancies.* Properties that look good have fewer vacancies because more people will be interested in renting a unit that is in good condition than one that needs lots of repairs.
- *Increased liquidity.* When a building is kept in good physical condition, it is easier to sell it when you desire. The better the condition of the property, the higher the resale value and the quicker it will sell in any market.

• • •

Now that you've got property management mastered, it's time to dig a little deeper into the mysteries of investment real estate. Everyone likes a good mystery, right? In the next chapter, you'll explore an assortment of fact-finding methods, including gathering the hidden clues about exterior and interior real estate conditions, uncovering seller motivation, and the puzzles of title and zoning as they affect real estate. You'll also learn to investigate properties first by looking from the standpoint of how the numbers work and then by going into the field with a magnifying glass to gather the necessary evidence that can make or break a deal. Put on your detective hats.

$$$

I Learned About Investing in Areas all Over the Country

I grew up in a blue-collar family where doing everything for yourself was a way of life. When I started investing in real estate, that attitude remained and I became a "hands on" property manager. I liked keeping a close eye on all my investments. I believed that if I wasn't looking out for them, then something bad was sure to happen and I would be in trouble. I finally realized that I could continue managing properties at a close distance, but I was limiting my possibilities.

Since I simply love to work with my hands and feel like I have more control over the profit in the property, I decided to physically manage the properties that were close to where I lived. But I began to discover something new. I learned that I could expand my real estate portfolio to other areas around the country and successfully manage them from afar. This was a novel concept for me. I started to learn how to let things go, begin to trust other people, and actually run the property based on the instructions I gave to the property managers. Once I finally understood this, I realized that I had the freedom to expand my real estate holdings to anywhere in the country while still keeping my investments safe and producing a profit that would continue to grow my wealth and financial future.

—LOU MEZA, REAL ESTATE AGENT AND INVESTOR

Inspections

Sherlock Holmes' Method of Discovery

> "People will try to tell you that all the great opportunities have been snapped up. In reality, the world changes every second, blowing new opportunities in all directions, including yours."
> —Ken Hakuta

Sherlock Holmes is a fascinating character. He could reach the most amazing conclusions about a person or an event simply by looking at the clues left behind. The truth is, most people could never interpret the clues good old Sherlock found because they didn't know how to look at them. What I call the Sherlock Holmes Method of Discovery is simply learning how to look at the clues you're given when evaluating an investment property and forming amazing conclusions for yourself. I always rely on this method of investigation when I first inspect a property. It's elementary, my dear reader.

FIRST THINGS FIRST: *Start with the Numbers*

In the last chapter, we established that buying investment property is similar to owning a franchise. Just like in any business, you constantly need to be familiar with how the numbers are affecting your bottom line. Ask yourself: can you pay the bills this month from the income that is coming into your real estate investment? Wise investors evaluate their properties by looking at the budget and profit and loss statements every month in order to create the greatest profits and keep the properties producing the highest rates of return for the money (or equity) that they have in the properties. This evaluation is critical to producing beneficial results over and over again.

Smart investors also take the time to look at the numbers up close and personal, just like Sherlock would with his magnifying glass. Factors such as the capitalization rate, net operating income, and price per square foot of the property should all be examined in detail. I'll show you how to do this and more (and the formulas that go along with it) in Appendix E.

> **DEFINITION**
>
> The Latin root word for many real estate terms is "CAP," which means money. There is *capitalization rate*, which means the amount of money you are getting for your investment based on the amount of money you have put into it. *Capital improvements* are the amount of money you need to put into the property. Whenever you see the prefix CAP, remember it is usually referring to money that you are getting or putting into a deal.

DON'T ALWAYS BELIEVE THE SELLER OR THE TAX RECORDS

I've always lived by the philosophy that you shouldn't believe everything you hear. This can be especially true with sellers of property. Sellers will not always be forthright in giving you all of the correct information about a property. In addition, you shouldn't rely on the information real estate agents tell you regarding the rents being collected. To get around the Pinocchios of this world, you'll want to look at several different forms of record-keeping. First, ask to see all of the lease agreements and rental records kept by the rental company or the owner. Compare the rents on the leases with what they say they are receiving. Next, you'll want to evaluate the tax records and see both the income and the expenses the seller claimed with the IRS. Finally, look at the profit and loss statements they are using to evaluate the purchase price. Most of the time these three ways of evaluating records do not match. Sellers will fudge things a bit by increasing expenses when reporting their taxes and reducing the income generated. Then, when trying to sell the property, they will do just the reverse and increase the income coming in and reduce the expenses. The most accurate reading will come from the actual books generated either from the seller or, better yet, from the property management company if one is used.

HOW TO PHYSICALLY EVALUATE A PROPERTY

When considering whether to purchase real estate or not, it is crucial that you investigate and analyze the current physical condition of the property. This allows you to create a solid plan for the necessary capital improvements that will cost money immediately after acquiring the asset. Wise investors make a point of knowing these costs *before* they invest. This way, they still have an option to get out of the purchase contract if they can't afford the necessary repairs.

Assessment of the interior and exterior of the building should be thorough. Be specific in what you are looking for, and take notes on what you observe. Attach a cost to each item that needs to be repaired in each unit of the investment property. This is where the Sherlock method of investigation gets exciting. Look for clues that are not specifically defined by the seller or the real estate agent about how well the property is managed and cared for.

Evaluate Exterior of the Property First

You should begin your evaluation with the exterior condition of the building. Don't be afraid to get down and dirty here. This is where your detective skills will come in handy. First, observe and evaluate the grounds and landscaping. Is there garbage scattered around the property? Do tenants take personal care of their exterior home environments? Exterior inspecting is where you get to be a little nosey without interfering with their personal space. Take note of how they are keeping the place up. Read the clues about how the tenants and current owner are taking care of the place. These items will impact the management costs and resale value of your investment in the future and tell you what sort of tenants currently live in the property. Next, as you continue your tour of the property, look at the following:

- *Roofs.* Roofs tell you a lot about the owner. If the roof is in need of repair, it may mean that the owner has not spent money on the inside of the property or they may be short on cash. Roofs are expensive items, but are necessary in the maintenance of your overall investment. A poorly maintained roof means that the owner has probably not maintained other essential items in the property. Be aware of this as your first clue.

- *Parking.* Check to see if there is enough parking for the tenants. Some cities have strict parking regulations, whereas others don't regulate parking. Look at the condition of the parking lot. Is the asphalt or concrete in good condition? Does it need to be redone? These are expensive repairs, so take the time to determine if it can wait or if it needs to be fixed right after purchasing the property. The next clue is to look at the condition of the cars in the parking lot. Are they run down and in poor condition or are they newer cars that are in good shape? These are good Sherlock clues. The newer the cars, the more disposable income the tenants have. If the cars are all in bad shape, then you may be in a low-income area, and you had better be getting a high rate of return or a good cash flow on the property.

- *Electric.* Evaluating the exterior electrical is critical to learning about the owner and tenants. How is the exterior electrical wired? Are there illegal connections for phone and cable? Illegal hookups are more common on rentals than owner occupied homes. You won't know if any illegal electrical hook-ups are from the owner or the tenants, but either way, it is a clue that something fishy is going on.

- *Meters.* It is important to notice if there are enough electric, gas, and water meters to go with the number of units advertised for the property. To meet building codes and zoning regulations, cities and counties often closely regulate the number of meters that are on properties. Cities and counties do not generally grant extra meters to a property other than those legally allowed. They will typically allow one extra electric meter for the exterior of each property as well as electric and water meters for common areas that are maintained and paid for by the owner. For example, if the seller is saying it is a four-unit building, but you only see four meters, you can suspect that something may be wrong, especially if there is exterior lighting in common areas. Some owners wire the common area exterior lighting into one tenant's personal meter without the tenant's knowledge. It is important for you as the owner to know when there has been an infraction like this.

- *Overall maintenance.* Look for details and information about how the previous owner managed and maintained the property. Did the owner take pride in the improvements that were made on the property? Were they done correctly, or were things left undone to deteriorate? Knowing this makes a difference when calculating the maintenance costs of the building, as well as when determining the purchase price you offer.

- *Building structure.* Evaluate the placement of the building. Is it set in the front or back portion of the lot? Is it possible to build other units on the lot? Will the area support additional rental units? What is the zoning and density of the location? The possibility of adding on to an existing property can be good incentive for a purchase.

Now that I have given you a brief description of how to put those detective skills to work, the form in Figure 16.1 will make your evaluation easier. Have fun, and like Sherlock, look for hidden clues that tell you about the property beyond what is obvious. Record as much information as possible because you will need it later when you are making repairs or negotiating the terms of the sale.

FIGURE 16.1: **Exterior Property Assessment**

Exterior Condition	Property Condition (poor, average, good)	Repair When?(Now, 6 mo., 1 yr., 3 yrs., 10 yrs.)	Cost of Repairs
Special features			$
Roof			$
Electrical			$
Meters			$
Cable and phone			$
Plumbing			$
Parking			$
Pools			$
Landscaping			$
Community facilities			$
Garbage areas			$
Windows			$
Outside doors			$
Garages/carports			$
Stairs			$
Siding			$
Foundation			$
Paint			$
Overall information			$

Interior Property Condition

By the time you are ready to look at the interior of a property, you should have come to a pretty good understanding of the owner through your fact-finding mission. You will know whether she was meticulous with managing the property or if things were let go. The information that you gathered about the exterior of the building will typically mirror what you will find in the interior of the building. On rare occasions, the outside will look bad when the interiors have been remodeled, but usually the owner will advertise any interior improvements that have been made. If nothing has been mentioned about property improvements, then you can pretty much bet that the inside will look similar to, if not worse than, the exterior of the building.

After you have evaluated the exterior condition of the property and it meets your approval, it is time to make an offer. Remember: when you are buying investment property, you will usually not be able to enter the interior of the property until you have an accepted offer. You must make your offer based on the numbers received from the real estate agent, the seller, tax returns, comparable properties, and your exterior evaluation of the property (if you are able to get all that data before you make an offer). You may need to make an offer based on the information received from the real estate agent. Make sure you add in the offer that you want to inspect these other financial records in more detail during the inspection phase of the transaction. Once you come up with a reasonable purchase price that you are willing to pay, you write an offer. If it is accepted (and it should be contingent on inspecting and approving the interior of the property), you will be able to get into the building.

Be sure to evaluate the interior of the building, unit by unit. Don't leave out any of the components of each unit in your inspection, especially electrical, plumbing, windows, curtains, carpets, kitchens, and bathrooms. Break it down item by item: Follow that loose wire, and flush the toilets. This is your chance to really check the place out, and you should take full advantage of it. It is always best to have a professional property inspector look at the interior and exterior of the units. Get the property inspectors to *really* inspect the property, even crawling around in the attic or in the basement. This will give you an expert opinion on the overall state of the property as well as tell you what needs immediate attention and what can wait. The clues you gather here will help you map out a plan for property improvements and costs associated with these repairs.

Because I gave you a form for your exterior inspection, it just wouldn't be fair not to give you one that will help with your interior inspection. By completely filling out the form in Figure 16.2 for each unit, you will have a record of which units are in good condition, and which need repair as well as the costs of those repairs. Make note of as much detail as possible.

FIGURE 16.2: **Interior Property Assessment**

Exterior Condition	Overall Condition (poor, average, good)	Repair When?(Now, 6 mo., 1 yr., 3 yrs., 10 yrs.)	Cost of Repairs
Special features			$
Interior paint			$
Carpeting and floors			$
Doors and hardware			$
Air conditioner			$
Heating system			$
Electrical			$
Windows and curtains			$
Laundry facilities			$

Bathrooms
  Toilets
  Sinks
  Showers
  Countertops
			$

Kitchen
  Sinks
  Oven/stove
  Counterops
  Refrigerator
			$

Bedrooms			$
Living room			$
Dining room			$
Overall information			$

Current rents	$	Current market rents	$
Future rents	$	Market rents in future	$
Year built		Increased income	$

ADD UP THE MAINTENANCE AND REPAIR COSTS BEFORE YOU CLOSE THE DEAL

Now the calculations and analysis begin. You should now have a clearly defined record of the interior and exterior condition of the property as well as attached costs for both the immediate necessary repairs and future repairs and improvements. You should also have a detailed report from the professional inspector and all of the records from the agent, tax files, and property manager. Crunch your numbers to see if the property makes sense for you to purchase. If the numbers make sense, the next step is to calculate whether the property will increase in value if you make all of these improvements.

Some improvements such as paint, landscaping, cleaning up, and carpets will immediately allow you to increase the rent, but don't forget that not all capital improvements will have this direct benefit. For example, improvements like repairing the roof, water heaters, and parking lot pavement won't increase the rental income but are still necessary. Determine which of your immediate and necessary repairs will increase rents (directly affecting the profit and value of the property) and which improvements must be done to keep the property functioning. Both types of capital expenses are important and should be calculated before you close your deal.

With all of your numbers in hand (and swirling around in your head), it's time to decide whether you still want to purchase the property and to determine if it meets the goals and objectives you have set up with your real estate plan. Remember those? If the property still makes sense to your overall plan and your ROE goals, then move forward and close the deal. Don't forget that when you are negotiating the purchase contract, you will want to know why the seller is selling the property, and if they will credit you for any of the necessary repairs. It is also important to know if the seller is willing to give some financing on the property so that you can more easily afford the property or get better institutional financing. You may also want to review the title report closely to see what has happened with the property over the years. This will also tell you about the owner.

PLANNING FOR IMMEDIATE CAPITAL IMPROVEMENTS

In an ideal world, once you close the transaction and own the property, you will have enough money to make the necessary repairs right away. As I've mentioned before, investors have the most motivation to make repairs within the first year of owning the property. They are excited about the shiny new pieces of real estate in their portfolios and are most familiar with the numbers because they have just run them. If you have the money and the time, keep the momentum going and make the repairs now. Don't forget to fill out the Alternatives for Profitability Form for each property (Figure 13.2) and try to stay on schedule for completion of the improvements. Don't get discouraged, however, if your improvements take longer than you thought. It can take up to a year or so to get a property turned around to the way you want it, especially if it has been poorly managed. You may need to get rid of some slow-paying or delinquent tenants and repairs can often cost more and take longer than anticipated.

The maintenance and management of a property can be overwhelming for some investors, especially in the early phases of your real estate plan. Take your time, get used to the property, stabilize your cash flow, and remember that all of this work is for your future. By paying proper attention to your property, you will be really happy with the results realized in the later phases of your real estate plan.

INCREASING PROPERTY VALUES WITH COSMETIC AND STRUCTURAL REPAIRS

Cosmetic and structural repairs, in addition to making a property more attractive, also increase the property's value. The time and money that you put into repairs and improvements will generally be worth the expense. However, be careful not to overimprove the property. On occasion, investors put too much money into their properties and don't calculate whether that improvement will make a difference in the rents or in the maintenance of the building. Try to remember that you are not improving the property to the condition that *you* would want to have in your own home. These are investment properties. Your tenants will not treat your property as nicely as they would if they owned it themselves. As a general rule of thumb, plan to spend approximately 5 percent of your gross scheduled income (GSI) for capital improvements for each property unless there is deferred maintenance and the property has not been kept up over time. In this case, the numbers may be greater than the standard 5 percent.

Once you've made the improvements in your property, you may see an immediate price increase when you increase the rents or decrease vacancy loss. This is a beneficial exercise as well as an inspirational exercise. It is important to see that your hard efforts have a direct correlation to your net worth. Make sure you keep track of what benefits and rewards you are getting for being so diligent and hard working. You deserve it.

Because you've already established that you are a hard worker who is well on her way to making millions, I want to make sure you stay on that path. In the next chapter, I'll emphasize the importance of not falling asleep or being lazy to the purpose and intentions of your real estate plan. You'll learn to keep your eye on the ball and discover how essential it is to review your real estate

> "Experience is not what happens to you; it is what you do with what happens to you."
> —Aldous Huxley

holdings annually. This will allow you to determine your next strategic move to sustain the rates of return on equity as determined in your real estate plan.

$$$

I Led the Family Into Financial Security

It was hard for me to take the lead, but I decided I would do it anyway. My husband and I have a really great relationship. We both work in jobs that we love and have small children at home who are involved in sports and many school activities. We lead busy lives with very little extra time to spare. I was concerned that the amount of money we were putting away in our retirement accounts and the stock market would not be enough to provide for our growing family and match the lifestyle we wanted to create in retirement.

My husband was not as concerned as I was, but we talked about it and agreed that if I would investigate this and take the lead, he would support my efforts. Soon after that, I heard Lisa on the radio and knew that what she taught was my way of investing. I wanted safety and security for my young, growing family. Within a couple of months, I bought an investment property according to my real estate plan. At first, I was surprised by how much work it took to learn about investment real estate and to handle managing tenants, but once I got some systems in place it didn't turn out to be as much work after all.

Today, my whole family goes out and looks at properties together. We have fun on these family outings and follow an easy step-by-step plan in examining and inspecting each property. My children have been especially helpful with these inspections. They notice things that I would never see! My husband is really proud of me, not only for the return on our investments, but he is thankful that I had the courage to act even when he was reluctant.

— B. Shimrat, Executive VP Consumer Products Company

Counting Your Net Equity Every Year

"Genius is 1 percent inspiration and 99 percent perspiration."
—Thomas Edison

Developing the skills to effectively manage your real estate takes time, so you shouldn't expect to become an expert overnight. One way to speed the process along, however, is to pay attention to each property every year and to practice good management skills over and over and over again. It takes the three P's: practice, patience, and persistence. All great athletes must practice, practice, and still practice more in order to be great. It is the same with creating wealth and making your properties more profitable. Remember what your old physical education teachers and coaches used to say: practice makes perfect, so go do one more lap around the gym!

Hot Tip

Managing the equity in your real estate portfolio is a 10 to 15 year process. You will need to take the necessary time to grow your real estate investments and continually stay aware of how your equity is working for you. Stay consistent, and you will produce the results you want.

MANAGING REAL ESTATE FROM THREE DIFFERENT ANGLES

In order to build your wealth through investment real estate, it is essential that you regularly evaluate and alter your properties to increase profits, reduce risks, and improve their marketability. It is really important that long-term investors understand that efficiently managing their properties as they grow and develop requires being able to look at their real estate from three different perspectives: the physical, the fiscal, and how the property relates to their personal value systems.

Managing the Property's Physical Condition

Managing the physical condition of your real estate portfolio can be the most physically and financially draining part of property ownership both for beginner and advanced investors. Learning the ins and outs of how to efficiently manage the physical buildings can sometimes take several years. In fact, many of the skills are developed through trial and error. Don't get too bummed when you make a property management error. This is very normal. You may let a tenant in that you knew didn't have good credit, but you needed the apartment filled, or you hired the first property managers you interviewed only to have them be duds. These things happen. The owner who accepts these mistakes and keeps going is the one who succeeds in the end. Just be sure to keep your intentions aimed toward creating properties that are in good physical condition and are rented at fair market value. This way, you will not only sustain your investment, but you'll also improve your profits.

Managing the Property's Fiscal Condition

Many investors believe that all they need to do to become wealthy is to buy real estate and build an empire over a 10- to 20-year period, and then before they know it, they will have reached all of their financial goals. They focus on one major objective: whether or not the property has a monthly positive cash flow, and if it is appreciating in value. These investors assume that if the property (or the entire portfolio) is making enough money each month to cover the monthly expenses, including the mortgage payments, then all is well with their real estate investments, and they are on their way to being rich, rich, rich!

Some of this is true, of course. An investor must always keep a steady eye on cash flow. If investors do not pay close attention, they will surely find themselves in financial trouble. But hopefully a little voice is shouting out from the back of your mind: "Wait!

Weren't there three other factors to consider? Didn't we already learn this stuff?" Yes, you did, and a big gold star to you for paying attention! While cash flow is important, it is only one fourth of the wealth-building real estate pie. Remember how you calculated the rate of return on equity (ROE) in Chapter 6? You learned how you needed to look at all four components: cash flow, appreciation, loan reduction, and tax benefits. This evaluation must be done each and every year that you own your property if you want to reach your desired goals.

DON'T FORGET

If you don't pay attention to all the equity that you are accumulating and growing every year, you stand the chance of missing out on creating tremendous wealth for yourself and run the risk of letting your equity get lazy on you.

Managing the fiscal condition of your real estate portfolio can be the most financially rewarding part of property ownership. But don't forget that it requires discipline and a willingness to analyze numbers in order to determine how these numbers relate to your goals and objectives. If you are sloppy or lazy in this phase of your real estate plan, you could lose hundreds or even thousands of dollars each month. Worse yet, hundreds of thousands of dollars can potentially be left on the table when a property is sold. That's a lot of money being wasted. The necessary skills during this phase require the services of professionals in the financial service industry: bookkeepers, accountants, attorneys, financial planners and of course, knowledgeable and well-trained investment real estate agents and advisors.

Managing the Property Owner's Value Systems

At all phases of property ownership, your personal values should be both considered and honored. Do not overlook the importance of maintaining a well-balanced real estate portfolio that respects your lifestyle, dreams, desires, and goals. Your portfolio should also take into account your tolerance for risk or lack thereof, as well as your personal tastes. When your values are in alignment with your real estate holdings, you are sure to produce more satisfying results. Owning real estate can be a lot of work, and there are many aspects of managing your property to juggle. So keeping emotional balance is crucial. Don't always go after the all-mighty dollar if that will conflict with your personal dreams and lifestyle. It is just as important to make financial decisions that support your value systems and lifestyle as it is to make financial decisions based on numbers or just getting wealthy.

MANAGING AN APPRECIATING MARKET AND YOUR ROE

Investors can be fooled when there is an appreciating market because they keep seeing their property values increase. This can be very exciting. Unfortunately, this experience of rising wealth can also be very deceptive. When investors keep all of their equity in a property and do not leverage it on other investments, the rate of ROE begins to drop. They receive what is called "diminishing rates of return" on their investments. In other words, the more money or equity you have in the property, the more likely the rates of return on equity that you receive will diminish.

Imagine this: you buy a property with little to no money down, get your desired ROE at the time of purchase, and are able to afford the loan with the amount of money you get on the rents. The market starts to heat up, and you experience lots of appreciation. You're happy and getting rich, right? Yes, you are getting rich, but how hard is your new money working for you to *keep you rich*, especially when the market begins to slow down or even decrease? To answer that question, now let's say that when appreciation increased rapidly, the value of the property went up a lot, and you have equity, you wisely increased the rents by 5 percent the first year. The mortgage payment stayed the same, the loan reduction was fixed, and the tax benefits remained the same. The only thing that significantly changed was the appreciation. So you would think that your rate of return on equity would increase right? Wrong, because you have so much of your own money into the property, now called your equity, you are still receiving about the same amount of benefit, except for the 5 percent increase in rents. This means that you have more money in and are receiving about the same amount of return out of the investment. That is a diminished rate of return on your money.

Remember the conversations about leverage from earlier chapters? So what happens when you own property in appreciating markets and do nothing with the money? Leaving properties underleveraged is a way to produce slow or sleeping equity on your investment. Your equity may be increasing, but at slower rates than it could if you were paying attention and moving the money around. It is in essence growing at a lazy rate and not working very hard for you. Are you beginning to see something here? Once again, although you have more money into the property, you are actually receiving *less* for your money. Your money is not working very hard for you; it is being lazy. Real estate returns actually begin to diminish when investors keep a lot of their equity in their properties and don't move it around into other investment opportunities. In order to reposition yourself and get your money working harder for you, it is necessary to take some of that equity out and refinance. Go put your equity into another property or exchange the property for a more expensive one. By increasing the amount of property you own, you will generate increased rates of ROE. When investors fail to stay active and really evaluate the rate of return they are getting on their equity, they lose out on the possibility of really improving their rates of return on their money.

DETERMINING HOW MUCH MONEY TO REINVEST AS THE ROE GOES DOWN

By now I think you understand that refinancing your properties and taking the extra equity out to reinvest is the main philosophy of this book. It is how you are going to continually achieve your annual rates of ROE. However, refinancing your investments must be done with a plan and strategy. I've see numerous investors make the rash decision to refinance on a whim that ended up costing them thousands of dollars. If they only knew that there is a prudent strategy to take when deciding to refinance, they might have saved themselves lots of money. Here's how you do it.

Strategic Refinance

Start by evaluating how much equity theoretically can be taken out of each piece of real estate or exchanged. Determine whether you are going to leverage the asset by 80, 75, 70, or 65 percent. You'll notice that the highest percentage of leverage I suggested was 80 percent loan to value. This way, if the market adjusts in the negative direction, you should still be able to sell the property if needed, because most real estate prices don't drop more than 20 percent for single-family residences and condominiums. It is always a good idea to refinance with this in mind: keep your property liquid for unexpected life events that might necessitate selling that piece of real estate.

Once you have the percentage of leverage settled, then determine if the refinanced amount will generate the ROE you are targeting to validate the expense of refinancing or exchanging. Sometimes it's just not worth it to refinance if you won't achieve the rate of return you desire. If you determine that it is, in fact, a good idea to refinance, look at the ROE and make sure you can afford this amount of leverage to sustain the property with the new loan amounts. If you can't afford the increase in loan payments, all of this strategy will come crashing in on you. Don't forget to always evaluate your ability to sustain that asset over time. It does no one any good to refinance and then not be able to pay the new mortgage payment even if the new ROE is within the targeted range. Take the time to look at a variety of different loan programs that are available to you and find one that will help you sustain and grow your real estate portfolio.

Some people get squirmy and nervous about incurring additional expenses on their personal residences in order to get their real estate investment portfolio going. Most people do not say to me, "I am so glad you had us refinance our house and increase our monthly payments." However, they wisely understand that it may cost them additional money from their active income to get their real estate portfolio started, and with that they are comfortable and happy. Investors who are on tight monthly budgets may need to buy their first investment property in areas that are slow growing, where appreciation rates are low, but cash flow is good. This is one way to get started in the game of real estate investing.

Keep in mind that you might have to change or alter your personal lifestyle to get a solid real estate plan established. Most wise and patient investors understand this. Making monthly contributions to an investment is expected in other financial planning fields in order to get rewards in the future. It is the same in real estate.

Knowing the Phases of the Real Estate Plan

Investors reinvest different amounts of equity at different phases of their real estate plans. In the early phases, most of the equity is continuously reinvested into other real estate assets. This is the time when leverage is really important and cash flow is typically minimal, and sometimes nonexistent. In the equity management phase, investors can alter the amount of leverage they use based on the purpose and intention of each particular piece of real estate and the overall performance of their entire portfolio. Sophisticated investors will determine how much equity they want to reinvest as it correlates to the goals and objectives stated in their real estate plans. Investors who are at the end of their plans are more likely to decrease the amount of leverage they are using so they can generate passive income for themselves (remember: less leverage equals greater passive income). These investors are nearing their desired goals and can afford to diminish their rates of ROE because they have been working their equity powerfully over a specific period of time.

Intended ROE Goal

As I've mentioned numerous times, investors should be making decisions about different pieces of real estate they own based the overall rate of ROE they have targeted in their real estate plans. When the average ROE is evaluated annually, investors have the freedom to underleverage certain pieces in their real estate portfolios based on different intentions of each asset in their plan. For example, you may want to underleverage a personal residence, a vacation home, or a home that you plan to retire to in the next five years. Taking less risk with these particular properties will make you feel more confident taking a bigger risk with other properties in your portfolio. You will know that no matter what happens, that property is "safe." You will always have a roof over your head; you are getting closer to your dream of not having to work for a living.

Risk Tolerance

Ask yourself how much you are willing to leverage on each property and how much passive income you want to generate. These are important questions to ponder when you are making decisions about what strategies to implement on your real estate plan. If you are conservative and don't want a lot of risk, then you will choose not to leverage very much. Don't forget, however, that less risk will more than likely lead to a lower ROE. In contrast, if you increase the leverage, you will increase the loan payment. This, in turn, decreases your cash flow and puts you more at risk, which may be uncomfortable to you. Respect what your risk tolerance levels are, and keep in mind that changing one of the factors will change the overall results of your entire portfolio. You will need to adjust many factors until you get the mix that is right for you.

Cash Flow

Some investors rely on the passive income (cash flow) from their properties to supplement their lifestyles. Others need to shelter some of their active income and would prefer to have negative cash flow properties. Determining which sort of investor you are is critical when evaluating how much to leverage your properties. It is really important to talk with your lender and your accountant when making these important investment decisions. Don't try to do this alone. You will save heartache and money by getting good advice. If you take money out of your investment every month in the form of passive income, it is more likely that you will be receiving a lower rate of return on your equity, and you are impacting the growth of your portfolio in the future. Make sure you understand that taking money out today and not keeping it in your investment may impact your future rewards and growth.

> **DON'T FORGET**
> **Real Estate is an Unregulated Investment Option.**
> While the stock market is regulated by the government and has penalties built in if investors take any of the benefit out of their portfolios before they have matured, real estate investing doesn't have these regulations. Real estate investors are therefore tempted to have their cake and eat it too by using the cash flow they get from their investments to increase their lifestyle, instead of reinvesting it. Doing this can ultimately shortchange their overall real estate portfolio, forcing them to reinvest more money or work longer in order to achieve the net equity they desire. Either way is fine, just be aware of the impact of taking cash out today.

SAYING NO TO CASH FLOW IN THE EARLY PHASES OF THE REAL ESTATE PLAN

There are countless investors out there who are interested in real estate investing because of the lure of cash flow. Many of them are already fantasizing about spending their cash flow dollars on new cars, clothes, and travel. What these investors fail to calculate is that if they spend their passive income today before they have developed enough net equity for themselves, they may be penalizing their future retirement portfolio potential. And *no one* is telling them this. I can't tell you how many times I've heard, "If only I had reinvested that property income instead of buying that (fill in the blank useless luxury item). Can you *imagine* how much I'd be worth?" Yes, I can, and that's why I'm stressing this point so much. The government regulates spending your passive income within the stock market, but does not regulate it for real estate investors. Many investors are blindly enjoying the fruits of their investments today without realizing how it is affecting their returns for the future.

"So," you might be thinking, "What's the big problem? This is great! No government, no regulation, immediate cash, this is a total score for me and my family!" Herein lies the problem. Many of my novice investors don't understand that if they take money out today and spend it, they won't have that money working for them and building into more money for their retirement. To which you respond: "Who cares! If I am investing, then I can have the benefits of both worlds. I can get appreciation built up over the years, have the tenants pay down the mortgage and get cash flow now so that I can supplement my current lifestyle. Yahoo!" Sounds good to me, but there are a couple of missing ingredients.

First, why are you spending your investment money today? I thought you said you were an *investor*. Real investors put money in today to be saved for tomorrow. Second, didn't you say you wanted to create a substantial net equity? Well, in order to do that you need to continually keep the ROE on your property at the levels you set up for yourself in your real estate plan. Keeping your ROE high usually means that you continually need to leverage, which usually means decreasing your cash flow. If you are playing your cards right, you shouldn't have that extra income to spend anyway.

Learn to regulate your rewards. Because the government isn't penalizing you for taking out your rewards early, let me remind you that there *will* be a penalty. It will take the form of less net equity than you planned, working at your job longer than you want, decreasing the lifestyle that you have been planning on, or taking more risk in your investments. And by the way, I would suggest that you learn to live within your means according to your *active* income, so that in the future you can have a life and a lifestyle that you really love.

Smart investors will keep all of their net equity, including passive income, working for them by continuing to leverage and reinvest the benefits back into their real estate plans. Let compounded growth take hold; give it the time that it needs to really work for you. Then, at the end of your real estate plan, you will be able to safely and securely live the lifestyle that you want. You may have to be patient and not get the rewards (or positive cash flow) out of your real estate as soon as you would like, but trust me, these rewards will be coming soon enough. With patience, persistence, and a clear understanding that you must regulate yourself, you will be on the road to making millions through real estate investing.

READING MONTHLY REPORTS AND OPERATING EXPENSES

Every month you should be reading the reports on your real estate portfolio and learning how you can improve its performance. Some properties will be performing efficiently whereas others may need extra care and attention because they are performing at levels below the market averages. It is important to remember that these properties are your means to creating lots of wealth for you and your family in the future and need your special attention all the time. It is like being a farmer and needing to tend to your garden in order to keep the weeds out. You want to give it proper nutrition and fertilizer so that your garden can grow and produce terrific fruits and vegetables. Practice good management skills through proper study of your monthly reports, and you'll be harvesting from your real estate portfolio before you know it.

MANAGING THE EQUITY IN YOUR PROPERTY

Sophisticated investors want to know how their money is working for them. Most investors have a general idea about how much income is coming in on their properties and what the expenses are, but knowing the specific details of how each property is financially performing is another matter all together and is very often overlooked. Some properties will be easy to manage and will have low expenses; others will have continually high vacancy rates, poor tenants, high turnover, vandalism, and late payments. Some will produce more income than you had expected due to rental increases or additional income from sources like laundry facilities, and still other properties will continue to underperform according to expectation. Every property is different, and each of those situations described above will affect the efficiency of the equity that you have in that property. Knowing which properties are performing well for you is your responsibility. Paying attention will help you decide which properties to keep in your portfolio, which ones need new management techniques implemented, and which ones you need to sell or exchange because they are not doing what you want them to do.

The more detailed information you have about how the property is performing, the better able you are to predict and adjust critical features within your real estate portfolio so you can continue to reach or exceed your targeted goals. For example: let's say that you estimate that the single-family residence you own is going to have expenses that are about 25 percent of the gross scheduled income (GSI). Unfortunately, when you get the actual numbers at the end of the year, you realize that you spent about 35 percent. This unexpected increase in expenses will affect the cash flow situation on your property. What did you do wrong? The key is to pay attention to the expenses on a *monthly* basis. This way, if you are off on your predictions, you can make the necessary adjustments as you go along. When you assumed that the expenses were going to be 25 percent and they ended up being 35 percent, you greatly affected your overall rate of ROE. Instead, by paying closer attention to those expenses, you can keep your property on track according to your budget. This is the equity management portion of your real estate plan.

NOT BUDGETS AGAIN!

You might have noticed that the dreaded word "budget" appeared in the last section. Yes, we need to revisit the idea of working with a budget once again. You thought you'd gotten that nasty task over with way back in Part Two, didn't you? Well, here I am bringing it up again. Sorry, but do you want to get wealthy or do you want things to stay just as they are? Yeah, I thought you'd choose wealthy. Good choice.

Most of you have put together your personal budgets and know where you are getting your money and how you are spending it. Now let's talk about creating budgets for your properties. The process is just the same as it was when you created your personal budget. In fact, you can even use the same form (Figure 4.1) that I provided in Chapter 4. Pay special attention to any variations in property management costs, adjustments in your loan (including any balloon payments coming up), and any changes to your income (increased rents or new laundry facilities, etc.). All of these factors will affect your budget and your profits, so make sure they are operating efficiently and are well accounted for.

Learning about managing a budget for each property will keep you from letting things fall through the cracks. When you are able to make monthly, quarterly, or annual adjustments through informed decisions, you will see growth in the amount of equity you are building up and an increase in the overall rate of ROE. This is what you are striving for isn't it?

When creating wealth through refinancing and watching your ROE, you must constantly be moving your assets around and reshuffling your real estate portfolio. It should be a fun process that creates all kinds of possibilities and options for the sophisticated and dedicated investor. In the next chapter, you'll discover how to make those moves. I'll discuss some of the alternatives you can use throughout your real estate plan to help you *make* and *keep* millions of dollars.

$$

Experienced Investor Finds New Ways to Make a Profit

I have enjoyed the pleasures of real estate ownership for over 30 years. My uncle suggested right after I got married that I should buy real estate to build wealth, and my wife and I have successfully done this throughout the years. In fact, we still own the property we first bought back in 1972. Once I discovered that I could increase my profits by regularly taking the time to determine how powerfully my equity was working for me, I took action, and it has made a tremendous difference. I've watched the value of my portfolio rapidly increase.

We now own a condominium in Hawaii as a seasonal rental and have bought land to subdivide. I have fun being a small builder/developer and landlord of multiple-unit properties. I have increased my real estate holdings by $1.8 million in a little over a year and have definitely taken my real estate portfolio to the next level. It has been personally rewarding and exciting to see my wife and kids begin investing with me, and we love the idea of doing this together as a family. It has made a difference in my family in a very positive way.

—RAVI BHOLA, MSEE, MBA, CORPORATE EXECUTIVE AND ENTREPRENEUR

Making Real Choices

Carrying Notes, Exchanges, Sales, and Gifting

"Success doesn't come to you...you go to it."
—Marva Collins, award winning educator

I nvestors who have been in real estate for a while have many different alternatives when it comes to making changes to grow and increase their wealth. Sometimes the options that are available can seem overwhelming and a bit confusing, but in reality, with a little bit of patience and practice, they are not as complicated as you might think. So let's try to unravel the mystery of these various options.

MOVING YOUR INVESTMENTS AROUND

One of the reasons I love investment real estate so much is that there isn't just one specific theory or strategy that you must follow in order to grow your real estate fortunes. You have the freedom to choose from a variety of different pathways, yet still arrive at the goals and objectives you have set up for yourself. However, one thing is constant: in order to make your real estate portfolio grow and prosper, you need to learn how to move your equity around to create the highest rates of return on your investment. Fortunately, to increase your net worth there are eight options from which you can choose: buying, selling, refinancing, exchanging, creating partnerships, carrying notes (or paper), inheriting money, and gifting portions of your estate to others.

Each of these methods should be used to increase the potential of creating higher rates of return based on how you move and transition your equity. As you know by now, buying property increases your overall net worth. The more you own, the greater your worth becomes over time. Because I already discussed the value of refinancing and creating partnerships in previous chapters, let's look at the rest of your alternatives in detail so that you can start producing the results that you desire.

MOVING THROUGH THE MAZE OF TAX LAWS
WITH 1031 TAX-DEFERRED EXCHANGES

When an investor sells an investment property, the sale can often result in an obligation to pay income taxes on the capital gain that the investor achieved while owning the property. A tax-deferred exchange is a tax deferral method set up by the IRS. The investor can sell an investment property (referred to as the "relinquished property") and use the proceeds from that sale to purchase a new investment property (called a "replacement property"). The gains made on the original investment will not be taxed at the time of sale. The taxes will be deferred to a later date when the investor sells and does not replace the property with another real estate investment through a 1031 exchange. Besides deferring the capital gain tax, exchanging gives investors the opportunity to reposition assets, change property types, increase leverage, and increase the depreciation deduction on their taxes. Exchanging also provides for estate and retirement planning, allows for relocation, accommodates property consolidation or diversification, eliminates or creates joint ownership, and reduces management obligations.

With so many benefits to exchanging, it should come as no surprise that the procedure is complex, so investors must seek professional legal and tax assistance to maintain the tax-deferred status on their investments. You cannot simply sell the property and purchase another without following the very specific rules and regulations governing the exchange. One wrong move, and you will have to pay all taxes due, especially if you miss the important deadlines.

Most exchanges involve three parties: the investor who is doing the exchange (selling and buying), the seller of the replacement property, and the qualified intermediary. In order to comply with IRS code, the investor will hire a qualified intermediary to oversee the exchange because the investor/seller is not allowed to have control of the proceeds at any time during the exchange process. See Figure 18.1 for a summary of the process.

FIGURE 18.1: **Exchange Flowchart**

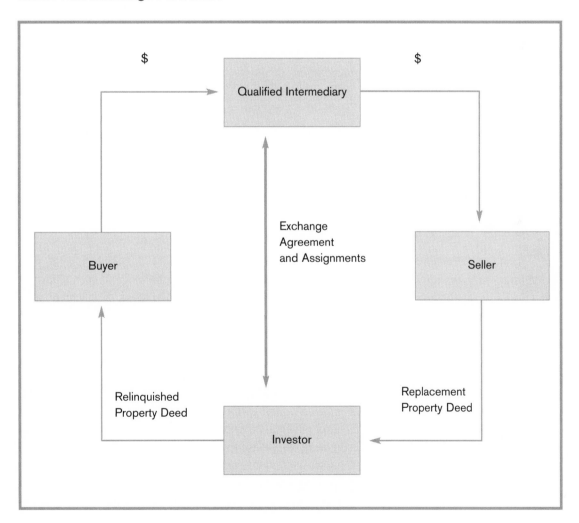

When qualifying a property for a tax-deferred exchange, several factors must be considered. These include:

- *Held for investment.* Property acquired for the purpose of immediate resale does not qualify. Replacement property that is sold immediately won't work either. Instead, a property must be held for a period of time for investment purposes. Investors who are looking to buy a property, fix it up and "flip" it usually won't qualify for a tax-deferred exchange.
- *Like-kind property.* Properties exchanged must of like kind. For example, selling land to buy a small apartment building qualifies, while selling stock to buy land does not. The like-kind properties must be investment properties in real estate.
- *Non-like-kind property.* Cash, stocks, and notes are all considered non-like-kind property. For example, if an investor accepted cash along with the replacement property, the cash would immediately be taxed while the replacement property's tax could be deferred.
- *Identification and exchange period.* An investor has 45 days from the close of the relinquished property to identify three possible replacement properties and 180 days to acquire all replacement properties. This is a simplified statement, so be sure to obtain the necessary information for your specific situation from the qualified intermediary.
- *Exchange requirements.* As a general rule, to avoid paying any capital gain taxes in an exchange, you should always attempt to:

   1. Purchase equal or greater valued properties.
   2. Reinvest all of the net equity (profit) in replacement property.
   3. Obtain equal or greater debt on replacement property. The IRS is more concerned that you transfer all of the equity from the relinquished property into the replacement property. Investors must increase the price or the debt with the replacement property in order to qualify for a qualified exchange. Remember: if you take out any of the equity during the exchange process, it will be taxed by the IRS.

- *Gain and tax obligations.* In order to determine if an exchange is feasible, you should know the amount of the gain you will have from the sale and the taxes that are due. There may be times when you decide to sell the property without the benefit of a tax-deferred exchange, but you must first know what your gain is and your tax obligation if you were not to use the 1031 tax-deferred exchange.
- *Investment objectives.* Once you know the gain and tax obligation, this information should be weighed against your investment objectives within your real estate plan. Do you want to stay invested in real estate, make other types of investments that may not include real estate, or even cash out your investment? Sometimes, it

is not in your best interest to defer the taxes due because you want to do something else with the equity from your real estate investment. The beauty of investing in real estate is that you have equity that you can work with to create many different kinds of options, and you have choices. That is a good problem to have. The longer you invest in real estate, the more options you will enjoy.

As I said, the 1031 tax-deferred exchange process is a complicated procedure, so be sure to obtain the expertise of a professional, qualified intermediary *prior* to the sale of the relinquished property. Many investors make large financial mistakes by not knowing the details of a 1031 exchange and by not getting sufficient financial advice.

STRAIGHT SALES

There may be a time when you decide that you don't want to own property anymore and that you are finished with property and equity management. You may get tired of managing your properties and paying close attention to your equity and just want to get out of owning real estate altogether. There may also be times when you are not able to successfully exchange a piece of real estate, so you opt to sell it through a straight sale. Or perhaps your tax advisor and financial planner advise you to sell the investment now and pay the deferred taxes. These actions mean that you will no longer be able to defer the taxes owed on that property and must pay the tax collector for all equities and gains made on that property, as well as all of the other properties preceding it that had deferred taxes in previous 1031 exchanges.

It is extremely important that you get excellent tax and accounting advice when you decide to sell your investment real estate, especially if you have been exchanging and deferring your taxes for many years. Many investors decide to quit owning real estate after being in the game for 15 to 20 years, opting to sell their real estate through conventional measures and pay all taxes due. They are thankful that real estate has been good to them and are happy to walk away from the sale of the property with a sizeable amount of net equity that they can either reinvest in a different market or spend freely on themselves. This is a perfectly reasonable way to look at things. Straight sales can be an excellent way to finish up your real estate plan. Just make sure that you know what you are doing so you do not get caught with an unexpected tax bill that can have serious consequences.

TENANTS IN COMMON (TICs)

Another method of keeping your money working for you by moving it around is an exchange option called TICs (Tenants in Common), which is more recently getting attention. These entities allow investors to exchange their proceeds into the TIC for at least six months so that they can continue to defer the taxes while looking for an exchange property that suits their investment needs more specifically. This option alleviates the time crunch dictated by the parameters of the 1031 exchange and provides a nice window for investors who are having a difficult time identifying a suitable replacement property to purchase. TICs are also great options for investors who want more hands-off real estate investment alternatives and prefer the guaranteed rates of returns that TICs offer. TICs have become very popular recently. They are becoming the choice for many sophisticated and mature investors who are near the end of their real estate plans and feel that getting the highest rates of return on equity is not as important as creating security and solid investments, or for investors who need a solution for the time restraints of the 1031 tax-deferred exchange process.

> ### DEFINITIONS
>
> *Carrying paper.* The seller offers to provide financing to the buyer so he does not need to come up with as much down payment and can secure more favorable financing terms from traditional institutional lending institutions.
>
> *First position* is the person or institution that will get paid off first when the property is sold or when there is a foreclosure on the property. This is the most secure position to be in when you are the lender. Position is determined by who records the loan or note first at the courthouse.
>
> *Second position* means that the person or institution will get paid after the first position has been paid. This is a less secure position than the first position, especially in a market that is declining or not appreciating rapidly. The security of the person in second position begins to diminish as property values drop. That is why investors pay more in interest rates and costs when securing second mortgages.

INSTALLMENT NOTES OR CARRYING PAPER

Many seasoned investors who are selling their investment properties are often interested in acting like a bank for buyers who are purchasing their properties. When the seller helps the buyer finance the property, it is called "seller financing or carrying paper." This type of financing works well for the seller for several different reasons. First, the seller is typically able to sell the property in a shorter period of time and at the price she wants by offering financing terms to help the buyer out. From the buyer's perspective, when the seller offers to carry a small loan for 10 to 20 percent of the purchase price, the buyer is able to get better financing terms from institutional banks and lenders that usually have more restrictive lending criteria for investors. It's a win-win situation for both sides.

The seller usually needs to carry the paper in what is considered a second position. This means that the institutional financing will be paid off first (referred to as being in first position) and the seller financing will be paid off second. The process of being paid off occurs when the property is sold again, and all the existing debt is paid off through the sale of the home or, less fortunately, when the property is relinquished through a foreclosure or there is a forced sale. Who gets paid off first, second, or third is regulated by who records the debt first, second, or third. The time and date of the recorded debt is what dictates the position.

Who determines position and how is it secured? It all boils down to how the paperwork is filed at the courthouse. Being in first position means that the loan being generated was recorded at the courthouse before any other loan or debt was recorded. The only debt that can bump a lender out of its position is a tax lien or a mechanics lien, both of which are more powerful than lender liens.

Liens on property are why lending institutions require that buyers and sellers purchase title insurance. Title insurance protects a lending institution by making sure that there are no liens attached to the person's social security number or to the property (such as unpaid property taxes) that would jeopardize the lender's position. Lenders will not create a loan for a buyer when a tax lien or mechanics lien has not been paid in full, unless a payment arrangement has been made with the government and the buyer is in good standing with tax arrangements and payments.

It's important to note that tax liens can occur after the lender has given the buyer the loan and recorded its first position. Even in this situation, the tax lien is still going to be paid off first. This is why banks, lenders, and sellers like to know what position they are in so they can regulate their risk factors when they decide to carry paper or make a loan. The amount of risk will definitely determine the amount of interest to be charged.

The second reason why sellers often consider carrying paper is that the government allows sellers to defer their tax bills on the gain from the sale of their property until they receive the principal from the sale. In these cases, the loan payments include both principal and interest payments.

DEFINITIONS

Tax liens are tax payments that have not been collected, such as income and property tax (local, state, or federal). When a person fails to pay taxes, the government will do whatever is necessary to recover the money that is owed. This can take the form of garnishing wages and attaching all assets with liens that will encumber the asset. When an asset is encumbered, it means that when a sale takes place for that asset, the lien must be paid off before the seller gets any of the proceeds at the sale. The government will put itself in first position when a property is sold or foreclosed upon to ensure that it is paid back first.

Mechanics liens come from contractors who furnish labor and materials for construction or improvements on property. A mechanics lien will arise when there is a dispute over an unpaid bill from the construction. Mechanics liens are a very powerful instrument that contractors use to guarantee that they get paid for services rendered through construction.

A third reason sellers are interested in carrying paper is that they can typically get a higher interest rate on their loans to the buyers than they could if they put their money in CDs or into the bond market through their brokerage firms or banks. As a result, the loan they are carrying for the buyer may be a better investment than taking that money out of real estate all together and putting it in a more passive income generating investment option.

TAKING MONEY OUT OF REAL ESTATE AND MOVING IT TO THE STOCK MARKET

Many investors get rather snobby about their investment arena of choice, whether it is real estate or the stock market. Of course, like anything, each investment vehicle has its particular benefits and its particular drawbacks. But one thing is certain, the more money you have, the better it is for you to have it in different markets. We've already talked about how important it is to diversify your portfolio within the real estate market. It is equally important that you diversify your portfolio *across* markets. For example, when your stock portfolio is doing really well, take some of your profits out and put them in the real estate market, and when the real estate market is doing really well, take some of your gain out and put it into the stock market.

This method of investment has the strength to carry you through all kinds of market shifts and conditions. You'll find that the overall performance of your entire financial portfolio will be very profitable and stable when money and equity can freely go between these two investment vehicles. I highly recommend this method to all of my clients. Don't get too protective over the stock market or the real estate market. There is enough money to be made for everyone in every investment option, so why limit yourself to only one of these markets? Try being a player in both fields to create stability, and you can win really big.

INHERITANCE AND GIFTING

Once investors have been implementing their real estate plans for about ten years, or one full real estate cycle, they will most likely have accumulated a lot of net equity, especially if they have been paying attention to the ROE and diversifying their real estate holdings. Usually the amount of net equity is quite substantial. When this occurs, it is important to pay attention to how you will be distributing this wealth. Talk with your financial planner and a competent tax attorney about how to protect and pass on the empire that you have worked so hard to create.

It's important to note that not only will you be gifting your wealth to future generations, but sometimes to the charities of your choice. As I've already mentioned, in the coming years, until 2020, the largest intergenerational transfer of wealth will occur with over $13 trillion passed on to the next generation. Therefore, it is not unusual for you to also be *inheriting* wealth or certain assets from your parents or relatives. Many of my investors will be inheriting wealth for which they need to become prepared. The same methods of distribution will apply for this newly acquired wealth. Again, be sure to get good tax and legal advice when dealing with these aspects of your real estate portfolio. I'll be discussing the distribution of your portfolio in much greater detail in Part Five.

You should now have a better understanding of all the various options you have in moving or transferring your equity. The purpose of defining this for you is so you can continue to make choices that will either produce more profits and higher rates of return on equity or give you options so that you can make lifestyle choices for yourself. The more you know, the better able you are to make powerful investment and personal decisions.

· · ·

In the next chapter, I'll start talking about the phase of your real estate plan that you've been aiming for: the exit strategy phase. I'll illustrate how you can convert your mature investment portfolio into a passive income stream that will last until the end of your days and on to future generations. I'll discuss selling assets, paying off mortgages, finding additional tax shelters, and protecting what you have worked so hard to create. This is the part you have been waiting for, and it can be lots of fun!

$$

Sophisticated Transactions Have Made Me Really Rich

I was a director in the movie business and climbed the corporate ladder in a short period of time. My career was on fire. I had everything money could buy: a nice house, a great car, and horses. Unfortunately, the long grueling hours took their toll on my personal life; I realized all I ever did was work. I wanted a different pace in my life, so I decided to investigate real estate. The market was good to me, and I made a lot of money in my first couple of years. Through the help and advice of an excellent real estate agent, I realized that I had a great deal of equity in my properties and needed to move it around if I was going to continue producing great rates of return.

This was a bit overwhelming and scary at first, but with help I was able to successfully learn about 1031 tax-deferred exchanges. I have used this tax saving method many times and have increased my real estate portfolio to over $5.5 million in a little less than three years. Having the knowledge and skill to successfully use some of these sophisticated maneuvers in real estate has taken a good real estate investment into an excellent real estate investment and given me a great deal of confidence in dealing with the more technical aspects of owning real estate. It isn't nearly as difficult as I thought.

—LESLIE SMITH, REAL ESTATE INVESTOR AND REAL ESTATE PLAN INSTRUCTOR

PART FIVE

Real Rewards:

The Millionaire Years

Real Income

Living on Passive Income

> "BE BOLD, make a stand for your life, and do what you dream about.
> This is where you will find the passion in life."
> —Kim Hecker, PBI Real Estate Investment Advisor

I've got some good news for you. All of the hard work you've been doing throughout your real estate plan is about to start paying off. This is the chapter where I begin using words like "exit strategies," "dream fulfillment," and "estate planning." You will finally get to have fun with the proceeds of the real estate empire that you have built. You may have even created enough net equity from all your investments, including real estate and the money you have in other financial markets. You are completely financially secure and can begin to live the life of your dreams. This will be the fabulous reality for many of you. Enjoy it!

WHY DO I WANT TO PLAN FOR MY FUTURE LIFESTYLE NOW?

Oftentimes, my clients say, "Lisa, why should I spend time now thinking about what I want to do in 10 to 15 years? What difference will it make? I'll just worry about that later when I have more time." My answer is pretty simple. You could have a decent life in retirement, or you could have an exceptional life in retirement. You choose. At the risk of sounding like a broken record, the more time you spend creating a full and balanced lifestyle (and I don't just mean money), the more meaningful and exciting your life will be once you stop working for active income and begin to create passive income.

Americans accept the fact that it's necessary to plan for financial futures. They put money away and study about investment theory, right? But as a culture, people don't spend the time planning their joys, satisfactions, and values for the future. In fact, if you even mention that you can influence or create the fun things in life with as much certainty as you plan your finances, people look at you strangely and dismiss this idea as unimportant. But there is nothing different about planning for your financial future and planning for your lifestyle future. I can't emphasize this enough. You will get tremendous results from both forms of planning. As an added benefit, you will keep your momentum throughout your years of investing if you have a clear vision of what net equity you are targeting and the lifestyle that that net equity will afford you. Plus, if you practice having a great life now that is filled with inspiration, you will be more familiar with this state of mind when you retire. Practice the art of living successfully both personally and financially so that when you have the time and the money, your life really *will be* amazing and you will already be familiar with it. Evaluate your lifestyle dreams every year just like you evaluated your real estate portfolio, and when making real estate plans, make sure you include some of those vacations and special events that you want throughout your real estate investing career.

True happiness comes from how you choose to live into your wealth. This is the heart of your real estate plan. The mechanics of real estate investing can be complicated, overwhelming, exciting, and lots of work. Living into your dreams and creating what you want should be totally fun and freeing. Try it out for a while, and see what shows up.

KNOWING WHEN YOU HAVE ARRIVED

It is not unusual for some of my clients to not know that they have actually attained their goals and objectives, especially when they start working with me. They don't realize that they have enough net equity to live the lifestyle of their dreams. These are usually clients so caught up in the acquisition and growth phases of their real estate plans that they forget to pay attention to creating a lifestyle that inspires them. Then, when they get to the end of their real estate plans, they are lost and bewildered about what to do with themselves. I've already discussed how important it is to plan for your dreams, and hopefully you won't become one of those lost souls. I've always found that the clients who take the time to plan ahead and think about what inspires them have the most fun while they are transitioning into the exit strategy. Believe it or not, there will actually come a time when you don't have to push your investments as much and can begin to make decisions that are not only about finances or how to make the greatest rates of return on your equity all the time. The key is to recognize when you are there.

LIVING THE LIFE YOU LOVE ON PASSIVE INCOME

For most people, transitioning from active income to passive income can feel awkward and a bit disorienting. Sometimes, they are so familiar with saving, scrimping, and restraining (all of which are characteristics that make for a good real estate investor, by the way), that having the extra money and being able to spend it is anxiety producing. They may even feel disoriented when they realize that they no longer have a title or job with which to define who they are. Some of this is natural and cannot be avoided. Fortunately, with good planning you can minimize this reaction and can actually find new meaning in your life during your transition. How does millionaire fit as a title? Do you think you could define yourself that way?

BEGINNING TO PLAN FOR USING PASSIVE INCOME

Not only is the mental transition to living on passive income tricky, but I have also found that many investors experience difficulties trying to convert their real estate from a net equity generator to a passive income generator. Here's the good news: you will not have to keep paying attention to the ROE like you did while your real estate portfolio was growing. Even better, now that your real estate portfolio is mature and developed, you won't have to continue carrying debt. You'll find that as you get older, it is more advantageous to have lower mortgage payments and a more conservative real estate portfolio that is not as leveraged. In the next few sections, I'll point out some ways that you can start transitioning your portfolios into passive income machines.

OWNING REAL ESTATE THAT IS NOT FOR ROE EXCLUSIVELY

There will be different times throughout your real estate plan when you purchase or hold onto real estate not because it is making a tremendously high ROE, but because you want that property for personal reasons. The closer you get to the exit strategy phase of your real estate plan, the more you will be making decisions based on your personal values. Now is your chance to finally liquidate the real estate that you don't like. Decide which pieces of real estate are working in your portfolio and which ones are not. You may determine that you don't want to own a piece of real estate anymore because it is too much of a headache or hassle, and you have other assets in your portfolio that are performing well for you. Living the life of your dreams should include minimal hassles and headaches. If a property has lots of troubles, especially as you approach the exit strategy phase, feel free to dump it.

You will still want to keep in your portfolio some real estate that is producing good income and some that is in markets that are based on appreciation. Both are important, but your debt service can be reduced to produce a good cash flow for you. Paying attention to ROE is less important because now you are focusing on cash flow for passive income purposes.

PAYING OFF MORTGAGES OR ACCELERATED PAYING DOWN OF MORTGAGES

Unlike in the earlier phases in your real estate plan when you wanted to leverage everything, this is the time in your financial life when you get to receive all of the benefits and rewards that you have worked so hard to create. It is usually a time when you want to pay down the mortgages and keep the cash flow coming in on the properties. You may decide to sell some properties that are low-performers and take the proceeds from that straight sale to pay down the mortgage on other existing real estate in your portfolio. Just remember: you will need to talk with your tax accountant and financial planner when you are selling off real estate that you have owned for several years because of the tax implications. I do not want you to have an unexpectedly large tax bill as you are navigating through this phase of your real estate plan.

The amount of passive income you are receiving each month should be the amount of money that you have been targeting from your real estate plan throughout the years. Remember that from early chapters? Your biggest problem may be how to spend the money that you are receiving every month from your passive income. It is a really exciting and fun time in life. You will be living off the rewards of your years of hard work. This is how it can really work for you. You have paid attention to your equity throughout the years, and now you get to have fun and spend it. Have fun. You deserve it.

SELLING REAL ESTATE, PAYING TAXES, AND RECAPTURING DEPRECIATION

There are several things you need to pay attention to when you are selling your real estate through a straight sale. As I discussed in the previous chapter, one option is to carry paper or notes to help defer immediate taxes. Make sure that you are legally protected and prepared to pay the necessary taxes that are owed. Strategically figure out ways to either defer or reduce them. Don't forget that the IRS has been allowing you to use your depreciation each year, and now you will be able to use this depreciation powerfully as you transition into generating and using passive income from your real estate portfolio. Unfortunately, you will need to pay a recapture tax for this depreciation when you liquidate or sell your property. This tax is usually about 25 percent of the tax benefit that you received, but it also depends on how long you held the property. This can have a significant impact on you if you are not careful with how you transition into your exit phase.

Make sure that you keep up on the ever-changing tax laws that will affect your tax liabilities as you begin to pay down your real estate portfolio and transition into passive income streams. Most local apartment associations are excellent about informing you of the current laws and changes of which you should be aware as a landlord.

BUYING VACATION AND RETIREMENT HOMES

Many of the investors that I work with buy vacation and retirement homes about five years before they have met their real estate goals and dreams. They begin to think strategically about where they want to move and what lifestyle they want. These investors move forward and buy low yielding, lifestyle real estate purchases so they can live in them later in life. This is yet another benefit to owning real estate.

Vacation real estate is one of the highest appreciating asset classes to own. The projections are that the baby boomers will be purchasing second homes and vacation homes in record numbers until the year 2020. The areas that are most affected by this demand are U.S.-based mountain areas with recreational facilities near by, like ski resorts and lakes, as well as anything near the water or ocean.

BEING PROTECTED BY KEEPING YOUR INVESTMENTS REALLY SAFE

Now is the time to *protect* what you have in your real estate portfolio. The larger the portfolio, the more you want to make sure that you have enough protection for what you own. This is also the time to reevaluate the skills of all your team members, making sure that they are qualified to successfully transition you into the exit strategy phase. These are the team players that are most important in helping you protect what you have worked so hard to create over the years. Take a look at your:

- *Accountants.* Make sure your accountants know a lot about investment real estate and about reducing or deferring as much of your taxes as possible. This is the time in the plan when you really want someone who is willing to take you to the next level. You will be moving a lot of your assets around through distribution, paying down debt, and selling some properties through straight sales. You will also have deferred taxes that can greatly affect your overall portfolio, so you need an accountant who can handle all of this with skill.

- *Attorneys.* Make sure that all of your assets are legally protected and that you have the appropriate title and vesting on all your properties. All legal documents should be signed and completed to avoid unnecessary taxation as you begin to distribute some of the assets in your real estate portfolio.
- *Bookkeepers.* Unless you like keeping the books on your own accounts, it is important to maintain good records and books on the real estate that you own. Your bookkeeper will account for how your money is coming and going, so be sure to hire someone you trust. You want to protect the money you've worked so hard to earn, don't you?
- *Property managers.* Your property managers are responsible for keeping your real estate running efficiently to produce passive income streams. You will still want to receive good reports from them so that you know how to increase the efficiency of your remaining property, even during the exit phase.
- *Real estate agents.* Real estate agents will be especially useful now because they can help you transfer some of your real estate through straight sales, exchanges and additional purchases that might benefit your family, improve your lifestyle, or fulfill a charitable contribution goal. Real estate agents will show you what is available and the many choices that you have.
- *Financial planners.* Financial planners should be hired throughout the development of your real estate plan. As your real estate portfolio has grown and developed, you should have asked your financial planner the complicated questions that will help guide you into wealth development. You should be planning years ahead of time for the distribution of your estate, gifting and the overall performance of your investment portfolio (including your other investment vehicles such as stocks, bonds, CDs, and savings accounts). Your financial planners should be your guides to fulfilling your goals and objectives as they relate to wealth development, asset protection, and taxation issues.

• • •

In the next chapter, you'll start to finalize your efforts by bringing you full circle to where you began, starting from a place of abundance and ending in a place of fulfillment. You'll learn how to have what you dreamed and planned for and pass on powerful messages for generations to come. I'll highlight the joys that are present at the exit strategy phase of your real estate plan and the wonders of living on the profits of the diverse real estate portfolio that you specifically created.

$$$

Financial Planners Protect Real Estate Investors

I am so glad that real estate professionals are teaching their clients more about making wise long-term real estate investments and the importance of protecting them. Almost all of my wealthiest clients own real estate in a variety of ways. Many investors fail to properly plan for the distribution of their estate, and this work should be done early on in the planning phases, long before an investor really needs them. I'm here to help them.

It is about time that financial planners, real estate agents, and investors work together to create long-term solutions for our clients that match up their dreams and aspirations. I love when everyone has one goal of working in the best interest of the client. It is a great feeling to know that I can help my clients realize their goal of achieving "enough" so that someday they are able to stop working and reap the fruits of their labor. If I do my job well, my clients will know when that day is coming long before it gets there.

—B. RYAN, FINANCIAL PLANNER/CFA

Finding Balance

Knowing When You Have Enough

"Two roads diverged in a wood, and I—I took the one less traveled by.
And that has made all the difference."
—Robert Frost

Now that you are at the end of your real estate plan and have created various streams of passive income for yourself and your family, stop, breathe, and reflect. Notice how hard you've worked for financial security. For years you have sacrificed and put aside the daily rewards of time, money, and resources in order to be financially secure. Let me be the first to tell you that the future that you have been working for has now arrived. The equity in your real estate portfolio is producing income to satisfy your plans and dreams, and there is enough money to do *whatever* you want. Congratulations!

THERE IS MORE TO LIFE THAN MONEY

It's important to remember that money is a means to an end, not an end in itself. Always keep in mind what you intend to do with the money you created. Because this is a book on real estate, I'll use a building analogy. Consider the money you've worked so hard to earn as the foundation for a building you want to build. If you've planned well and used the right materials, that foundation will be strong and steady and support just about any type of building you can imagine. The building you choose to build upon that foundation is the life you've dreamed about. Everyone will have different types of houses built on this sturdy and strong foundation. No two houses will look the same. The important thing is that it is *your* building, and it belongs to you and your family. Make it everything you desire. Remember: there are no dress rehearsals in life. Have fun, make some mistakes, laugh, cry, and be fully alive. Take the time to appreciate what you have and be thankful for both the little things and the bigger things that life brings to you. Take stock of what you value, and remember to cherish the people you love.

WHO SAYS YOU CAN'T HAVE IT ALL?

There may have been people along the road to your success who have told you that you can't have it all. They probably suggested that you stop dreaming and take your head out of the clouds. These are usually people who are not motivated to do what it takes to have it all. They most likely have not taken the time to set up a plan and evaluate their goals and dreams and have never sought outside help or advice to make their lives really wonderful. Don't listen to people who don't have what you want. Instead, talk to people who *do* have what you want. Then, emulate what they have done, and you're sure to get what they have. I promise you, it is within your reach. You just have to be willing to be great and go for it. Real estate investing is a marathon not a sprint, so be prepared to stay in the game for the long haul.

SEVEN SECRETS TO SUCCESS

To achieve the life you desire, you must follow your heart and your mind. These seven secrets to success will lead you on the path toward reaching those goals. Make sure that you:

1. *Have balance.* Creating balance in your life takes time and focus, but it is very possible and well worth it if you are willing to do what it takes to get it. You will operate with more joy and satisfaction if you have balance in your day and in your life. Strive to create balance just like you created financial security for yourself.
2. *Have your dreams.* Oftentimes adults feel as though they need to put their dreams aside because they are getting older or because life threw them one too many

curve balls and somehow their dreams passed them by. Disillusionment sets in, and they give up on those dreams that once meant so much to them. It is important to continuously strive for your dreams. Do what it takes to make your dreams a reality, no matter what obstacles or hurdles get in the way. The obstacles are the adventures of life. I would much rather live life fully and accept the bumps that come along for the ride.

3. *Give to charity.* Many people feel that the time to give to charity or give back to society will come once they are financially established. This is not always accurate. Your habits of charity and giving back should be established when money and time are tight and you have to sacrifice to make payments to the charities of your choice. This way, you will learn to make it a priority when things are going well and when things are not going well. Charitable giving can be some of the most enjoyable money you'll ever spend, and volunteering can be some of the most satisfying time for you. The rewards are not monetary; they are life fulfilling and often life changing. Start developing an appetite for giving, and you will be amazed at how you will experience your life. Your gift of money or time will also have an impact on the world and your environment. No gift is too small or insignificant. Some investors love the fact that they can work toward creating this in their lives when they never thought it would be possible to really have a lasting impact on others. Because of their diligence with their real estate plan, they are able to enjoy this part of life.

4. *Have hobbies.* Make sure that you plan for hobbies that really excite you during your everyday activities. If you are too busy to do some of the activities that you really enjoy, then set up special time that allows the creative and satisfying side of yourself to come out. Do not forget that hobbies are fun and healthy for everyone. Work hobbies into your schedule and make them one of your priorities in having a balanced and happy life.

5. *Spend time with family and friends.* The older I get, the more I value my family and my friends. Without them life is dull, boring, and meaningless. I love my family and encourage you to rekindle those relationships with the people that you really care about. Spend time now with the people that mean the most to you because you never know how much time you'll have with them. Time together will bring you satisfaction and love that can never be replaced, no matter how much money you have.

6. *Go on vacation.* Make sure that you plan to go on vacation at least once or twice per year (if not more than that). You will find that even minivacations can recharge your batteries and give you the strength you need to face your "real life circumstances" once again. If money is tight, don't let that stop you. Go camping

or find other creative and inexpensive ways to get out of town. It's sure to boost your energy and renew your spirit.

7. *Make sure you travel.* I find that it's really important to travel to new places and see how other people live their lives. I love to explore my wonderful state, my country, and the world every chance I get. I've learned so much about myself simply by observing other people in their own environments. Traveling introduces you to a variety of cultures, reminds you of how big and amazing our planet actually is, and shows you new ways of thinking and perceiving the world in which you live. Stretch your boundaries by going on an adventure. You never know what you'll discover.

THE CIRCLE OF LIFE: BEING CONTENT AND HAVING ENOUGH

It is important to learn to be happy with your life regardless of whether you have financial security or not. You will want to work on being content at all phases of your real estate plan. This includes learning to be grateful for all that you have and knowing when you have enough so that you can finally stop chasing after your goals. For me, enough is when I have planned out a lifestyle that really reflects my inner desires for financial security, family, travel,

> **DON'T FORGET**
> You will know when you have enough net equity because you will be analyzing and evaluating your portfolio once a year.

charity, and continued wealth. When I have a plan and work it accurately, I will be annually evaluating the growth and strength of my real estate portfolio, and I will know when I have met the goals I have established. When I have reached my net equity goals and have reviewed my real estate plan with my financial planner and accountant who give me the green light to retire and live off the passive income, I will know that I have enough.

It is a larger task to be satisfied and learn to be content than it is to learn to create money. By following the methods in this book, making money will naturally happen. Many investors rush into investing as though it will satisfy all aspects of their lives, but the truth is you need to focus on creating happiness and contentment within yourself. Although it takes just as much work as making the money, you'll find that this is the most satisfying part of your real estate plan.

BEGIN TO CREATE BALANCE IN YOUR LIFE NOW!

Look at the wheel in Figure 20.1. Each of its eight sections is a part of your life that helps you create balance. Pull out your colored pencils or markers and color in the percentage of goal attainment for each of the sections. For example: if you feel comfortable with your family life and most of your dreams are accomplished, you might darken 90 percent of that section filling it in from the center parts to the outer rim of the circle (there is always room to grow and improve). If you want to be in great physical shape, but never work out and are overweight, then darken just

DON'T FORGET

You should fill out the Wheel of Balance and Dream Worksheet each year when you are evaluating your real estate plan.

FIGURE 20.1: **The Wheel of Balance**

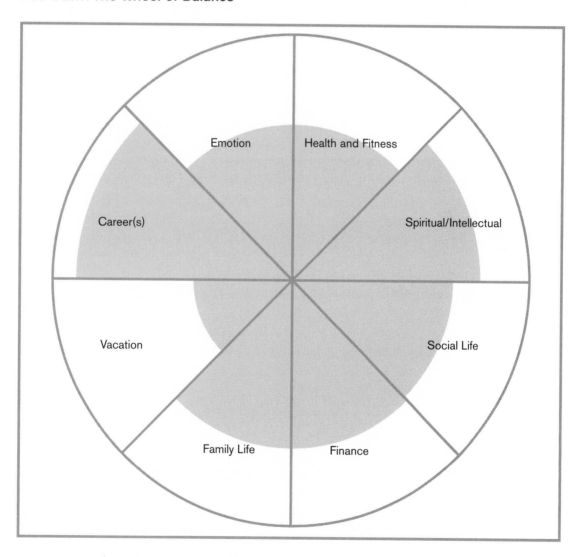

> **Hot Tip**
>
> Just for kicks imagine the wheel of balance exercise is the wheel you are driving your life with. As this example demonstrates, when your life isn't balanced you have a bumpier ride.

10 percent of the health and fitness section. Do this for all of the sections and don't worry about being precise. This should this be fun and informative.

Now that you have evaluated how your life is balanced, create your dreams for the future. The dream worksheet (Figure 20.2) is used every year by investors so that they can begin to define and write down what they are committed to. This will change each year. Investors want to focus on growing wealth for financial freedom and the dream worksheet helps investors grow and develop their personal dreams. Give it a try. You will be able to play around with what life will look like for you as you are building your real estate fortunes. Don't forget about

FIGURE 20.2: **Dreams Worksheet**

Be as creative as you can about your dreams in the following areas. Do not eliminate something from this worksheet just because you don't know how to accomplish it, or because it doesn't immediately make sense. Have fun thinking BIG.

Health and Fitness. What do you want your health and fitness levels to be? _____

_____

Vacations. Where do you want to go? How long, how much will it cost and who will go? _____

_____

Family Life. What does it look like? How do you feel in it? Who is with you? _____

_____

Social Life. What's fun? Who enjoys doing things with you and how often? _____

_____

Career(s). What salary, position, or title would you like? Are there any changes you'd like to make? At what age will you retire? _____

_____

FIGURE 20.2: **Dreams Worksheet**

Spiritual/Intellectual Life. What does it look like? Who do you share it with? What inspires you and how do you inspire others? _____

_____

Money in the Bank. How much do you have? How much do you plan to have and when? What will you use it for? _____

_____

Real Estate. What do you own? When will you buy and what will you buy? _____

_____

---

the intangible things in life. They will become the gold far more valuable than any material wealth that you will create. Remember: money is only a means to an end, not the end by itself. Don't get lost in those two concepts, or you may miss out on the things that really matter the most.

• • •

In the next chapter, you'll learn how to pass on your legacy to your children and your children's children. I'll discuss the importance of giving back with joy and making a social difference in the world in which you live. You'll also learn to put your commitments in writing and actually make those dreams come true. You're well on your way!

$$

If I Can Do It, Anyone Can Do It!

Real estate has been really good to me, and I have been really good to real estate. I have been investing in real estate since the mid-1980s. I have seen the boom markets and the bust markets. It has not always been easy, but I've always taken seriously my responsibilities in owning properties and managing them for long-term growth. There have been times when I really thought I was crazy holding onto my real estate because of all the problems with tenants, lowered rents, high vacancies, and lost property values, but somehow I knew that with every downturn of the market there was a stronger upswing coming. My belief that real estate was one of the best investments available kept me going.

I am so glad that I persevered. I have seen so many of my business partners and friends bail out of owning property at the first sign of trouble, and today they do not have nearly the wealth that I have. I have the freedom to do anything I want. I can continue to work or quit working and live off the passive income generated from my properties. Either way is fine. I am living my life just the way I'd always imagined I could. If I could make real estate work, then any of you can as well. Just get going, and make it work for you today. The sooner you get started, the quicker you will be able to reap the rewards of your decisions.

—JMAR, REAL ESTATE AGENT/PROPERTY OWNER/ENTREPRENEUR

A Legacy of Real Financial Intelligence

"The miracle is this—the more we share, the more we have."
—Leonard Nimoy

Now that you've finally made it to the end of your real estate investing road, it's time to reflect on the journey. The exit strategy phase of your real estate plan is designed to guide you in mapping out and defining the most valuable aspects of your life and what you want to preserve for future generations. This is the time to create a legacy of real financial intelligence that is long lasting and compelling for the people you love and the things that you cherish.

PASSING ON POWERFUL MESSAGES

Once you have mastered how to grow your wealth and produce the results that you desire, you can pass on what you have learned. Some of the messages passed down with inheritance have little to do with growing money, but are about managing and giving money away. The messages you pass on can vary from what you want your heirs to do with the wealth that has been preserved for them to what values you'd like your heirs to adopt.

Most investors get so caught up in building, creating, and protecting their wealth that they forget to ask themselves what they want to do with the wealth they have created. How much will they leave for their children or relatives? What will be donated to charity? These are important questions that should be discussed early in the development of your real estate plan, but they will have special significance during the exit strategy phase.

The questions you ask yourself can be very powerful if you take the time to look into what you really want passed on as your legacy, but they can sometimes also be disturbing for people who don't want to think about the inevitable situation of their lives. Unfortunately, the reality is that everyone is going to pass away eventually, and how you leave your fortune and estate can have a lasting impact on a lot of people. Why not have a say in how that happens? At the same time, you can teach your family about financial management and giving through how you distribute the assets in your estate. The questions in Figure 21.1 might get you thinking.

MAKING A SOCIAL DIFFERENCE AND GIVING BACK WITH JOY

Social psychologists have reported that people over the age of 60 begin to adjust their attention and focus on life away from themselves, becoming more concerned with society and social matters. They start focusing on the younger generations and how they can both give back to others and contribute to the community at large. It is a natural evolution of the developmental process for people to contemplate charitable contributions and give freely later in life, especially since they are more likely to have the time and resources to devote to giving. This social awareness becomes more prevalent and important for real estate investors who will probably be in their 50s, 60s, and 70s when they finally reach the exit strategy phase of their real estate plans.

Mapping out your contributions can be fun and creative for those who choose these avenues of expressing their interests. Some of the planning should begin to take shape in the middle of the equity management phase of your real estate plan.

DISTRIBUTION OF YOUR ESTATE

Good estate planning is essential when you have developed a diversified real estate portfolio. You will want to plan the distribution of your estate with a good estate attorney.

FIGURE 21.1: **Focusing on Your Legacy**

1. What memories do you want people to have of you in 50 to 100 years? _____

_____

_____

2. You can have a lasting impact on the people you love and care about through strategically using your real estate plan. What actions would you take now that will impact others in the future? _____

_____

_____

3. Passing on a legacy has tremendous power. What do you want your legacy to look like? What values would you like passed on? What do you want people to learn from you? _____

_____

_____

4. How much money do you want your heirs to inherit? Do you want to have any say in what they do with the wealth they inherit? _____

_____

_____

5. When giving money to your heirs, are you going to wait until they are in their 20s, 30s, 40s, or 50s before they can have the proceeds from your estate? _____

_____

_____

6. Are you going to wait until you are gone before dispersing your estate, or do you want to give your family some of your estate while you are still alive? _____

_____

_____

7. Do you plan on contributing to society from the abundance you have created? What are some of your favorite charities or ways that you would like to influence the world? _____

_____

_____

Most estate planners agree that it is better to distribute most of the assets in your estate before the time of death. You can avoid certain taxes and create longevity with your specific estate planning. Proper planning for the distribution of your estate can save you hundreds of thousands of tax dollars and keep it within the family where most people would like it to stay. It can also help you pass on important messages to your children, grandchildren, and great grandchildren.

Don't forget that a well thought out estate distribution plan can influence the purchase of some of your properties in the earlier phases of your real estate plan. Some time during the 10 to 20 years that you are buying real estate, you may decide to buy a piece of property that is located near a hospital or institution to which you would eventually like to donate. Or perhaps you may want to purchase a home that is located in a particular part of town where you can make an impact on the community or donate the home to a charitable organization. Proper planning now can save you a great deal of hassle later on and inspire you to create more in your real estate portfolio.

YOU CAN HAVE A SAY FOR THE NEXT 50 TO 100 YEARS

Older civilizations around the world, such as in Japan, do not hesitate to plan out 25 to 50 years in advance. These cultures have more patience and endurance than our fast-paced, fast-food culture. They are more familiar and comfortable looking at the future and making plans for it. Some families in these cultures have even planned their estates (empires) well into the next century. Sadly, Americans are generally more shortsighted. They usually do not have a plan for the year, let alone 5, 10, or 20 years ahead of time. Break out of that mold, and use this time to expand your influence and direction from the abundance that has been created through your real estate plan.

MAKING A COMMITMENT

Planning for your future is an ongoing process, and it begins with the present. The form in Figure 21.2 is designed to inspire you to make some specific commitments. Keep your commitments short and definable so that you will accomplish them. After you write down each commitment, share it with someone so you increase the odds of accomplishing it. Fill in four different commitments that you want to achieve within the next three months after reading this book. Be as specific as you can. You want your commitments to be measurable and placed in time.

> This real estate plan can even work for the investor who has little to no money to start with. You can get started with as little as $3,000. Just get started!

FIGURE 21.2: **Commitments**

Example	
Your Name:	Jane Doe
Commitment 1:	I want to get my financing in order and have loan approval on my first investment property by the third week of May.
Commitment 2:	I want to learn about investing in three different areas around the country by the second week of June.
Commitment 3:	I want to select a property with an ROE of 20 percent to purchase by the third week of July.
Commitment 4:	I want to be in escrow by the fourth week of August on an investment property.

Your Name:

Commitment 1:

Commitment 2:

Commitment 3:

Commitment 4:

Keep it simple, set in time, and measurable. This is a get-into-action form.

YOU CAN REALLY DO IT!

Remember that small time investors can make it *BIG* in real estate because of leverage and the ability to buy properties at discount and fix them up for a profit. Most property owners who invest in real estate can earn between $30,000 and $150,000 per year and still create a healthy real estate plan through strategic purchasing and property and equity management. The beauty of real estate is that the art of leverage works for larger properties in the same way that it works for smaller properties. Even better, the rates of return are the same for both large and small investors. No more excuses! Get out there and invest!

BEST WISHES AND HAPPINESS

As you reach the end of this book, I want to take the opportunity to say that it has been my great pleasure to share with you what I have learned and passed on to many investors throughout the years. You are now equipped with all the necessary information that you need to make a fortune in real estate investing. I hope that you have discovered some practical investment techniques to implement so that you can create these results in your own life. Most importantly, I hope that you now realize that you can make and *keep* millions of dollars through safely and strategically investing in real estate. The key is to build your wealth slowly so that you will keep it. Then later in your real estate plan, you will be able to gracefully grow into your wealth.

May you have everything that you dream about and keep reaching for the stars. You are worth it! Keep up the good work.

$$

Charity Work Is Our Life, We Use Real Estate to Secure Our Future

We love what we do. We live and work by the U.S. border and serve the people of Mexico by working for a small church. Our income is dependent on the donations and generous gifts of others. We have a humble existence and that is okay for us. It may appear odd to others, but we're already living the life of our dreams. We have been living this way for years, but started having a growing concern about how we were going to support ourselves when we stopped working for the church in Mexico. Real estate investments seemed like a good option for us. We decided to partner with our son who lives in Wisconsin and began our investment career with him.

Together we bought a house in our hometown that has two units—a large single-family residence in the front and a smaller studio in the back. We decided to rent out both units with a positive cash flow while we continued working and living near Mexico. We now have a place to live when we retire from our current service work. We will be near our children and grandchildren and have an inexpensive place to live while receiving a small income from the front house. Living in the studio will be just fine with us. We could not be happier that we took the risk to start getting ready now for what was going to happen in the future. We are thankful that our son has seen what we did and wants to continue buying properties so that he can start earlier with his wife and kids to achieve their dreams. Our legacy will continue through his family's investments.

—CARL AND KATHY, MISSIONARIES IN MEXICO

Appendices

Where Should I Buy?

> *"Invest in your mind and learn how to acquire assets and you will be choosing wealth as your goal and your future. The choice is yours and only yours."*
> —Robert Kiyosaki and Sharon Lechter

With so many markets from which to choose and with each in a potentially different stage of its market cycle, deciding where to buy property can be a bit anxiety inducing. One way to relieve this anxiety is to take a look at the trends in a particular geographical region you are considering. You'll want to seek professional advice within each region, but it is also crucial that you know how to select these areas by yourself.

It's important to note that the information contained in this appendix can only reflect the time that this book was written. A region can be hot one year and quite cool the next, so I highly recommend that you keep up on the most current information and trends.

Southern California

The Southern California region has done fabulously since 1997. The market has been on a steady incline and home values have skyrocketed, so that this area is now one of the most expensive places to live in the country. This means that cash flows are hard to come by without putting too much money down, which will inversely affect your ROEs and diminish the overall rates of return on equity. However, the gains through appreciation have been spectacular, so having some of your real estate holdings in Southern California can be very valuable for growing your long-term wealth in real estate. Southern California can be broken into five different markets:

1. *Los Angeles County.* LA County is a growing and thriving metropolitan area. The amount of commerce that comes out of the Los Angeles area is phenomenal. The prices have not gotten too out of hand (relatively speaking) and some good investment opportunities still exist in that market.

2. *Orange County.* Orange County is one of the most expensive counties in which to live both in Southern California and across the country. It is difficult to find properties that make financial sense for investors in the single-family residence and condo markets. The high cost of entry (due to appreciation) and the low cash flows generated for rents make sustainability an issue of concern. Some commercial properties are still profitable and working for investors.

3. *San Diego County.* Next to Orange County, San Diego County is one of the most expensive places to own real estate in the country. The prices are high, and the rents don't keep pace with the cost of buying investment properties. Seasonal rentals are doing well along the coast, and downtown properties have continued to perform well. Typically, more seasoned investors are able to stay and invest in San Diego County. However, making the monthly payments becomes tricky if investors do not have either lots of cash for a down payment or lots of disposable income monthly to make the negative cash flow work for them.

4. *Riverside County.* Currently, Riverside County is the best county in Southern California in which to invest. It has experienced some of the highest appreciation rates in the entire country. The costs are still reasonable, and the rents are more closely related to the cost of the building. On the downside, property values may not climb as high as other regions in Southern California due to the lack of high-paying jobs. High-paying jobs directly influence property prices and rental rates and are more often found in Orange, Los Angeles, and San Diego counties.

5. *Imperial County.* Lots of new home building is currently going on in Imperial County. Higher vacancy rates and lower costs of entry make this an interesting market to keep your eyes on. Pay attention to what industries are moving into this area and how long the houses are staying on the market.

Central California

Overall, California has been a great state for economic growth. It has been producing jobs and products consistently for the past 40 years. Many investors love keeping their money in the state of California just for that fact. The diverse economy continues to fuel real estate growth and demand, which in turn continues to generate amazing rates of appreciation.

- *Bakersfield, Fresno, and Modesto.* All of these areas show signs of growth and expansion over the next 10 to 20 years. The prices are not as high as the Southern California markets or the San Francisco Bay area, so investors can get in with more reasonable prices and better cash flows. There is still plenty of land, so tremendous growth is both possible and expected. Keep your eyes focused on these areas.

Northern California

The San Francisco Bay area saw its heyday in the 1970s, 1980s, and 1990s. Eventually, the area got so expensive that people could not comfortably live there. As a result, the job market began to change, and good workers started leaving the area seeking a more reasonable environment in which to live and work. They moved to areas such as Southern California, Colorado, the Southwestern states, the Northwest, and the Southeast region of the country. Properties finally started declining in value in the early 2000s due to the changes in stock market values and the bursting of the dot.com bubble. Sacramento has continued to show signs of solid growth and development and expansion is expected in these markets.

Northwest Coastal Region (Washington and Oregon)

In the 1980s and 1990s, this region experienced growth and an expansion of its population, but since 2000, the economy has declined and has not been doing very well. Many people in the 1980s and 1990s liked the home prices, job opportunities, and natural beauty in these areas, but have come to dislike the damp and cold weather. In addition, the job market was greatly affected in 2000 by the dot.com industry fall, which tightened up those exciting job opportunities. These areas are having a hard time recovering from the economic shifts that have occurred, and many people are leaving.

There has also been considerable government regulation that has limited much of the development in this area. Environmentalists have a great deal of pull and influence in these areas, which typically slows land development and growth and increases building costs. Exceptions can be found in cities like Ashland, Oregon, that have colleges and special attractions that lure people to these areas. Such cities have done well and continue to attract people who want the Northwest lifestyle, yet also want some culture and activities. The latest news shows that Seattle and Portland are about to turn around as well.

Northwest Region (Utah, Idaho, Nevada)

This region continues to draw people and investors into its marketplaces and has been experiencing tremendous growth and development in the past five to ten years. Jobs are locating there to fuel the health of these economies, and the region appears to be stable and growing. Salt Lake City, Utah, and Boise, Idaho, have been reported to have good real estate values and tend to produce stable properties that will be able to show cash flow and slow and steady appreciative growth.

Colorado

This area of the country is experiencing new growth. With the recreational activities and ski resorts as well as affordable housing, I would keep my eyes open for this region. Indicators are strong for this region.

Sunbelt States (Arizona, New Mexico)

The Sunbelt states have experienced tremendous growth with the expectation of baby boomers moving to where it is warmer and land is inexpensive. Because of this, developers have built tremendous inventory. Unfortunately, baby boomers are not moving as quickly as expected, and the vacancy rates have been high in some of these newly developed areas where growth and mass movement was predicted. This area is especially popular with investors from Southern California. Prices have skyrocketed in some of these markets due exclusively to the money coming from the California markets and beginner investors. These conditions have created an extremely "hot market" that will be directly affected when real estate values in California begin to wane and go in the reverse.

- *Phoenix and Tucson.* Appreciation rates have been exceptionally high in these cities, mostly driven by out-of-state investors. The expected growth in these two cities is good, yet current investors continue to complain that vacancies are high and appreciation rates a bit false due to the rush of investors pushing up the prices. The conclusions on what to do with these markets are mixed. Some experts say it is a great investment area whereas others are more hesitant about the long-term growth and sustainable appreciation in these regions. If you already own in these areas, keep what you have, but pay attention to what is going to happen in the next two to three years, especially with the job market diversification and opportunity as well as money coming in from California.

- *New Mexico.* This state has been experiencing good job growth and population growth in recent years. The growth is not as rapid as in Arizona, but it's steady. I would recommend investing in cities like Santa Fe, Albuquerque, and Las Cruces. They seem to be expanding and growing at a steady even pace. The larger multiple-unit buildings produce great cash flows in these regions.

Texas (Dallas, Fort Worth, Austin, Houston)

Texas can fall under the Sun Belt region, but it has its own specific solid information. Buying property in Texas has some drawbacks, such as high property taxes, sometimes up to 3 percent to 3.5 percent annually. Even reasonably priced properties suddenly get more expensive when the property taxes are high. Make sure you ask about the taxes before you sign the contract. They will greatly impact your ability to sustain the property as the market adjusts over time.

- *Dallas/Fort Worth.* This area has had a tremendous downturn over the past four years. The large corporations in this area laid off many employees, and the foreclosure rate skyrocketed. Expectations are that Dallas is coming out of its slump and will be a good investment area in the upcoming years. Many people are concerned that because there is so much open land, the developers will continue to build and the existing inventory will not rise in value very quickly. I am not as concerned about this. People still like being close to schools, parks, employment opportunities, retail stores, and cultural hubs. I think this particular market will show tremendous signs of growth over the next several years.
- *Austin.* Many investors have gone to this diverse and vibrant economy over the past several years, so expect inflated prices. There are many colleges and universities in the area that have kept this city stabilized while the rest of Texas goes through its extreme highs and lows. Pay attention to high vacancies and increased damage to the properties due to the high demand for student housing in the area. Austin has several attractions that have brought many people into the area to retire. It is a great city with lots of potential for years to come.
- *Houston.* This market has been growing and vibrant over the past several years as well. Housing prices are reasonable and can make investing there attractive for out-of-state investors. Investors who go into this market report that the numbers work and that you can find viable investment properties that are sustainable with cash flow and will experience good appreciation.

Florida

Florida is getting lots of attention and media coverage these days. Developers are building new homes at unbelievable rates, and people are moving there in droves. The expected growth rate is terrific over the next two decades. However, pay attention to the tax base in Florida. Properties are reassessed each year, and the tax payments typically increase every year as well. The assessors will usually evaluate the property to about 85 percent of the true value, but this annual increase in taxes can take away those expected cash flows and put beginner investors in jeopardy. Appreciation will be great, but the ability to sustain it will be compromised due to taxes. This is especially true for commercial properties where rents increase incrementally according to the lease contract. Small business owners may be forced to move due to the increased taxes for which they are accountable when on triple net leases.

Mexican Gulf Coast (Florida, Alabama, Mississippi, Louisiana)

This is often referred to as the "forgotten coast," lagging behind other large coastal areas in attention. Investors are just beginning to wake up to this area's investment and lifestyle possibilities. The numbers work very well and the investment opportunities are plentiful. A word of caution: be aware of the amount of coastal condos that are being built. No one can be certain if the baby boomers and Generation Xers will in fact move into these high-rise buildings. There may be an oversupply of this product on the market, but only time will tell. It is fun to watch what will happen in this region of the country. The real estate prices have gone haywire since hurricane Katrina. Housing prices in the surrounding areas have risen quickly due to the increased demand and lack of surplus. The increased number of tropical storms may turn people away from moving to these regions.

Northeast Region

The Northeast is highly populated, and the prices have been competitive and much like the California markets. Business is vibrant and diverse in this region due to its immense population. Recently, prices have appreciated at such tremendous rates that it has become difficult to hold onto properties due to cash flow constraints. It is recommended that investors own some property in areas where appreciation has been high (such as California and the Northeast Coast) and then make sure they diversify their portfolios into other markets where the cash flow is better to help balance out a real estate portfolio with sustainability. You may see some greater appreciation or resurgence in these markets because of the incredible population base that feeds and sustains them.

Central States

The Colorado area has been growing in momentum over the past several years and is now positioned to be a great area with expected job growth and population increases. Properties are cash flowing with a steady appreciation rate.

Midwest

The Midwest has slow appreciation growth, but rental properties in this region produce steady income. This is a good product to have for the long-term investor who wants slow consistent growth that generates cash flow. The properties may only appreciate at 2 to 4 percent per year, but they *will* cash flow. These are gentle and easy properties to put into your real estate portfolio. This region has also experienced a lot of economic recession due to factories and manufacturing moving out of the area and going overseas. But slow and steady growth is projected for this region. There is also contradicting information about the migratory patterns of seniors within these areas. Some have predicted that the baby boomers will leave these regions in search of warmer weather. Interestingly enough, some of these expected migratory patterns are not occurring, and people are choosing to stay closer to family and friends rather than move to warmer regions. This will be interesting to watch to over the next ten years. What will happen, no one really knows.

Rust Belt Region (Ohio, Pennsylvania, Michigan, etc.)

This region has experienced tremendous job loss and economic depression recently. As a result, many of the cities and towns have become run down. There has not yet been a resurgence of jobs to flood the economy. Appreciation will be lower in this region, but pay attention to good discounts and positive cash flow properties. Flat real estate markets are predicted in this region except in some of the larger cities where a resurgence of downtown living and mixed-use living is taking off. The buildings that are in high demand are city lofts where workspaces are on the first floor and living quarters are on the top floors. These have been growing in popularity across the country, but especially in this region where the inner cities have been growing and experiencing development.

Southeast Coast (North and South Carolina, Georgia, and the Virginias)

These areas are really growing and developing. Jobs have moved in, the weather is attracting many people, and the prices are affordable. Many investors are going into Atlanta and the Carolinas because of the diverse economies, affordability, and mild weather conditions. The appreciation rates in these areas are predicted to be high, yet the entrance costs are still more reasonable than some other highly appreciative areas across the country. Pay attention to these regions for high appreciation, job stability, and lifestyle advantages.

• • •

As you can tell, we could probably write a book about each of these different regions. Each city and location has its own unique features, benefits, and deficits. Begin to investigate these areas for yourself and run the numbers. If the numbers work, buy the property. It's as simple as that. Pay attention to the health of the economy so that you will know if the property is going to be paying dividends in cash flow or appreciation. Remember: you do not have to find the hottest market. Simply find properties that meet your overall plans and objectives. It is more important to get into the game of real estate investment than to worry about whether you have found the perfect market. Have fun and buy up a storm!

Questions to Ask When Evaluating an Area

*"Some men see things as they are and ask 'why'?
I dream things that never were and ask, 'why not'?"*
—George Bernard Shaw

When going into an area to determine if it is good for investing, it is important to quickly assess market conditions. Remember: municipalities (or any kind of government) regulate all kinds of things like the development of jobs, housing, and taxes for an area. They have tremendous influence over the growth and development of a region. Use the information that follows to help with your assessment of particular areas.

City Economic Development Department

Because the stability of an area is dependent on having well-planned strategic growth, developing cities usually have an economic development office or have someone responsible for managing the economic growth of the region. The following are some questions you'll want to ask when you meet with these officials:

- What is the expected growth of business in your city over the next year, five years, ten years, and twenty years?
- What companies, corporations, and industries is the city or state trying to attract or reduce? How are you marketing or attracting these businesses to the area?
- Do you have local community colleges or universities that will train the current residents for the jobs you are attracting to the area?
- How is the city economic development department working with other parts of the city government?
- Is there support for the ideas that you are trying to promote? What are the difficulties you face in accomplishing your goals?
- Are the local citizens excited about the new growth, or are they resisting change?

Chamber of Commerce

The chamber of commerce is not usually a governmental office. It is funded through membership of the local merchants and businesses who are interested in networking, promoting, and sustaining the economic growth and commerce in their area. You'll find that some chambers are very active and have solid membership whereas others can be weak and are struggling. Chambers that are strong can market and promote an area to attract upcoming economic development, which is important to know as an investor. Some chambers do a terrific job promoting and attracting new business to an area as well as maintaining and keeping existing businesses. The activities of a local chamber of commerce can sometimes be a telling feature of the focus of a city or region. Make sure to drop in on the local chamber and chat informally for a while. It will be well worth your time. Chat about:

- How many businesses are in the area?
- How big is your membership?
- What types of businesses are you trying to attract?
- What kinds of people are stopping by to talk with the chamber?
- What types of people are being attracted to the area—seniors, families, and businesses?
- If I were to come into the area, what would be the difficulties I might encounter when starting a business or trying to work with the city officials?

- What is great about the area?
- What are the problems in the area?

City Planning Department

City planning departments regulate what type of land is being developed, the zoning that will be granted, time frames for building, fees, and other government regulations. In other words, planning departments regulate the specific physical building of a community. They make sure that the citizens are complying with the regulations of the city planners, and that they are complying with local building codes. If you can set an appointment with the city planner or one of her associates, you will have an invaluable interview. Here are a few questions to ask:

- What plans do you have for city or county infrastructure such as highways, water, sewers, and schools?
- How are you planning to pay for the infrastructure necessary to support the new growth in the area? Will it be funded through the builders and developers or through the citizens by property, income, and sales taxes? Or will it be funded by special assessments?
- What are the tax structures (or rates) in your city or county?
- Do you expect any changes in the current rates? Are these changes being supported or rejected by the citizens?
- How many permits are pulled at this time?
- What types of permits are out? What kinds of commercial projects? What kinds of residential housing permits and what size of homes?
- Is there a city redevelopment plan? How much is it? May I buy one?
- Are there strict zoning requirements?
- Are variances difficult to obtain?
- Is there a city zoning map? May I see it?

City Building Department

City building departments are the operational side to the city planning department. They work with developers, builders, homeowners, contractors, engineers, architects, fire departments, water departments, and utility companies, to name a few. The building department officials will be the people with whom you will be dealing when completing a new home or building a new commercial building. Inquire about:

- How long does it take to get building plans approved through the city?
- What are the fees and costs for building a single-family home, condo, multiple unit, or commercial property?

- What types of reports, such as engineering, architectural, grading plans, and perks are needed to complete the building process?

Housing and Urban Development (HUD)

This department processes the housing needs in the region, mostly to lower-income and special-needs individuals. They regulate Section 8 housing, which provides government subsidized housing to those who need government assistance. HUD also provides low-cost loans and grants to owners in areas that are run down. Most large cities are interested in improving the areas that have become run down over the years, so federal and local government money is generally available. In fact, they are often very eager to give this money to owners at low or no interest to make specific improvements in areas that are designated as redevelopment areas. But buyer beware, government money is fickle! Sometimes it is available, and sometimes it is not. Even when it is available, it is often not marketed or promoted very well because no one in the HUD department has time to advertise or solicit owners or investors to use the money that is available. It's important for you to know that if the municipalities do not spend the money or give it away, they will lose it for the next year. You could be helping them out, but you must get to the right people who are "in the know" and will be able to tell you if there is any money available for improvements. Here are some questions to ask:

- Are there any government low-interest loans or grant money for redevelopment in the area?
- What are the requirements for converting my investment property into a Section 8 property?
- What are the benefits for the owner to have Section 8 tenants?
- Will I be able to charge market rents for my properties if it is a Section 8 property?
- Do you have a shortage of available properties that serve the Section 8 renter?

Residential Real Estate Agents

Talk to real estate agents and have them send you information about the new area before you go to visit. If you like the agents, and they are familiar with investment real estate, set appointments to meet with them for no more than two hours to look at the best investment properties they have available. If you are still interviewing other agents, make it shorter, maybe 30 to 40 minutes, to get a feel for the area and for how well they know the market. Make sure they are familiar with the area and can advise you about investing and being an out-of-area property owner. Ask them:

- How long have you been in the real estate business?

- What specialty or subspecialty do you have?
- Do you sell investment real estate?
- How many investment properties have you sold in the last two years?
- What are the best investment types of property in the area?
- What would you suggest an investor look at in your area?

Commercial Real Estate Agents

Contact a couple of commercial agents to gather information about commercial property and multiple unit properties. They will have invaluable information about the growth of businesses in the area and how investors are making money through owning commercial real estate. Find a commercial agent that is willing to work with you. Commercial real estate agents typically like to work with investors who are buying larger properties with bigger price tags, often over a million dollars in value. Make sure that you are ready to invest and have your money available when you meet with them or they will most likely not take you seriously. When contacting a commercial real estate agent, ask them some of the following questions:

- How long have you been selling commercial property in the area?
- What is the demand for commercial property at this time?
- What kinds of commercial property do you have in abundance?
- What kinds of commercial property are in high demand?
- What are the local CAP rates of multiple-family units and commercial property?
- What is happening with the raw land in the area? Is there a demand or surplus?

Land Developers and Builders

When you go into any area, look at what the land developers are doing and look at what the builders are promoting and marketing. Profitable and strong national and local building developers spend lots of money promoting and marketing their inventory. Go visit the model units, and inspect the quality of work. When you speak with the salesperson, ask him the following questions:

- Who is coming into the area and looking at moving into the area?
- How many units do you have on the market?

> **DEFINITIONS**
>
> *Land developers* take raw and vacant land with no improvements and subdivide the land to prepare it for the building developers. They add utilities such as electric, water, cable, and telephone and put in sewer pipes, streets, curbs, and gutters.
>
> *Building developers* come in after the land developers have finished their job. They build the houses or add improvements to already completed properties.

- What are the standard market times to sell the homes you are promoting?
- What kinds of houses are people looking at buying?
- From what parts of the country are people coming here?
- Are they young, old, well-to-do, or bargain hunters?
- What size housing are they most interested in at this time?

Property Managers

Property managers are among the most important players on your team. They will be able to help you manage the growth and development of your real estate portfolio. Take extra time selecting these people for your team. Ask some of the following questions:

- What are the local rental rates per square footage?
- Have these rates changed much in the past several years? What are the typical rental rate changes in a good market? What percentage do they increase per year?
- When the rental market declines, how much do the rents go down? What percentage should be expected in a declining market?
- How much do you charge to manage residential monthly/yearly leases?
- How much do you charge to manage residential seasonal rentals?
- How much do you charge to manage commercial long-term leases?
- Are there additional marketing or management fees of which I need to be aware?
- Do you take a mark up on the repairs that are done on the property? If so, what mark-up rate do you charge?
- Do you send me monthly reports on the property in Quicken or Quickbooks accounting program?
- Will you send me digital photos of the property every six months?
- What are the shortages or surpluses in the residential and commercial rentals?
- What have been the standard vacancy rates over the past ten years?
- How much of a fluctuation in vacancy rates does this area experience typically?

• • •

Now that you have all of these questions, you will be able to comfortably go to any market and evaluate it for yourself. Good Job. Have fun! Be Profitable. Buy Property.

Know Your Economy

"The more power you have over your money, the more money will be attracted to you. It's how you think about it, feel about it, and invest it."
—Suzy Orman

In the world of long-term investment real estate, paying attention to the economy can save you tens of thousands of dollars and countless sleepless nights. This is due to the fact that unlike the securities market that responds instantaneously to consumer confidence or fear in the market place, real estate values and rental rates adjust slowly over time and move in wave-like patterns rather than in high peaks and valleys. The slow moving waves of real estate give investors the advantage of having both long-term visibility and the ability to forecast movements within the real estate market more accurately and profitably. Investors who pay attention to the real estate market patterns and cycles can make strategic moves when key economic indicators move in any direction, choosing to liquidate or maintain their real estate holdings based on national or regional economic data.

Real estate is a slow moving asset because it provides residential housing and commercial buildings for human beings. As you may have noticed, humans by nature dislike change. Most people don't decide to sell their homes and move over a weekend. It usually takes people about a year from when they begin to talk and think about moving until they are actually in their new homes. This slow movement works to the advantage of busy investors. They can read the market and make decisions based on their long-term strategies and goals much easier when they have time to contemplate, decide, prepare, and then act. Because the data that they need to research reacts slowly, they do not have to be on their computers valuing their investments every day. Instead, they can look at their real estate values and ROEs every quarter or six months and have a good indication of the health and well being of their investments and of markets around the country where they might consider buying.

Forecasting and Visibility in Investment Real Estate

The following descriptions of macro and micro economics reveal ways that real estate investors can use the economy to help them read and interpret real estate market information effectively so that they can both predict how the market will change and how to improve the performance of their investments. This is what I call being able to accurately forecast real estate market trends and patterns and having clear investment visibility. When learning about economics and using historical data and statistics, remember that no one can predict the future with 100 percent accuracy. You can never be sure whether or not the future will respond as it has in the past. People use past data to help guide them on what have been typical and normal patterns so that they can determine what might happen in the future. Investing will always have its risks. Being more informed and knowledgeable gives you more options, but never guarantees your investment results. Now go out there and have fun learning about the power of macro and micro economics!

Figure C.1 demonstrates the intricate web of these economic indicators and how they influence long-term real estate investing. These factors should be considered when determining the health and viability of a real estate market.

UNDERSTANDING MACRO AND MICRO ECONOMICS
Macro Economics

Macro economics is the study of how large economic forces impact the health and stability of an economy. It is the "big picture" view of how the economy works. Following are some of the key forces that affect real estate portfolios.

FIGURE C.1: **Economic Indicators**

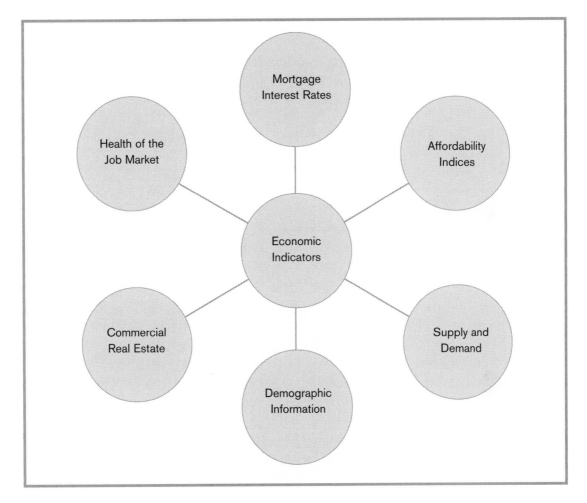

Recessions or depressions. Recessions and depressions occur naturally in all economies around the globe. Developed countries such as the United States, Canada, Australia, New Zealand, parts of the African continent, and most European countries have sophisticated economies that are regulated by a centralized government system. These governing systems help regulate the flow of currency and the sale of goods nationally and internationally to protect an overall national economy from large swings in inflation and resulting recessions. A government's ability to safely and accurately control the flow of money into and out of the economy can steer the nation out of a depression and into a recession or move the nation from a recession into a healthy flourishing economy. This is why knowing the national unemployment rates, the cost of certain goods, and what the government is saying about the overall health of the nation is important to investors.

Nationally based loan interest rates. The Federal Reserve regulates the loan interest rates according to the overall health and well-being of the national economy. Long-term investors should pay special attention to these interest rates because they directly influence the number of real estate sales and the rise of or decline in property values. For example, if you live in an area that is depressed and there is talk of increasing the loan interest rates, you may be heading for more declines in property values. But, if you live in an area where the economy is healthy and the interest rates are decreasing due to a national recession, then your local market is likely to continue experiencing an increase in property values. Remember: when one part of the country is experiencing a recession, other parts of the country may be having a boom market. This is exactly what happened to Southern California in the late 1990s and early 2000s. The nation was experiencing a recession, and the local economy was booming. The Feds needed to stimulate the rest of the nation, so they continued to lower interest rates to encourage spending, which stimulates job growth and generally improves the economy. In Southern California, the state economy was booming yet the national interest rates continued to drop, fueling the appreciation rates of the real estate because properties continued to be more affordable with these low interest rates.

Wartime. In the early phases of war when the safety of our homeland and the world in general is unknown, people's sense of security and willingness to take risks are hindered. As a result, the national economy is impacted. If war occurs, real estate values can decline or even come to a standstill because the pool of buyers shrinks until consumer confidence returns. Property that is held in areas immediately around military bases will go through high vacancy rates during wartime due to the military personnel going overseas to fight. When the war ends, housing demands increase around military bases and landlords and property owners are once again happy. Military personnel are generally good tenants and pay their rents in a timely manner. It must be all of that discipline. If they don't pay on time, you can contact their commanding officers and make sure that they pay or they get in trouble. Not bad as a guarantor for the rent being paid on time!

Demographics of the nation. Demographics define who is living in an area by age, race, and education. It is pertinent to define the specific housing or business needs of these groups. The statistics gathered through the Census Bureau every ten years help cities, states, and the nation track and plan for growth and development. A decline or growth in the number of people in any given area will impact the job market and spending habits of the residents in these areas, which in turn affects the overall economy. When the country has an increase in the number of retired people or there is an unexpected increase in the number of births, it has long-range effects on the economy in the following ways:

- *Health.* When the nation has a growing population of seniors, the increased costs of health care need to be addressed and accounted for from an economic perspective. Federal and state medical benefits may not cover this growing demand as the general population ages and begins to retire. The cost of Americans living longer has not been accurately accounted for, and how to fund these growing medical needs still remains unanswered. Most retirement plans have not been sufficiently funded to cover these increased health care and long-term assisted living costs. The nation may be looking at a tremendous national deficit to cover the medical expenses that the baby boomer generation will need in the next 20 years.

  Why bring this up when discussing real estate investments? Because the national deficit and the cost of supporting the increased medical benefits will affect all Americans and their ability to spend, save, and invest in the future. Keeping an eye on how the government plans to solve some of these difficult problems will definitely impact your future real estate investments and the amount of money that will be in the market for housing, job growth, and retail spending.

- *Social security.* Not unlike the country's health crisis, the instability of social security benefits will also have a large impact on the national economy over the next 20 years. Americans correctly fear that their social security benefits will not be enough to support their current lifestyles when they stop working. As a result, they will need to rely more on their investments (passive income) to live the lives to which they have grown accustomed. The largest of these investments is usually a family home. Most seniors tend to sell their larger homes after their children have left because they don't need the space anymore. Some prefer to use the proceeds from the sale to fund their retirement dreams, while others wish to supplement their retirement portfolios by redirecting some of their equity into new investments such as real estate or very conservative investment funds within the stock market. Commercial and residential real estate is greatly affected by where seniors get their income. Residents who are dependent on social security benefits require local commercial real estate that supports lower priced services (i.e., discounted retail centers and medical facilities). In contrast, seniors with investment portfolio money (meaning they have planned well and put money away throughout the years and now have more disposable income to spend) want real estate that offers amenities and retail centers that are geared towards the specialty items requested by the affluent.

- *Wealth.* The amount of wealth that is accumulated or held by individual Americans is important to know so that their future spending habits and lifestyles can be estimated with some degree of accuracy. Currently, over 68 percent of Americans own their homes and have most of their wealth held in the equity of their homes, but they are not using this equity very powerfully to help them with retirement needs. Americans will also be experiencing another new phenomenon over the next 20 years, when more money will be transferred from one generation to the next at levels that have never been experienced in history. With so much wealth being transferred, the money will need somewhere to go. This will impact the demand for investment opportunities over the next 20 years as the new generation looks for places to reinvest their inherited dollars. Many of these heirs will have little experience in managing and keeping the money they inherit. This highlights the importance of having a good solid financial education and a variety of investment opportunities to fill this growing consumer need in the next 20 to 30 years.

- *Migratory patterns.* It is important to know how groups of people are moving in or out of the state or region. The information about these migratory patterns helps officials, developers, and real estate investors strategically plan for the movement of these large groups of people. Knowing whether an area is experiencing population growth or decline dramatically impacts commercial and real estate investment demands and profitability.

- *Cost of goods for construction and building materials.* An increase in the cost of building materials greatly affects the cost of real estate. Currently, America has experienced an increase in cement and wood costs, which has driven the price of real estate up and decreased the profit margins for the developers. This increase in material costs is usually passed on to the buyers directly. An increase in labor costs usually indicates that the housing market is healthy and that there are not enough laborers to keep pace with the demand for construction workers. In contrast, a decrease in labor costs suggests just the opposite—the economy is not doing well and that there is an overabundance of workers looking for employment. This usually results in a slowing in new building construction starts and an overall sluggish economy.

Micro Economics

Micro economics takes a look at each of the individual sectors of the economy and studies how they operate. Unlike macro economics where the economy is analyzed on a broader scale, micro economics (micro meaning small) examines the economy on a more local or regional level. Below are several of the factors that will affect your real estate portfolio on a micro level.

Local and regional recessions and depressions. Much of the information described in the national macro economics section applies in the same way to local and regional recessions and depressions. It is important to add, however, that most areas will naturally cycle in and out of recessions about every ten years. This doesn't mean that you should leap out of any market just because it is experiencing a recession, but make sure you protect your investment by knowing the depth of the recession and what local officials are doing to stimulate the economy. It is also important to look at what tax and government incentives officials are offering developers and corporations to move into the area and bring affordable housing and jobs into their economy. Recessions can greatly be altered or even prevented when the central government is proactive in bringing new business into the area.

Local or regional disasters. Real estate prices and rental income can be severely impacted by natural disasters that occur in a market. Earthquakes, hurricanes, and tornadoes can not only destroy property in an area, but they can keep people from wanting to move there for fear of such disasters occurring again. It is impossible to predict or be prepared for these unforeseen events.

Age. Knowing what age groups make up any market is crucial information for real estate investors to have. Different age groups require different types of real estate, so it is important to recognize when an area is experiencing a great deal of growth in its population. This knowledge will influence the types of real estate that are currently needed and will be needed over the next 10 to 20 years. Pay attention to areas that have rapidly changing demographics, like Florida, California, parts of the Northwest, and parts of the Southeast.

Seniors. If you know that you are buying an investment in an area that is attracting and retaining seniors, you want to have properties that address their needs and contain services designed specifically for them. This includes single-story homes, good medical facilities, and diverse recreational and educational facilities.

Youth. If an area is attracting lots of young families, be sure to research the local schools (elementary, secondary, and college levels). You should also know which larger national retail stores are moving in and be aware of any small parks and recreational facilities nearby.

Diversification of the job market. Whether or not a job market is diverse is one of the most important factors to consider when deciding to purchase real estate in any particular area. Look for a job market that contains a good mix of types of small businesses, medium-sized companies, and large corporations. Industries go in cycles, just like real estate does, and a local market puts itself in unnecessary danger when it is too dependent on any one industry. An example of this phenomenon can be found in the rust belt region of the United States where the local economies were heavily dependent on manufacturing. When the manufacturing companies could not be competitive with the world markets, they moved their factories overseas or to the South where labor costs were cheaper. Now these markets and economies are deflated and depressed, and they have been unable to produce a diversified job base that will stimulate economic growth and development. Buyer beware of an area that is overly dependent on one industry (for example, all biotech, space technology, tourism, telecommunications, manufacturing, or medical facilities).

Unemployment rates. The unemployment rates of a particular area are key to determining the stage of the real estate cycle of that area. When unemployment rates are high, it is likely that the area is in a declining real estate market.

Affordability indices. Economists use affordability indices as one of the most critical factors to examine when determining where a market is in its real estate cycle. Affordability indices are defined as the average number of people who can afford the average priced home in the area. Areas with high affordability indices are good places to buy real estate because the cost of purchasing the property is lower and the cash flow on the property is usually more reasonable and will sustain the purchase of the property. When affordability rates fall as low as 12 to 14 percent (meaning the percentage of the population can afford to buy the median priced home in the market), it is a strong indicator that real estate prices may not continue to climb as rapidly as they have in the recent past. In fact, they will most likely begin to decrease. Certain factors such as a low supply of and high demand for existing or new housing can delay this natural decline in pricing.

Supply and demand. Supply and demand is also a critical factor when looking at any real estate market. This indicator describes a consumer's housing needs in relation to what housing is currently available for sale in the market place. Too much demand and not enough supply drives prices up while the opposite situation drives prices down.

New housing starts. Paying attention to new housing construction (called housing starts) tells investors a lot about the overall health of the economy. When new houses are built, it is usually a good indication that the economy is healthy and can provide a great economic boost. When new housing construction stops, there is trouble brewing in the job market. New housing makes up a huge part of any economy through the cost of goods and materials, hiring construction workers, and all of the business generated through real estate sales.

Existing housing for sale. The existing housing for sale is usually managed through real estate brokers and agents. When there is a lot of new home construction in a local market and an overabundance of existing housing for sale, it is likely that the homes for sale will sit on the market for longer periods of time. There are only a certain number of housing units that are needed in an area at any given time. The lengthening of market times for selling properties is one of the first indicators that the prices of homes will be declining in the near future.

Permits being pulled. The number of permits being pulled (issued) in an area tells you what the developers are predicting will be profitable for them in the next couple of years and how many new units will be available. Be sure that you also look at what types of permits are being requested and have been requested for the last two years. Take note of whether the permits are all for large single-family residences, multiple units, condominiums, commercial property, or retail spaces. This will indicate what will be coming on the market soon. For example, if there is a demand for a particular kind of real estate, such as small office spaces, and you are thinking of building or buying a small office, take a look at the permits being pulled. This will tell you about your competition, what will be coming onto the market soon, and the supply and demand, all of which begin the cycle with permits.

Commercial real estate. When you follow what is happening with commercial real estate, you will know what is happening with commerce. It is a leading indicator of what is occurring in the job market.

Types of vacancies. Looking at what type of vacancies there are in an area can be an excellent indicator of the health and well-being of its overall economy. For example, a lot of vacant retail strip centers with for rent signs or high vacancies in larger office spaces are signs that the local economy is not doing very well. You can assume that there was an expectation of larger businesses moving into town or larger companies were already in town and then moved out. In contrast, it is the first sign of a rebounding or recovering economy when an area has an increase in demand for small office spaces, especially if the market is recently rebounding from a depressed economy. It can be an especially good sign when small business entrepreneurs start moving into small offices that were formerly parts of larger corporations and had become foreclosures. Small business owners who take their business to the next level will stimulate the economy and benefit everyone. Commercial realtors can be excellent resources to help wind your way through the vacancy maze and help you discover what types of commercial real estate are currently available.

The Psychology of Investing

"Whatever the mind of man can achieve and believe it can achieve."
—Napoleon Hill

There are many people who have truly wanted to invest in real estate for several years, sometimes for over a decade, yet have not been able to pull the trigger and actually get over their analysis paralysis. They take investment courses and look at property, but for some reason they *still* do not own investment real estate. It is not uncommon at all for people to become frustrated with themselves because they can't seem to break this cycle, no matter how much they want to. Sadly, they begin to believe that they will never be able to achieve what they so desperately want and become despondent and upset.

Does this sound familiar to any of you? If it does, you are not alone. Investing in real estate is really scary for a lot of people. It almost freezes them. They want it, but feel that it is out of their reach. People who invest in the stock market do not go through nearly as much anxiety and apprehension as they do when thinking of investing in real estate. And rightly so. The stock market is more hands-off, and if you want to sell your stock, you simply call your stock broker or go online and get your proceeds within a couple of days. As you have now learned, that is not how real estate functions. It is much more labor intensive, but also much more profitable if handled correctly.

When I was taking clients out as a real estate agent to show them investment real estate, I regularly experienced a frustrating phenomenon I called "I want to . . . I need to . . . but I just can't, so show me some more properties please." That occurred more frequently than I would like to admit. I would meet with a client, they had the money and would tell me what they wanted to buy. I would find them the property. It met their goals, but for one reason after another they did not pull the trigger. It was very fascinating to me. I was a top sales agent for residential real estate and helped many people to buy their personal homes, but when it came to investing, I continued to experience a wall of resistance that could not be penetrated. Some clients would react the same way no matter how much we talked about it, no matter how many properties I showed them, and no matter how smart the investment was. They *still* wouldn't buy.

After being frustrated with a particular client one day, I asked if we could do a mini experiment to see if we could get her to break through this wall that was keeping her from moving forward toward achieving her dreams. She looked at me strangely, but trusted me enough to let me try something new. I explained to her that I had a Masters in Counseling and Human Services, and I was familiar with art therapy techniques and working with children to express themselves. She looked at me weirdly again, but agreed. So off I marched to my office and arrived several minutes later with an arm full of items: colored markers, pens, pencils, crayons, and white paper. I told her we were going to play for a little while.

It was time to try something new and radical with this generous client of mine. I couldn't bear another day of clients not buying real estate when everything was right for them. I asked her to pick her favorite colors and to draw a picture of her mother. I requested that she draw how her mother related to her own dreams and to her own money. She was not allowed to use any words and had to draw a picture no matter how artistic (or artistically challenged) she was. Gleefully, this client agreed and began to draw a picture of her mother.

Many people ask me why I require that no language be on the paper. My answer is simple; most people have been writing and telling people about their families for years. It is a very familiar story, but this knowledge is kept in place through language. However, very few people have *drawn* how things are and how they remember their lives. It can be very powerful because you are tapping into a wisdom that is more unfamiliar and unknown. I have personally found that more breakthroughs occur through drawing because it is all new information to work through and the client does not have as many known and loved defenses using this medium.

These exercises have made a profound impact on many of my clients and students, but not everyone likes the touchy-feely nature of this exercise. That is why I have kept it at the back of the book, for the brave souls who are interested in this part of their human development. The goal should be to have fun and draw away to your success and prosperity. Here are some key factors to remember when beginning to draw:

- Use colored markers or crayons; have fun using a variety of colors.
- Have four sheets of blank white paper or use the forms in this book.
- You can not use any words of any kind, drawing only please.
- Do not worry about your artistic ability, just have fun and play around.

First, try drawing a picture of your mother (see Figure D.1). Many people do not know their birth mother or haven't had a female role model in their lives. If this is your situation, try to think of the closest mother figure that you have. It is just the modeling that is important and does not have to be a biological parent. Let your creativity flow.

FIGURE D.1: **Mother Role Model: Genetic Mapping**

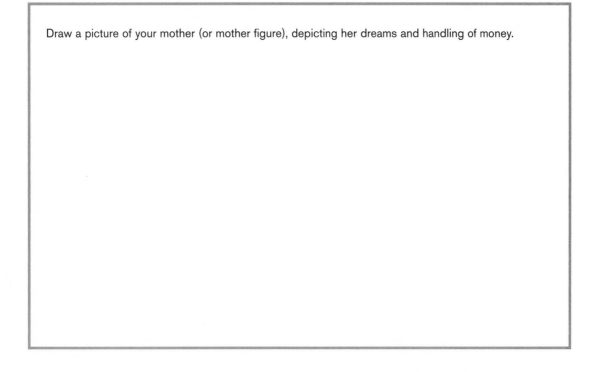

Draw a picture of your mother (or mother figure), depicting her dreams and handling of money.

Now that you have completed your drawing, how was it? Did you discover anything new or unusual? Did you discover anything that surprised you? Answer the following questions to get more information from your drawings:

- What were the valuable things that your mother dreamed about?
- Did she get what she dreamed about?
- How did she handle her money?
- Did she save and invest?
- Did she spend all of her money?
- Did she travel and have her dreams fulfilled?
- Did she give her money away to the family and children?
- What did your mother teach you about money and dreams?

Ready for some more discoveries? Let's keep going! Now draw a picture of your father or father figure (see Figure D.2). Remember: if you don't know your biological father, it is okay. Just use the male figure that you consider the most like your dad.

FIGURE D.2: **Father Role Model: Genetic Mapping**

Draw a picture of your father (or father figure), depicting his dreams and handling of money.

Now how was that? Did you discover anything new? Did you find out anything about your father that you didn't know before? Did you have any new insights that are surprising to you? Answer the following questions to get more from the drawing you just completed:

- How did your dad express himself with his money?
- Did he complete his dreams in his life?
- How did he tell you about his dreams and his goals?
- Was he secretive and shy about his dreams?
- Did he teach you about financial management and growing your money?
- Is he happy now?
- Does he have what he wanted or dreamed about?
- What did he value and how did he tell you about it?
- How have you integrated his values and ways of handling money and dreams into your present life?
- Do you see any similarities or patterns?

Next, I invite you to draw a picture of how *you* handle your money and your dreams (see Figure D.3). Have fun and draw away. Be creative!

FIGURE D.3: **Who Are You Now?**

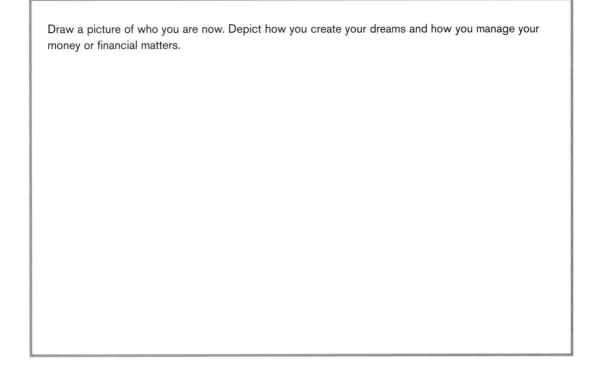

Draw a picture of who you are now. Depict how you create your dreams and how you manage your money or financial matters.

Did you discover anything about yourself? Any new revelations? Answer some of the questions below and see what your drawing reveals:

- How are you currently handling your money?
- How are you currently handling your dreams?
- Who are you most like? Your mother or your father?
- What are your fears about investing or dreaming?
- What are your excitements and joys about investing and dreaming?
- What did you discover most about yourself through this exercise?

Don't blame your parents for anything that appeared in your pictures. This is simply an exercise that will get you in touch with what you remember about how you grew up. You have the power to change anything, no matter what your background was. You are a dynamic and wonderful human being.

Remember that client who first let me experiment with her? As silly as she thought it seemed, drawing herself and her parents helped her understand the ways her family approached money and investing, and she finally began to buy investment real estate. It really worked for her and gave her an in-depth understanding that her reactions to investing were more than just about numbers and real estate. In fact, she discovered that there really was a psychological influence to investing.

She realized that her mother had unfulfilled dreams and was sad about her financial situation, but never did anything about it. Instead of moving forward in her dreams, this client's mother always kept her money hidden and would never invest it. My client drew a picture of the mattress where her mother put all her money and a sad face about not having her dreams met or fulfilled. My client was really touched when she recognized that she had been experiencing the same emotions personally. From this simple exercise, we learned where some of her behaviors and patterns were coming from. Her mom was not able to get past her fears and invest wisely or create dreams that satisfied her. This is very common among many investors.

We then looked at the drawings of her father and how he related to his dreams and handled his money. Feeling stuck and apprehensive, my client was more reluctant to start drawing her father and didn't know what to draw. Tempted to use words, I instructed her that she would get more out of the exercise if she just drew. She reluctantly proceeded. Soon she began to draw a picture of her father. He had invested in many projects and owned several small businesses and stores, a true entrepreneur who was very financially successful and independent. She began to realize that she had never noticed that she behaved more like her father in her various careers, but still was frightened and scared like her mother in her investments. She started to see that she was acting like both of her parents. Of course, it's natural and normal for people to be like their parents. This is what was modeled for her as a small child. But now, as an adult, she could powerfully *choose* who she wanted to be. Her future did not have to be based on her past, but on whom she wanted to grow like and become.

This was her breakthrough. She realized that her past experiences were pulling her back and she didn't want to resist anymore. She knew that if she was going to move forward and finally buy some investment real estate she would need to separate herself from her mother's experience and fears of letting her money go out from under the bed. She didn't want to control or change her mother; she just wasn't going to act in fear anymore.

In order to set this new reality into cement and make it more powerful, I asked this generous and brave client to do one more exercise. She gladly said yes and was off drawing her final picture. This time she drew herself in the future. When she was finished, she had drawn a picture of who she wanted to be in the future. It was a woman with many different businesses and investment properties who was happy having a life full of dreams and happiness. She was liberated. Soon we went out, and immediately she decided to buy her first investment property. She was now like her father in investing, yet still honored her mother's strong love for family and security.

Now create what you really want for your future. This is the most exciting step in this exercise. In Figure D.4, you get to determine and draw who you want to be, based not on your past and not restricted by your present, but on what you see as possible in your future. This is your chance to show the world what your life is going to look like. Don't forget: people who have a vision of where they want to be are more likely going to get there than people who are not interested in being specific. Be bold, be extraordinary, and direct your life in the direction of how you truly want to be. You have the power, now use it effectively.

Did you learn anything about yourself that will change the way you invest or handle your money? Did you experience a breakthrough or have a better understanding of how you respond to your money and your dreams? I have used this exercise in my classes and with many of my clients who find themselves stuck and unable to buy investment real estate no matter what they do. At first, some of them are nervous to do this exercise, but most are really glad they took the time and find it to be very powerful for them. They find that they can truly have the freedom to achieve whatever they want no matter what was in their pasts, and that they can rely on their own personal insights and power to control their future investment careers.

Over the course of several years of working with my clients, I have learned some hidden truths and would like to share them with you. Look at these hidden truths only after you have done the exercises above or you may influence your drawings.

- Notice if your parents had clearly defined dreams or not. If your family never spoke about or nurtured their dreams, it may initially be more difficult for you to start dreaming and drawing, but that will come soon enough.

FIGURE D.4: **Who Will You Be?**

Draw a picture of who you want to be. Let the drawing depict how you create your dreams and how you will manage your money and financial matters.

- To free yourself from your past, just start dreaming and telling people what you are going to do. Talking about your dreams will help you turn them into reality. If your family talked about dreams and fulfillment, it will be easier to move into investing and creating an exciting life.
- If you saw that your parents were poor money managers, very frequently you will not see them with any hands in your drawings. People who are drawn with hands are typically able to grow money, receive money, and give money. Over and over again I have noticed that the clients that came from families with lots of wealth had defined hands in their drawings.
- Typically, parents who gave their money to their children instead of investing it placed most of their values on family and relationships. Again, the fulfillment of their dreams was not based on money or investments, but in having a strong family. Many of these parents associated investments with the opposite of strong family values. If this sounds familiar to you, you may have a harder time beginning to invest.

Evaluating Investment Properties

"Spend as much time investigating the investment as you spend earning the money that you are thinking of investing."
—Brian Tracy, author

T he task of evaluating investment property can be complex, but it is well worth the time you put into it. Here are several different factors you should examine before you even walk through the door:

Age

The age of the property will definitely influence its value or future cost. This factor needs to be assessed when either purchasing property or when determining whether to keep, exchange, or sell it. You should evaluate all capital improvements needed on the property before and during ownership so that you can compare these extra expenses to newer properties that may not need additional improvements to produce the same returns.

Capitalization Rates of Return

This is the percentage rate of return received on an investment, based on the income generated from that investment after all the expenses have been paid. Buying a property with a high CAP rate means that the property is producing good income (cash flow) based on the price that you paid for the asset. Properties that are less expensive to purchase and have strong income will have higher CAP rates. Keep in mind that properties with high CAP rates may not see as high rates of appreciation as lower CAP rate properties. Experiencing lower appreciation does not mean the area or property will not rebound or change for the better. You could buy a property in a deflated market that is just about to rebound and you will be able to capitalize on all the new appreciation in a short period of time. Properties that experience quick appreciation are usually in diverse economic environments that have just recovered from a downturn in the economy.

Properties that have high CAP rates are usually located in lower income neighborhoods or in the middle parts of the country where the prices are more reasonable and the rents are more in line with the cost of the building. Receiving higher CAP rates can also mean you will encounter more difficulty on the property (a higher risk can sometimes come from low-income areas) and lower property values.

In contrast, properties that have lower CAP rates are often found in more expensive and desirable neighborhoods where the property values and the incomes of the tenants are higher, but the rents do not typically cover the cost of buying the property. These kinds of properties are usually located along the coasts of the United States. Investors who have a lot of equity and want to buy safe and secure real estate investments will purchase some of their properties in more expensive, low CAP neighborhoods even when they know they will receive lower income. This is because these properties are usually lower risk (due to the neighborhoods in which they are located).

CAP Rate = Net operating income ÷ Purchase price

Cash on Cash Returns

Many investors evaluate property based on what cash-on-cash returns they are getting for their investments. This simply means that they want to determine how much cash flow they'll get each month from their investment based on how much money they put into the investment.

Percentage Cash-on-Cash Return = Cash flow ÷ Cash invested

Gross Scheduled Income (GSI)

Rental income that is scheduled to be generated each year as well as income from other sources such as laundry or parking combine to form your gross scheduled income. GSI is also referred to as potential gross income.

Gross Scheduled Income = Number of units @ $_____ per month =
$ _____ x 12 months =
$_____ annual rental income + any other income from property

Effective Gross Income

This is derived by totaling potential income (gross scheduled income) from all sources, then subtracting vacancy and collection losses. Collection losses are the costs associated with having to collect lost rents, evictions, and attorney fees for delinquent tenants.

Effective Gross Income = Gross scheduled income − Vacancy − Collection losses

Gross Rent Multiplier (GRM)

The gross rent multiplier formula is used for determining new property values when rents are increased. It is especially useful when purchasing rental property that is under-valued in rental incomes. Don't forget: an increase in rental income directly affects property values.

Gross Rent Multiplier = Purchase price ÷ Gross scheduled income

Purchase Price

The price of a property is calculated by multiplying the gross scheduled income by the gross rent multiplier. It is important to realize that determining the value of investment real estate is based on the income that is generated from the property. Comparisons to similar properties that have sold in the area will also influence the price, but ultimately, property value is determined by the amount of rents collected in relation to the price being asked.

Purchase Price = Gross scheduled income x Gross rent multiplier

Net Operating Income (NOI)

The income that is generated after deducting all of the operating expenses, but before deducting for income taxes and loan interest payments, is your net operating income.

Net Operating Income = Gross scheduled income − Operating expenses

Operating Expenses

Operating expenses will include items such as taxes, utilities, maintenance, management, insurance, and reserves, but will *not* include loan payments. Property expenses increase for three main reasons: there are more amenities offered at the property, the property is located in a less desirable area and there are more maintenance costs, or the property may experience higher vacancy rates.

Price Per Unit

Calculating the value of a property by price per unit is effective, especially when you are looking at multiple units. This is a quick and easy way to assess property values based on per-unit costs. It is common to evaluate investment property with terms such as "price per door." This method of evaluating property helps investors compare how much they are paying per unit (door) to what is being paid in other areas across the country.

Price Per Unit = Sale price of property ÷ Number of units on property

Price Per Square Foot

Both the overall value of the property and the purchase price are influenced by the amount of square feet the rental property has. This method of evaluation is used when determining whether or not you are renting the units at market rate, and if there is room to increase rental rates to increase the profit and property value.

Price per Square Foot = Purchase price ÷ Square footage

Rental Rate

Comparing the market rental rates is valuable when assessing a current property's condition and performance. Knowing if rents are below market, at market rates, or higher than average will help determine monthly rental income and the likelihood of filling vacancies when they occur. This understanding can also give an indication of the property's current value and expected value once rental rates have been adjusted.

Rental Rate = Total rent per month ÷ Square footage of living space

Vacancies

Vacancy rates will vary widely depending on the market and economy where you are buying property. Usually a particular market will not see vacancies that go higher than 10 to 15 percent in any given cycle. Higher vacancy rates are typically an indication that there is poor property management in place, the market is experiencing tremendous economic difficulties, the property is in need of repair compared to the other properties available, or the rents are too high. Maintaining and keeping your investments viable is directly related to keeping vacancy rates low.

Glossary

Accommodator. A person or entity that manages the paperwork on a 1031 exchange transaction, knows the timelines and specific requirements of the IRS and the exchange process, and holds the money or proceeds that have been distributed from a 1031 exchange to accommodate the seller during the complex requirements of the tax deferred exchange.

Accountant. The person responsible for taking the details of the money flow (details are usually from the bookkeeper), files annual and quarterly reports for the IRS, provides tax saving ideas, and determines how to increase profit margins for personal or business uses.

Active income. Income that is generated from wages and salary for work that requires attendance or participation in order to be paid.

Acquisition phase. The first phase of real estate investing that is marked with high anxiety, fear, anticipation, and excitement.

Adjusted gross income. The amount of income an individual receives from wages or commissions minus specific deductions such as IRA contributions, alimony, moving expenses, and capital loss deductions.

Affordability index. The average number of people in a given area who can afford the average priced home in the area.

Aggressive. A measure of intensity or risk that one is willing to take when investing with a more profitable and risky outcome.

Annual cash flow. The amount of money that is received from all the income on the property after all expenses have been paid for the entire year.

Annual operating expenses. All of the expenses for operating the property plus the vacancy rates for the entire year, not including loan payments, only the expense for operating the property for the year.

Apartment Association. An organization that represents the needs of apartment owners, usually providing legal services, monthly meetings, current events, and tax laws, as well as other important information for property owners.

Apartment building. A set of individual housing units that are in one building owned by a person or entity called the landlord or owner.

Appreciation. The growth in value over time.

As is. The owner sells a property with no improvements, and the buyer accepts the property in its current condition with no improvements or warrantees.

Assessors Parcel Number (APN). A number assigned to a single parcel of land (any kind of real estate) by the state or county assessors office. All parcels of land, no matter how large or small, have an assigned APN. New APNs are assigned when land is subdivided.

Attorney. Person or entity that advises the investor about laws and regulations, and who may represent the owner in a dispute when mediation, arbitration, or court is needed.

Baby boomer generation. The largest generation (76 million) within our current population, born between 1942 and 1962.

Bad credit. A term that defines the past history with credit worthiness and payment history that is not favorable for the borrower. The credit report shows that the borrower has an unfavorable track record of paying bills on time or maintaining his or her obligations.

Banker/lender. A person or institution that lends money.

Bookkeeper. Person or company responsible for inputting details regarding money coming in and out of the company or personal account. The bookkeeper is responsible for keeping track of the categories and organization of the flow of money.

Budget. Projected amounts of money in various categories used to determine expenses and income for personal or business uses. These projected numbers are usually compared to what income and expenses actually occurred. This method of comparison improves the growth and profit of both personal and business wealth and development.

Building developer. Person or entity that builds houses or adds improvements to already completed properties after the land developers have prepared the land.

Business owners. Person or entity that owns a company and is not employed by others.

Capitalization rate (cap rate). The percentage rate of return received on an investment based on the amount of income generated from that investment after all expenses have been paid.

Capital improvements. Money or resources needed to make improvements to a building, structure, or business of real estate.

Carrying notes. Owners who finance a portion of the buyer's purchase in order to receive a monthly payment for the loan.

Cash flow. The balance of cash that the property generates after all money is collected from all sources, expenses are paid, and loan payments are made.

Charitable contribution. The act of giving money, resources, or time to a nonprofit organization or cause that is given freely without expectation of return. This is part of what investors do at the end of their real estate plan.

Codes, covenants, and restrictions (CC&Rs). The regulations and bylaws of associations that defines lawful actions within the association that govern how homeowners and managing entities interact with each other.

Collateral. Using additional security such as real estate, coins, or jewelry as a pledge for the payment of a new loan.

Commercial property. Property that is zoned specifically for business use and does not house people for the purpose of living and sleeping.

Compound interest. Interest that is calculated on the accumulated unpaid interest as well as on the original principal.

Condominium. Property that is owned in collection with other homeowners where the owner owns the interior space of his or her unit and also owns an undivided interest on the exterior of the building, plus all common area in the complex or development.

Condominium conversions. A process where owners and developers convert existing apartment buildings into condominiums. There is one APN for an apartment building, and after the conversion there is one APN for each condominium.

Consumer debt. The revolving debt for cars, trucks, boats, furniture, and miscellaneous items that are owed by a person.

Contractor. Person who makes repairs and additions on a building or may build the structure from the ground up.

Counter-intuitive. The opposite of what is expected, against the natural thought process.

Credit counseling/debt relief services. Financial advice and support to assist customers to strategically manage their debt and spending habits.

Credit risk. The degree of probability that a loan will be paid on time according to the terms of the loan agreement.

Debt reduction plan. A strategic plan of action that focuses on paying down debt in a particular order and set time.

Debt service coverage ratio. The amount of debt on a property compared to the amount of projected income generated by the property.

Declining real estate market. A real estate market that is experiencing declines in price and value.

Default. Legal process taken when an owner is not paying his or her loan payments as agreed upon in the terms of the lender's note. The notice of default states that the borrower is not living up to the loan obligation and specifies what steps the borrower must take to avoid foreclosure.

Depreciation allowance. A taxable benefit the government allows investors to use with investment real estate. The government assumes that the building and structure will deteriorate over time and allows a tax benefit for this deterioration against the owner's tax returns each year. This benefit does not apply to homeowners' primary or second homes.

Diminishing rate of return. A decline in the return on investment over time.

Discounted properties. Properties bought below market value, sold at a discount.

Discretionary funds. Money that is left over at the end of the month or year after all expenses and obligations have been met. There is no specific obligated use for these funds.

Dissolving partnerships. The process of ending or exiting from a partnership according to the terms of the partnership agreement.

Diversify. Including a variety of properties in a variety of regions across the country in order to create a stable and balanced portfolio.

Domestic reorganization. A couple, whether married or living together, splitting up and moving away from each other.

Down payment. The amount of money a buyer uses to purchase a property.

Dreams. Inspiration for what really matters in one's life. The contemplation of what ignites the spirit and soul of an individual to perform at levels never thought possible and to have things never imagined before.

Economic forecast. Ability to read the future of the market with some assurance and accuracy.

Effective gross income. The total of all potential income (gross scheduled income) from all sources, minus vacancy and collection losses.

Equity. The amount of money, appreciation, cash flow, loan reduction, and tax benefits an owner has dedicated to/invested in a property at any given time.

Equity management phase. The second phase of real estate investing that requires more complicated transactions and lasts for the longest period of time.

Escrow. Term used in several states to describe the neutral party that is managing the real estate sales or refinance transaction from a nonbiased position. This entity handles all legal documents, title reports, insurance policies, loan documents, county recording processes, and home warrantee policies, etc. for both seller and buyer.

Estate planning. The process of mapping out how an individual or family wants to distribute wealth after death. It includes tax savings strategies, charitable contributions, and inheritances.

Exchanges. A technical term that means a tax-deferred exchange for real estate investors. This term indicates that the owner is exchanging one investment property for another property that meets specific IRS codes and regulations.

Exit strategy phase. The last phase of real estate investing, when investors are living off of passive income generated from their investment portfolios. This phase is most concerned with producing income and protecting assets and distributing to heirs and charities.

Expenses. All the costs of owning and managing property, which can include mortgage payments, management fees, maintenance, utilities, taxes, vacancy, capital improvements, rental, and collection loss.

Fear. An emotional experience that intensifies situations making them more frightening and risky than they should be in reality.

Financial objective. A goal that is set to meet a financial target, which includes specific actions designed to produce expected results.

Financial planner. A qualified person who specializes in assisting investors to strategically manage their money for the purposes of growth, protection, estate distribution, and security

Financial responsibility. Being accountable and following through on obligations and commitments. Paying attention to financial matters as they relate to current and future obligations and dreams.

Financial security. Having peace of mind due to proper financial planning.

First position. The person or institution that gets paid first when property is sold or goes to foreclosure.

Fiscal condition. The financial status and health of a person, organization, or business.

Fixer uppers. Properties that are in need of cosmetic or major repairs to bring them back to conditions comparable to the area. This term is typically used to indicate that the buyer is buying the property at a discount or wholesale, and will improve the property and sell it immediately for a profit.

Foreclosure. Properties that have been taken from a buyer by a bank or lending institution because the owner failed to make payments on the bank note as promised.

Franchise. A business model that is duplicatable and has a proven record of performance and sales.

Functional obsolescence. The building as it was originally designed does not have usefulness for its current function or purpose. Older buildings usually become outdated after 30 to 40 years

Future value of investment. The value of money in the future as it relates to a current investment choice.

Generation X. The generation of people born between 1963 and 1983. Although still not as large a group as the baby boomer generation, they constitute about 13 percent of the entire US population.

Gross rent multiplier. A formula used for determining new property values when rents are increased.

Gross scheduled income (GSI). The rental income expected to be generated by the property, based on the tenants' leases, rental contracts, and asking rental prices.

Hard money lender. A person or institution that will loan money to a borrower who has no credit, bad credit, and/or no collateral. The rates and fees are expensive because the risk of the loan is greater.

Home equity line of credit (HELOC). An open line of credit against equity in a property.

Home owners association. A governing body elected by home owners to regulate the by laws and agreements regarding the common area owned by all the owners within the association. The amount of ownership for the common area is an undivided interest for all the home owners, and the voting rights are equally distributed among the members of the association.

Improvement. The building or structure on a parcel of land (this language is used for tax purposes).

Inheritance. Money or assets received by family members or others at the time of death through the distribution of the estate.

Insurance agent. Person or organization that represents the consumer regarding the services and products offered through the insurance company, including updating policies as their needs for protection change.

Intergenerational transfer of wealth. The amount of money that will pass down from the older generation to the younger generation.

Investment clubs. Gatherings and meetings for the intention of discussing and sharing ideas about investment strategy, theories, and knowledge.

Investment mastery. The ability to understand and participate in investment transactions with exceptional skill and superior techniques resulting in increased profits and stabilization of the investment.

Investor's tax rate. The owner's income tax rate determined each year when income tax returns are filed. This includes both federal and state personal income tax rates.

Internal Revenue Service (IRS). The government organization that collects taxes from income, sales and property.

Land. Property that does not have any improvements or structures on it, often used for agricultural purposes and parking services.

Land developer. A person or entity that takes raw land with no improvements and subdivides the land to prepare it for building developers, usually adding utilities such as electric, sewer, water, cable, telephone, streets, curbs, and gutters.

Lease options. Contracts between an owner and a buyer where the buyer agrees to pay a fee to have the option to buy the property they are leasing by making monthly payments towards the down payment of the property.

Legacy. A statement, purpose, or money that is passed on to future generations long after the benefactor has ceased to exist.

Leverage. The use of other people's money to acquire the full value of an asset. The use of a small amount of money to get the benefit of an asset of larger value.

Liability. Responsibility to make payment and to obligate money, time, or resources to an entity or organization based upon an agreement between the parties.

Lifestyle. The way a person chooses to live that inspires, depresses, or fulfills them. Lifestyle takes into consideration values, financial condition, desires, and family situation.

Litigation. Lawsuit that goes to court or to arbitration to resolve a dispute.

Loan payments. The amount of money that is paid for borrowing money (usually monthly or biweekly) which typically includes both interest and principal payments.

Loan reduction. The amount that the principal is reduced with the loan payments.

Loan to value (LTV). The ratio of the amount of debt service or loan is against the total value of the property.

Long-term sustainable wealth. Wealth that is created and kept in a person's possessions after many years. Wealth that is grown and protected for years to come without hesitation or concern.

Low-income areas. Areas that provide housing for low-income populations, usually accompanied by higher crime rates and increased maintenance issues.

Maintenance. The upkeep of property, such as termite inspections, furnace and heater filter changes, landscaping, roof, electrical, and plumbing repairs, and any seasonal treatments.

Market rents. The rents collected that other comparable rental units are receiving in the area.

Market value. Properties that sell for the prices that other comparable homes are selling for in the area.

Mechanic's lien. A recorded instrument that is placed against the owner of a property when a contractor is not paid for services rendered.

Mentor. A role model or person willing to teach as set of skills desired by another.

Monthly contribution. Amount of money that sometimes must be contributed to the investment to maintain the debts and obligations on the property.

Monthly homeowner fees. Community monthly maintenance fees that are charged to the homeowner of an association to cover expenses such as exterior lighting, security, landscaping, parking, pools, club houses, etc.

Multiple unit apartments. A structure or building that has more than one housing unit per building and only one APN for all the buildings and units on the parcel.

Negative amortization loan. An adjustable rate loan that does not pay off any of the principal and does not pay all of the interest due on the loan. The difference between what is owed and what is paid is added to the principal balance. Rather than decreasing, the amount owed for the property increases over time.

Negative cash flow. The property does not produce enough income after all expenses, taxes, and debt service are paid. The owner usually needs to contribute money monthly to keep the property going due to lack of sufficient funds being generated from rents and other income sources.

Net equity. The amount of total equity available to an investor after closing costs, taxes, and recapture fees are paid.

Net operating income. Income that is generated after deducting all operating expenses, but before deducting for property taxes and loan interest payments.

Original contribution. The first amount of money that an investor places into real estate investing with the goals and objectives established in the real estate plan.

Parcel. A portion of land that usually has been subdivided from a larger piece of land.

Partnerships. The collection of money, time, and resources to purchase, manage, and improve a venture with specific divisions of ownership and differing roles within the agreement.

Passive income. Income that is generated through investments where effort or participation is not required in order to be paid.

Penalties. The cost of selling an investment early, or breaking one of the agreements in a contract. The penalty is usually related to extra loan points, interest that is due, and/or the amount of some of the tax shelters and benefits originally expected.

Permits. Government documents that allow developers and builders to begin their construction, expansion, and/or growth plans.

Portfolio income. Income that is generated from investments held in the stock market produced from dividends, annuities and royalties.

Present value of money. The value of money in today's currency. The amount of services and products that can be purchased with a specific amount of money invested.

Probate sale. A real estate sales transaction that requires a court order and court action designed to protect a deceased person, used when a deceased person fails to have a Last Will and Testament drafted to express intentions regarding the distribution of the estate. The court acts as the guardian and protector of the deceased person's estate.

Proceeds. The amount of money distributed to the owner at the end of the sale of a property.

Property manager. A person or company that is responsible for managing investment real estate for owners for a monthly fee. They are accountable for collecting rents, supervision of repairs, tenant selection, evictions, advertising, and providing paperwork to the owners.

Qualified intermediary. Neutral entity that holds the proceeds from a 1031 exchange that acts as the go-between from the seller and the buyer so no taxable event occurs with the sale of the relinquished property.

Rate of return. The amount of reward or benefit received for placing a specific amount of money in an investment for a specific period of time. The amount of growth on an investment with specific terms and conditions usually defined in a percentage rate.

Real estate agent. Licensed person who is qualified to buy and sell real estate for another person or entity for a profit and is also able to advise and make assessments about the value and condition of real estate assets.

Recapture tax. Tax that is due when a property is no longer exchanged and is sold. There is a 25 percent recapture of the tax benefit of depreciation.

Refinance. The process of acquiring a new loan for more money, or at better rates and terms, which in turn pays off the existing loan on the property.

Reinvestment. Placing the benefits or rewards (cash flow, etc) from the investment back into an investment to accelerate the growth of the investment.

Relinquished property. When the first property in a tax-deferred exchange is sold, all of the proceeds from this sale are deposited into another investment property to avoid taxation on the gain from the sale.

Replacement property. When the second property in a tax-deferred exchange is bought, all of the proceeds from the relinquished property are deposited into this investment to avoid taxation on the gain from the sale.

Return on equity (ROE). The rate of return on an investment after cash flow, appreciation, loan reduction, and tax benefits are calculated and evaluated every year.

Risk. The process of potentially losing something you have for getting something better and more valuable than what is currently possessed.

Risk tolerance. Comfort level to manage or experience certain levels of risk as it relates to rewards and benefits.

Second contribution. The second amount of money that is placed in investment real estate that is not related to the original contribution. The second contribution must be money that has not already been accounted for in the original contribution calculations (it is not the equity growth generated from the original contribution). It is money not related to the original contribution such as bonuses at work, inheritances, refinance from a property not related to the original contribution. The expected rate of return on equity is in addition to the original contribution expectations.

Second position. The person or institution to be paid after the first position has been paid.

Single-family residence. A structure or building that has one housing unit (typically called a home). There is one building and APN on the parcel.

Sophisticated investor. A seasoned real estate owner who has knowledge and experience with a variety of real estate transactions, including management, maintenance, budgets, and tax saving strategies.

Standard percentage improvement value. A percentage of the total property value that is used as a standard measure to arrive at the improvement value and land value of a parcel of real estate.

Straight line depreciation. The formula used to calculate the number of years to depreciate an asset. The typical number of years to depreciate residential investment properties is 27.5 years, and 39 years for commercial properties.

Strategies. Methodology and system for making decisions and actions.

Stock broker. A person who assists investors in purchasing or selling individual stocks, mutual funds, bonds, money markets, CD, and/or other products.

Success coach. A person who is committed to assisting people to accomplish their goals and dreams.

Supply and demand. Consumer's housing needs in relation to what housing is currently available for sale in the market place.

Sustained rate of return. A rate of return that must be met consistently in order to meet the established goals and objectives.

Target. A specific place that one moves towards with intention and purpose to fulfill a desired goal.

Tax assessor's ratio. The ratio between land value and improvement value on the property tax records.

Tax benefits. The benefits an owner enjoys for owning real estate, including depreciation, loan interest, and operating expenses.

Tax lien. Instruments that are recorded against an owner when the IRS has not been paid.

Tax records (property). Recorded documents from the tax assessors office that distinquish the value of real estate through either the land value or the improvement value.

Tax savings. The amount of taxes (state and federal) that can be saved by taking the taxable benefits for owning real estate and multiplying that number by the investor's income tax rate.

Tenant. Person or company who pays rent to use one of the units owned by the investor.

Tenants in common (TICs). A common investment vehicle that brings investors together to share in the ownership of real estate without having to physically or fiscally manage the property. Because there is a manager of the TIC, this investment has few management issues and concerns.

Timeshare. A type of vacation property that is owned by a collection of people or entities that own only a fraction of the entire property. The owners' times allotted to use the timeshare are usually no more than one to two weeks per year. Annual mainte-nance fees are assessed, and the property can usually be traded for other like kind properties around the world.

Transaction. Business deal that is time related, has a specific intention or purpose, and usually is related to the sale or purchase of real estate.

Triple net leases. Commercial real estate term that indicates that the tenant pays the owner for all taxes, maintenance, interior improvements, and utilities. The owner is only responsible for the debt service on the property and exterior improvements.

TUMMI. Acronym for what is covered in the operating expenses of a property: T = taxes, U = utilities, M = management, M = maintenance, I = insurance.

Underleveraged. Real estate with a small loan on it compared to the total value of the property. Properties that have at least 50 percent equity are considered underlever-aged properties.

Underwriters. People who look at the details of the loan package and ensure that the cri-teria established by the lender or institution are met and followed.

Unrealistic expectation. Outcomes that are predicted that are not based in sound busi-ness reasoning. The predicated outcomes are too aggressive and not as likely to occur.

Vacancy rate. The amount of time that the property experiences loss of income due to no tenants occupying the unit.

Vacation homes. Properties that are owned by one or sometimes several owners that are located in areas that attract visitors. These homes are generally located by bodies of water, golf courses, mountains, and ski resorts.

Vested interest. A person or entity that has a legally binding financial interest in an asset, who has something to gain (money, status, or personal value, etc.) through involvement with a transaction or investment.

Zero-down financing. Financing terms that allow the buyer to have no money of his or her own invested in the purchase of the property. All of the money to acquire the property is borrowed.

Zoning. The government's regulation that determines the types of properties (commer-cial, residential, or agricultural) and actions (business, pets, or residential services) that can legally take place on the land.

Index